THE VANISHING MES

THE VANISHING MESSIAH

THE LIFE AND RESURRECTIONS *of*

FRANCIS SCHLATTER

David N. Wetzel

UNIVERSITY OF IOWA PRESS

IOWA CITY

University of Iowa Press, Iowa City 52242
Copyright © 2016 by David N. Wetzel
www.uiowapress.org
Printed in the United States of America

Design by April Leidig

No part of this book may be reproduced or used in any form or by
any means without permission in writing from the publisher. All reasonable
steps have been taken to contact copyright holders of material used in this
book. The publisher would be pleased to make suitable arrangements with
any whom it has not been possible to reach.

The University of Iowa Press is a member of Green Press Initiative
and is committed to preserving natural resources.

Printed on acid-free paper

Library of Congress Cataloging-in-Publication Data
Names: Wetzel, David N., author.
Title: The vanishing Messiah : the life and resurrections
of Francis Schlatter / David N. Wetzel.
Description: Iowa City : University of Iowa Press, 2016. |
Includes bibliographical references and index.
Identifiers: LCCN 2015033813 | ISBN 978-1-60938-423-4 (pbk) |
ISBN 978-1-60938-424-1 (ebk)
Subjects: LCSH: Schlatter, Francis, 1856-1896? | Healers—
United States—Biography. | Healers—United States—History.
Classification: LCC RZ232.S35 .W48 2016 | DDC 615.8/52—dc23
LC record available at http://lccn.loc.gov/2015033813

— To —
Richard

CONTENTS

Preface and Acknowledgments, ix

PROLOGUE
Where the Mirages Are Born, 1

———

PART ONE
The Life of the Harp: A Biography

ONE
The Denver Cobbler, 19

TWO
Pilgrimage, 35

THREE
The Desert Messiah, 51

FOUR
Healer of the Multitudes, 67

FIVE
"Father takes me away," 91

SIX
Winter Retreat, 105

———

INTERREGNUM
Into Mexico, 119

———

PART TWO
The Hand of the Harper: A Biographical Quest

SEVEN
"These men were imposters," 133

EIGHT
"Look at my face," 149

NINE
The Sparrow's Fall, 163

TEN
The Days of Daniel, 177

ELEVEN
"A True Account . . . ," 191

TWELVE
God's Leading, 205

EPILOGUE
Francis Schlatter Cyclus, 219

APPENDIX
The Evidence Trail, 223

Timeline, 231

Notes, 233

Survey of Prior Works, 265

Index, 271

PREFACE AND ACKNOWLEDGMENTS

MY INVESTIGATION into Francis Schlatter's known life and its shadowed legacy began in 1989 when the publications department at the Colorado Historical Society (known today as History Colorado) decided to publish an annotated collection of letters from the 1890s. One of the letters, written in October 1895, mentioned Francis Schlatter, and I asked my intern to research him for a footnote. I'd read about Schlatter years earlier in Gene Fowler's *Timber Line*, a highly literary rendering of Colorado's past, when I joined the historical society in 1980. The intern came back with a good description of Schlatter's healing ministry but ended it with the curious statement that the healer might have died in an insane asylum. I knew this didn't square with Fowler. But when I looked at *Timber Line* again, I realized that Fowler knew nothing of Schlatter's fate—and so covered his ignorance with an appealing metaphor.

I decided, at first, to find out what happened to Schlatter—and only that. But as my speculative pursuit of the healer's posthumous life went forward, I became aware of how dependent my research was on chance and contingency. The very next discovery might bring my work—of days, months, and years—to an abrupt end. My colleagues understood this, yet they offered unstinting help and advice at every step. In that respect, above all, I want to thank Mary Ann McNair, at once an advocate and loyal skeptic who never wavered in her generous support of the project; my wise colleague David Fridtjof Halaas; my astute detail warden, Clark Secrest; and my developmental editor, Larry Borowsky. Special thanks also goes to Rick Manzanares, who accompanied me to Mexico in 1998 and has remained a valued adviser. Other friends and colleagues who read parts of the manuscript, exchanged ideas, or offered help are David von Drehle, Luther Wilson, Stephen J. Leonard, Judith Gamble, Richard Kreck, Joe Roberts, Katherine Kane, Joe Dean, Peg Ekstrand, Steve Grinstead, Modupe Labode, Paul D. Mitchell, Kate LaHue, Faye Christensen, and Kate Meadows, whose writer's salon group in Kansas City gave me valuable commentary. My immediate family members, especially my brother, Jim, and my son, Richard, gave support and advice. And I would be remiss without acknowledging, posthumously, the enduring support of my wife, Jodi, and friend Calvin C. Clawson.

Researchers with whom I exchanged information about Francis Schlatter's life are Tim Blevins, head of special collections in the Pikes Peak Library District; author Conger Beasley Jr.; author Gil Alonso-Mier and his assistant Jean-Philippe Marie dit Moisson; researcher and author G. Weston DeWalt; and translator Emily Ivanova.

Many people assisted me in the wide-ranging but essential work of research, which encompassed finding sources, giving advice, and suggesting avenues of investigation. They are: Mme. Jose Ries in France; Helen Cleaveland, Jim Clayson, Shirley Fredricks, and Chris Potter in England; John L. Hatch and Rubén Beltrán Acosta in Mexico; Pat Norris, Beverly Coss, Ann Goodpasture, Donna Miner, and Katharyn Wunderley in the Midwest; Kelly Gatlin, Marla Riley, Jake Snyder, and M. Susan Barger in New Mexico; and Irene Quinn and Roger A. Stedman in Colorado. Special thanks to Susan Brookman, who spent hours researching newspapers in Santa Fe, and Norene Roberts, who did the same at Smith College in Northampton, Massachusetts. Ralph Juhnke in Kansas City graciously offered his services as photographer.

Initial funding for this project came from a 1992 travel grant from the Colorado Endowment for the Humanities (CEH), which allowed me to visit, among other places, Good Samaritan Hospital in Cincinnati. There, with the assistance of staff in the medical records office, I uncovered a pivotal document in my investigation, the hospital's patient record book for 1896. Incidentally, although my visit predated today's federal Health Insurance Portability and Accountability Act (HIPAA) privacy laws, the hospital acted in accordance with HIPAA's provision that historians and biographers be allowed to view the records of patients who died more than a half-century earlier.

That 1992 research trip to historical societies and repositories around the Midwest and into the South included the Chicago Historical Society, Ohio Historical Society, Indiana Historical Society, Tennessee State Library and Archives, Maury County (Tennessee)

Library and Archives, Alabama Department of Archives and History, State Historical Society of Missouri, and St. Louis Mercantile Library. Later I expanded my search in repositories such as the Center for Southwest Research at the University of New Mexico, New York Public Library, New York City Municipal Archives, Philadelphia City Archives, and the Miamisburg and Canton, Ohio, public libraries. I could not have done this work, however, without visits to the Library of Congress in Washington and the National Archives and Records Administration (NARA) in Washington, D.C., Denver, and Kansas City.

The greatest bulk of information and assistance, however, has come from the Western History Department of the Denver Public Library, including current and former staff members Coi Gehrig, Brian Trembath, Bruce Hanson, and Phil Panum, and current or past staff members in the Stephen H. Hart Library of the Colorado Historical Society (History Colorado): Patrick Fraker, Rebecca Lintz, Barbara Dey, Karyl Klein, Jay DiLorenzo, and Michael Wren. This book could not begin — or end, as it does, of course — without a special appreciation for the Museum of New Mexico in Santa Fe, and to Diana DeSantis and Orlando Romero.

William Keel in the Department of Germanic Languages at the University of Kansas generously offered his time and expertise in examining language patterns in *Modern Miracles of Healing*, as did Rudi Hartmann, a native speaker of German and professor of geography at the University of Colorado–Denver, and Ellen Quinlan of Denver. I also thank the forensic experts identified and discussed in the appendix: Robert Pickering, formerly of the Colorado Museum of Nature and Science; Barry Bullard, formerly of the Institute for Forensic Imaging; forensic artist Stephen Mancusi; and Robert M. George of Florida International University. My deepest appreciation, however, goes to the late Michael Charney of Colorado State University, who undertook this project freely and energetically — and gave me reason to pursue it early on.

The efforts of all these friends and advisors would have amounted to nothing, however, had I not found a publisher willing to entertain a "footnote" historical figure, as the second *People's Almanac* categorized Francis Schlatter in 1978. The University of Iowa Press, under the direction of Jim McCoy, has given the healer a congenial home —

and me the comfort of knowing the project was in good hands. I especially want to thank two people among them: acquisitions editor Elisabeth Chretien, who saw merit in an unconventional approach to the traditional domain of historical biography, and managing editor Susan Hill Newton, who shepherded the book through production, including enlisting the exceptional skills of editor Bob Burchfield and designer April Leidig.

Finally, I want to express my gratitude to the institutions that nurtured me — the University of Utah, where I learned the craft of writing, and the University of Minnesota, where I found in the American studies program a subject on which to write, guided and inspired by my mentors: Mary C. Turpie, Mulford Q. Sibley, and David W. Noble.

THE VANISHING MESSIAH

Where the Mirages Are Born

— 1895 —

O
N NOVEMBER 13, 1895, a normally quiet and subdued neighborhood of Denver played host to a bustling scene, as thousands of people from across the region patiently waited in line
to be touched by a renowned healer. Every day for the past two
months, Francis Schlatter, a former cobbler and Alsatian immigrant,
had laid his hands on multitudes of people, performing astounding
feats of healing by his very touch. By mid-November his fame had
spread across the country, and trainloads of the sick and injured
poured into Denver, seeking a treatment or cure from this Christ-like
figure. On this particular day, the healer placed his hands on some
five thousand people who walked by a small cottage where he stood
behind a picket fence. A double line passed down the street, turned
the corner, passed along another street, and then turned another
corner. From there it disappeared from view.

This, as it happened, was Francis Schlatter's last day in Denver
—and the end of his brief, sensational career as the New Mexico
Messiah, or simply the Messiah. But nobody who stood in the long
lines, or among the milling crowd of observers, had any idea he
would be gone before midnight. A photographer, William White,
caught the afternoon scene and later captioned his photograph
"Francis Schlatter—Last Hour Treating in Denver." But White had
no foreknowledge of the event that would forever mark the healer's
legacy.

The next morning, at sunrise, as the smell of fresh coffee and rolls
drifted from the vendors' tents, pilgrims who had camped overnight
in the surrounding lots took their places in line. Soon others from
throughout the city joined them, and by six o'clock at least five hundred people waited for the day's healing sessions to start. Then, at

FIGURE I. Last photograph of Francis Schlatter's healing sessions
in Denver, taken a few hours before the healer disappeared on
November 13, 1895. Schlatter can be seen treating the crowd directly
above the carriage at the far left in the image. William A. White,
Library of Congress, LC-USZ62-105410.

about seven o'clock, a man emerged from the home in which the
healer was a guest. He silently handed the first person in line a note.
Others quickly gathered to read it, and cries and moans suddenly
broke the stillness of early morning; the healer had vanished in the
night, leaving behind just the note, and giving no indication of where
he had gone. As the news of the healer's disappearance passed down
the street and through the neighborhood, the disciplined and hopeful line disintegrated into swirls of betrayed sufferers who sobbed,
railed in anger, or simply shook their heads in disbelief.

The pandemonium increased and spread as newly arrived pilgrims, stepping off trolley cars that bore signs reading "This Car
for the Healer," learned that Schlatter was gone. A small crowd of
distraught pilgrims surged toward the picket fence where the healer
had stood, nearly trampling it, but were pulled back by cooler heads
and hands. Still, a few people managed to yank off a picket or two as
relics or keepsakes. Others momentarily laid handkerchiefs on the

fence and platform where the healer had stood to absorb his miraculous healing power. This was all they could take away from the place that had once been called the New Mount.[1]

News of the disappearance traveled back into the city from the little wooden cottage that had been Schlatter's home for two months. It sat on a tree-lined street in Highlands, an old upland suburb rising above the South Platte River west of downtown Denver. Some eighty thousand people had passed by the healer here since mid-September, and another twenty thousand or so had seen him before that in Albuquerque, where he had first appeared after emerging from the New Mexico desert. As the story went, two small boys had come across a man lying on top of a "black mountain"—Tomé Hill—a few miles south of Albuquerque, his hands raised to the sky.[2] Frightened, they ran back to their home in Tomé, and he followed them into the village. From there he wandered from town to town along the Rio Grande, and his reputation as a *curandero*—a healer—spread rapidly.

But Schlatter was more than a healer. With his long, shoulder-length hair, rich beard, and clear blue eyes, he evoked the image of Jesus Christ. More than that, his humility, generosity, and temperament embodied all the virtues of Christ, and he asked for nothing in return for his healing work. "I have no use for money," he said. When someone insisted on paying him, Schlatter quickly turned the coins over to a poor bystander.[3] It was said that he brought back a small child from death twice, only to lose the child a third time.[4]

Schlatter treated everyone—no matter their race, nationality, or station in life. He took no credit for healing them, for it was the Father, the word he always used for God, who did so. Nor did he ask for a confession of faith or doctrinal creed, only that sufferers believe that the Father would heal them. But he acknowledged being the divine instrument through which they were healed, and when anyone asked him if he were the Christ, Schlatter said "Yes."[5]

By the time he began healing in Denver, in mid-September 1895, his fame had traveled across the country, buoyed by curious reporters whose news stories reverberated along the wire services. Mail poured into the post office, and Schlatter tried to answer every letter—for he believed that anything he touched would have the same healing effect as his own hands upon a sick or suffering pilgrim. When he touched each person who stood before him, he raised his head and said, "Thank you, Father." He took each person by the hands and squeezed tightly, even small children—who never cried out in pain.[6]

Every day Schlatter stood behind the picket fence, bareheaded in the sun or rain, and treated the line of sufferers while bystanders filled the street, standing among carriages in which the infirm or disabled waited for the healer to visit them at the day's end. Vendors set up tents here and there to sell sandwiches, popcorn, watermelon, and lemonade. The scene was part carnival, part worship service, but overall a sense of quiet expectation and hope filled the air.

As October passed into November, the crowd numbers grew. The healing sessions would not last forever, and there were rumors that Schlatter would take his ministry to Chicago on November 16. Newspapers repeated the date of his scheduled departure, and trains brought hundreds of anxious pilgrims into Denver from around the West and Midwest. The healer spent less time with each person— down from a half a minute to just a few seconds. The ministry seemed to be building to a crescendo, for many who had scraped money to come to Denver did so because Chicago was out of the question.

And then he was suddenly gone.

Twenty-four hours after William White took his photograph, the scene was one of desolation. It looked like a field that lay barren of everything but the scattered remnants of crowds after carnival tents had been removed. Newspapers across the country, notified immediately through the wire services, carried stories of the healer's disappearance and the pathetic scenes of grief and disappointment that followed it when he failed to appear at his usual place. "From that time on," *Denver Post* reporter Joseph Emerson Smith recalled years later, "he totally disappeared. Every now and then a report from some distant isolated point told of his passage and was published, to be immediately discounted."[7]

A half-century after Schlatter's disappearance, almost nothing remained of his legacy. Healers appeared from time to time, some with Rasputin-like beards and others with black robes and amulets, all calling themselves Francis Schlatter. But they were widely dismissed as imposters, set apart by their very pretensions from the simple humility and charisma of the New Mexico Messiah. Meanwhile, the collective memory of Denver's great healer faded into what Gene

Fowler, another former *Denver Post* reporter, called "old men's legends." Fowler knew only that the healer had ridden off on a white horse, making an appearance here and there before vanishing "as though taken to the skies above the Bad Lands, where the mirages are born."[8]

Indeed, by 1945, fifty years after his disappearance, one of the most sensational healers of the nineteenth century was all but forgotten. And no wonder. In that time the world had undergone remarkable change — from the birth of the automobile to airplanes, steel-girded skyscrapers, motion pictures, psychoanalysis, jazz, Einstein and Freud, insulin and penicillin, and two horrendous world wars. Yet at the end of World War II, so far removed from the height of Schlatter's great fame, two New Mexicans whose lives he had indirectly touched met in Santa Fe to share their mutual interest in him.

One party to the meeting was Agnes Morley Cleaveland, author of *No Life for a Lady*, a vivid memoir detailing a young girl's coming of age on the New Mexico frontier, which brushed the best-seller lists in 1941. In it was a chapter entitled "The Healer Comes to Datil," a brief account of Schlatter's three-month retreat on the family's isolated ranch after his dramatic disappearance from Denver. Agnes Cleaveland's host in Santa Fe was Edgar Lee Hewett, the director of the Museum of New Mexico, which was situated in the Palace of the Governors. Hewett had very recently published *Campfire and Trail*, a memoir of his life as both a teacher and archaeologist. One of its chapters, entitled "The Copper Rod," offered the first solid account of Schlatter's death for a generation of readers otherwise ignorant of his fate.[9] Joining the two writers was Cleaveland's son, Norman, who had served during the war in the Army Air Corps.[10] What brought them together was undoubtedly related to Francis Schlatter, the final months of his life on the Morley ranch, and his untimely death.

Agnes Cleaveland, born Agnes Morley in New Mexico Territory in 1874, was the eldest child of William and Ada Morley. Her father, a celebrated planning engineer for the Atchison, Topeka & Santa Fe, lost his life in a shotgun accident when Agnes was nine. A year later, in 1883, her mother married Floyd Jarrett, who persuaded her to invest in a cattle ranch and build a substantial two-story log home that became an oasis of culture in the isolated village of Datil, New Mexico, 150 miles southwest of Albuquerque. Then, after a year or two, he abandoned the family, taking a good deal of Ada's wealth and leaving her to bring up three small children.[11] She held on to what she could financially and kept the ranch going.

Thus Ada's daughter Agnes and her younger siblings, Raymond and Loraine, came of age living in two different worlds that embraced both the lessons taught in eastern boarding schools and the hard realities of the frontier West—the vast distances, the isolation, the rough-and-tumble cowboy life, and the unpredictability of weather, animals, and passing strangers. Some of her most memorable tales in *No Life for a Lady* were of eccentric visitors, including a few outlaws and one silent, fearsome-looking cowboy who asked to use the piano, then played exquisitely before thanking her mother and quietly walking away.

But the most unusual visitor by far was the healer Francis Schlatter, who arrived on a cold night in early January 1896, shortly after Agnes had left for college at Stanford. The healer appeared without warning at Ada's front door, led by one of the ranch hands, and asked to come inside. She didn't hesitate, for she knew him by sight. She had gone to Denver in the previous fall expressly to see the healer—to stand in line for hours just to receive his touch.

Ada was baffled to know how Schlatter had found his way to her ranch—across formidable mesa country in deep snow. All he said was, "The Father has directed me to a safe retreat. I must restore my spiritual powers in seclusion and prayer."[12] The healer stayed there for the next three months, and when not engaged in wide-ranging discussions with Morley about the state of the world, he remained alone in his upstairs room swinging a heavy copper rod shaped like a baseball bat. The rod, he said, was necessary to maintain his spiritual strength.

Over time, observing the purity of Schlatter's mind and character, Ada Morley abandoned her well-constructed belief in New Thought—the idea that God was spirit, love, and will—and came to accept Schlatter's personal connection with the Father, the living God of the Bible, whose voice spoke to him continuously. She proposed publishing a book on his life and divine mission. He agreed— and even offered the title: *The Life of the Harp in the Hand of the Harper.*

Meanwhile, he said, the Father had commanded him to go into Old Mexico, to await a divine summons. Then he gave Ada a prophetic hint of what was to come. As Agnes told it, he said: "You will have what will seem to be certain evidence of my death brought to you. The world will laugh at you for rejecting—but reject it! I shall not be dead. I will return to Datil. The Father has told me that Datil is the place He has selected for New Jerusalem. Wait for me."[13]

Ada Morley did wait—for nearly twenty years. When someone showed her a newspaper clipping that told of a skeleton found under a tree in Chihuahua, along with a strange copper rod and a Bible with Schlatter's name on the flyleaf, she didn't believe it. "He told me to expect this," she said to Agnes. "He is not dead. He will return."[14]

He never did.

In 1945, sitting with Edgar Hewett at the Museum of New Mexico, Agnes Cleaveland knew why. Between them lay Schlatter's copper rod, an artifact that almost single-handedly confirmed the healer's fate in spite of his promise to Agnes's mother. The rod would have perhaps remained lost forever if Edgar Hewett, a college president–turned–archaeologist, hadn't come across it in Mexico by chance in 1906—as he also did Francis Schlatter's unmarked grave.

"Under a lone pine tree on the eastern slope of the Sierra Madre in Chihuahua," Hewett wrote in *Campfire and Trail*, "a few yards west of the Piedras Verdes river, there is an unmarked grave which, if known a generation ago, would have been a shrine to thousands."[15] At the time, Hewett was conducting archaeological fieldwork in northern Mexico. One day his Mexican guide halted his horse at a spot near the village of Casas Grandes. Here, the guide said, he had come across the body of a dead man ten years earlier. It was in the middle of winter, and very cold. The guide, just a boy then, thought the man had frozen to death. A large white horse stood hobbled nearby. The boy ran down to notify the village. An inquest party came and buried the body on the spot.

As the guide told his story, Hewett listened politely, then became more interested with each detail. He asked a few questions—about the man's appearance, his possessions, and the horse. He was a large man, the guide said, with a beard and long black hair. The boy also saw some of the man's possessions—a fine western saddle, a Bible, and a copper rod, shaped like a baseball bat, inside a leather holster.

By the time the guide had finished his story, Hewett suspected who was buried there. In 1895, while a student in Colorado's Normal School in Greeley, Hewett became intrigued by newspaper accounts of Schlatter's healing sessions. Occasionally Hewett rode the train to

Denver to observe the healer at work. He was fascinated by the cures Schlatter produced. "I have never tried to explain it," he wrote in *Campfire and Trail,* "couldn't if I tried. I can only say it was the most astonishing thing of its kind that has ever come to my notice."[16]

Hewett asked his guide if any of the objects remained. Yes, the guide said. He took Hewett to see the *jefe politico,* the town's mayor, who willingly showed the archaeologist the Bible, saddle, and copper rod that Hewett's guide had mentioned. The Bible bore the name of Francis Schlatter on its flyleaf, the saddle carried the mark of a Denver manufacturer, and the copper rod testified unequivocally to the healer's identity. Hewett's chain of evidence was complete.

However, after examining the objects, Hewett decided to keep the entire episode a secret. In 1906, even though a decade had passed since his disappearance, Schlatter's image as a Christlike healer still resonated with former pilgrims and disciples. Hewett didn't want the healer's copper rod turned into a sacred relic, his unmarked grave dressed up as a shrine, or Casas Grandes turned into another Lourdes, its picturesque streets crowded with cure-seeking pilgrims. So he merely thanked the *jefe* and left. That night he wrote up the episode in his book of "campfire notes" and went on with his archaeological research.

Sixteen years passed. By now Hewett had become a well-known southwestern archaeologist and teacher. He traveled widely throughout the Southwest, conducting excavations and training a generation of leading American archaeologists. In 1922 his investigative work took him back to northern Mexico, and he decided to look up the *jefe politico.* He found him at home, he said, and the old man remembered their earlier visit. Hewett asked the *jefe* if anything remained of the healer's effects. No, the man said. The saddle was worn out, and the Bible had long since disappeared. "But ah, *si! The copper rod!*" He brought it out from a back room for Hewett to examine again.

The rod looked the same as it had before. "My interest was restrained," Hewett wrote, "but obvious."[17] The rod was a significant historical artifact, and Hewett obviously wanted it for his collection. But he decided not to offer the *jefe* money for it. Instead, as he was leaving, he asked if there was anything he could do for the town. Yes, the man replied. They needed a schoolteacher for the fall. Hewett immediately wrote out a check to bring one up from Chihuahua.

Months later a heavy package arrived at the archaeologist's home in Santa Fe, wrapped in gunny sacks and tied with string. Its return address was hidden in a fold, and Hewett had no idea what it might be. But when he unwrapped it, he was bowled over. Here, on his desk, lay the copper rod of the healer Francis Schlatter, an unexpected gift from the *jefe* of Casas Grandes.

Hewett quietly placed the rod in the collections of the School of American Research, which shared space with the Museum of New Mexico in Santa Fe's Palace of the Governors. There it remained in obscurity until he published *Campfire and Trail* twenty-one years later, confident that the memory of Francis Schlatter had faded to the point where it would be safe to resurrect the healer's mysterious relic.

The 1945 meeting between Hewett and Agnes Cleaveland at the Palace of the Governors marked an important shift in Francis Schlatter's legacy. As Hewett showed the seventy-one-year-old Cleaveland and her son, Norman, the copper rod, he told them of his need to keep its existence a secret. "It was feared," Norman wrote years later, "that Schlatter's disciples might make difficulties for anyone known to be in the possession of the Healer's rod."[18] But, undoubtedly, Hewett also wanted to keep the rod unknown to imposters who had exploited Schlatter's name and reputation in the early decades after his disappearance and rumored death.

Cleaveland's and Hewett's accounts of the healer's last months bore an even greater effect on his legacy in the decades following 1945. Together they satisfied at least two generations of authors, scholars, and researchers that Francis Schlatter had died peacefully in northern Mexico in 1896 and lay in an unknown grave near the Piedras Verde River. Thus it's remarkable that no one in all that time became puzzled over the contradiction between the two admittedly secondhand accounts—Agnes Cleaveland's of a skeleton under a tree and Edgar Hewett's of a freshly dead body on a riverbank.

— 1990 —

The Palace of the Governors sits on the north side of Santa Fe's main plaza, a centuries-old anchor to the changing commercial life of the square. Its broad portal, supported by a colonnade of wooden posts, offers shade in most seasons to scores of Indian artisans who sell their jewelry, pottery, and textiles to passing tourists. On the building's upper face protruding vigas cast narrow sundial shadows across the white stucco facade. In the semidarkness of the porch below, red- and green-painted doors and windows accent the building's block-long expanse. Built in 1610, the palace has undergone several face-lifts—most recently in the early twentieth century, at the behest of Edgar Lee Hewett. Instead of an old Territorial porch with Spanish-style posts, he wanted it to feel as timeless as the earthen pueblos scattered around Santa Fe.

As I approached the palace, walking through the plaza on an early afternoon in May, the building's simple architecture struck me as both dignified and welcoming, so unlike the austere neoclassicism of most American government structures. It no longer functioned as New Mexico's seat of power, but it still served in an official capacity as the state's museum. It was here that Hewett kept his office for some three decades as director of both the School of American Research, which was dedicated to advancing southwestern archaeology, and the Museum of New Mexico. I would have liked to explore the museum, and its exhibits. But I was there for one thing only—to see the healer's copper rod.

I entered through the east side of the building, off Washington Street, where stately wooden double doors led to the museum's library. Light from high windows bathed the room, and a few researchers sat at four long study tables. I told the librarian who I was, and he called the museum's curator of history, Diana DeSantis, who showed up a few minutes later. DeSantis took me into the back hall and down a staircase to the museum's basement. We entered a spotless conservation lab, where she had arranged some of the museum's artifacts relating to Schlatter, mostly pictures. Then she said, "Would you like to see the copper rod?"

"Yes, very much," I said.

DeSantis unlocked a door to a large storage room lined on both sides with sturdy shelving. At first glance, the room looked like a home for unclaimed objects. Museum curators, I knew, preferred to keep like with like—and here, as we passed along the shelves, was a hodgepodge of textiles, pieces of furniture, albums, framed pictures, and a few *santos* and *retablos*. I figured the storage room was little more than a holding cell for artifacts waiting to be cataloged or conserved before finding a proper home—except for the copper rod. It struck me, when I saw it, as a permanent orphan.

The rod sat at the front of a chest-high shelf, apart from the other objects, as if abandoned. I approached it with a temerity that surprised me, and studied it for a few minutes, hovering over it. I noticed many scrapes and scratches along its surface, some long and deep, and a distinctive bend in the middle, as if it had been slammed hard against a tree. At its narrow end was a series of raised ridges that formed a handgrip, and a weathered leather strap fit neatly into a custom-made rectangular hole in the bottom. The rod widened gradually from that point, like a baseball bat. Its top had a strange depression, as if molten copper had collapsed into a fissure when the rod was cast.

"You can lift it, if you'd like," DeSantis said encouragingly. "But be careful—it's heavy."

I hesitated. I'd come to see the rod, for sure. But I hadn't actually thought about holding it in my hands. I almost declined—but knew I'd always regret not touching an object that Schlatter had held. Not only that, the rod was a huge mystery. Clearly the healer intended it for some purpose—no doubt a spiritual one—and I believed that the rod held some kind of clue to the mystery of his life.

Slowly I took the handle in my right hand and rolled the rod across the shelf, letting it fall into my left. That was a mistake, for its weight almost took my hand to the floor. With exertion, I kept it in the air, and slowly grew confident that I wouldn't drop it.

"My God, it *is* heavy," I said.

"Believe it or not," DeSantis said, "it only weighs thirty pounds."

"Thirty pounds of copper," I said, raising and lowering it gingerly. "I can't believe that the healer tossed this around like a piece of wood."

She smiled.

It suddenly occurred to me that I hadn't come with any questions about the rod, and I began to feel ridiculous just holding it in my hands. Gently, but with some effort, I replaced it on the shelf—and felt relief. For several minutes my hands seemed lighter and more buoyant released from their burden.

One question—or thought, rather—did come to mind right then. But it would have been disrespectful to express it, especially

FIGURE 2. Francis Schlatter's copper rod. As the
most mysterious object associated with the healer, the copper
rod was long believed to have had spiritual properties.
Arthur Taylor, courtesy Palace of the Governors
Photo Archives (NMHM/DCA), 67152.

at that moment. A month or two earlier, when I first began my research on Schlatter, DeSantis had steered me to Agnes Cleaveland's
and Edgar Hewett's accounts. Now, as I stood only inches from the
healer's copper rod, I realized that Edgar Hewett's venerable story
was a piece of fiction. There had been no body, no hobbled horse,
and the boy hadn't run down to tell the townspeople of his discovery.
There was no unmarked grave on the banks of the Piedras Verde
River. No—other than the fact that Hewett undoubtedly saw and
examined the healer's possessions, all of it had been a product of his
skill as a raconteur—a campfire tale.[19] He had wrapped his story
around the copper rod just as the *jefe* had done with burlap, hiding
its mystery within.

   As I made my way back across Santa Fe's plaza, I marveled at
how suddenly my understanding of things had changed—including
Hewett's story. At the nearby New Mexico State Library that morn-

ing, by sheer accident, I'd found the earliest reliable account of the discovery of Schlatter's remains. It had appeared in the *El Paso Times* of June 6, 1897—and, so far as I knew, no one in the past fifty years or more had come across it.

The account went like this.

On May 28, 1897, four El Paso prospectors riding up Tinaja Canyon in the Sierra Madre met a rider on his way down. He was a Mormon cowboy named McGren, and he likely belonged to one of the polygamist colonies in northern Mexico that eluded federal prosecution in the States. He was on his way to report a death. While out on the range, he'd spotted a saddle and gear hanging from the limb of a tree. As he rode closer, he said, he realized that it was some kind of camp, and then he saw a human skeleton under the tree. He offered to take the prospectors there.

What they found when they arrived was remarkable—something like a physician's anatomical skeleton laid to rest. It sat on a rotten blanket with its spine reclining against the trunk of the tree. A bony right arm fell across its chest, and the right knee was raised as if the man, before he died, had propped up his leg before falling asleep.

Straddling the limb of the tree was a new Denver-made saddle, a bridle and rope, and a white felt hat, all protected by a slicker. On the ground, next to the trunk, lay saddlebags, a pile of clothing secured with some books, a bunch of letters bound with a rubber band, and a canteen half filled with water. The prospectors found a Bible containing an inscription to Francis Schlatter from a Denver friend, Clarence Clark, and a Spanish-English dictionary bore the phrase "Con complimente, su amiga, Ada Morley Jarrett. Datil, N.M., 3-24-96."[20]

The four men immediately recognized the identity of the dead man, for Schlatter's name was widely known throughout the Southwest. Not only that, his famous copper rod lay next to the skeleton. Otherwise, there was no sign of violence, struggle, or unusual cause of death. The scene looked peaceful. The healer's horse had apparently wandered away.

While the prospectors loaded the man's belongings onto their pack horses, McGren burned the blanket and dug a shallow grave. Then they buried the skeleton, marked the site, and descended the canyon. Following the Piedras Verde River, they made their way to Casas Grandes, fifteen miles and a good day's ride away.

When they arrived in the village, the prospectors met with the *jefe político*. He might have known them, for one of the men, Richard Caples, had been mayor of El Paso and a veteran gold prospector in Mexico. The *jefe* took charge of the healer's effects and had them photographed at a local studio, Sexton and Faine's. The prospectors purchased a print of the photograph to carry back to El Paso. It would serve as proof of the healer's identity. But the men were in no hurry to return. For one thing, they wanted to learn the cause of death — though lightning strike or starvation seemed the best possibilities — and they questioned some of the villagers.

Eventually, the prospectors found another Mormon cowboy who turned out to be an important eyewitness. The previous November, he said, he'd come across a long-haired man riding a white horse in the vicinity of Casas Grandes. Later, from a distance, he saw the same man sleeping beneath a tree, his horse grazing nearby. Not wanting to disturb him, the cowboy rode on, but he later recognized the man's horse in an Indian village.

The account in the *El Paso Times* was straightforward and factual, the information reported by reliable eyewitnesses — all of them known residents of El Paso.[21] Nevertheless, it contained a curious — one would even say astounding — coincidence. Both the second cowboy and McGren bracketed the circumstances of the man's death: one was there shortly before it occurred — if the man had died of a lightning strike, that is — and the other had discovered the remains. It was as if each of them was corroborating the factual reality of the other.

But the factual reality, I suddenly realized, was suspect in itself.

How could anyone who died in the wild, and whose body was left to the ravages of nature, leave behind a pristine, untouched skeleton — with one arm peacefully resting on a rib cage, with one knee casually upraised, lying on a blanket, and surrounded by objects neatly arranged and undisturbed? As far as I knew, complete skeletons are rarely found in the wild. Coyotes, wolves, and buzzards get to them quickly — or any carnivorous animal drawn by the scent of death. In the frenzy of feeding, the pile of clothing and books next to the man's body would have been scattered here and there — as would his clothing, flesh, and bones.

Among several possibilities that came to mind, the most compelling one pointed to a conspiracy — at least between the two cowboys.

But not a conspiracy of murder. The improbability that a decomposing body would end up as a pristine articulated skeleton suggested just the opposite. It looked, instead, like a conspiracy to prove that a death had taken place there when it hadn't.

Could Schlatter have arranged to have his death staged? If so, how? The most reasonable explanation, it seemed to me, would be that the cowboys removed a desiccated skeleton from an old grave, probably from a local cemetery. Then they could have placed Schlatter's effects neatly around it at the top of Tinaja Canyon. The area was remote but accessible to the two cowboys, who wandered that range, and McGren could select the timing of his "discovery" when a party of prospectors or others came along.

Suppose I was wrong. Suppose that by some freak of nature the wolves and coyotes were not prowling the Sierra Madre that season. Suppose the two Mormon cowboys actually did find themselves at that lonely spot, months apart, purely by chance. Suppose Schlatter had fallen victim to a lightning strike, or even starved himself to death, believing that God would raise him up to establish New Jerusalem, only to have deceived himself, or met an untimely fate, and his bones left moldering atop Tinaja Canyon. What then?

If death somehow overtook Francis Schlatter in Mexico, that would have been a shame, not only for Ada Morley but for the unanswered questions of history. But if he had walked out of Mexico leaving the evidence of his death behind him, that was a mystery worth pursuing. If he *did* live on, not simply to go into oblivion but for some larger purpose, I was sure the clues to his motives—if I ever found him—would lay buried in the facts of his known life.

PART ONE

THE LIFE

of

THE HARP

A Biography

CHAPTER ONE

The Denver Cobbler

Father was preparing me for what was to come.
But I had the power to heal before I left Denver.[1]

FRANCIS SCHLATTER

FRANCIS SCHLATTER arrived in Denver for the first time on September 19, 1892—by railroad, perhaps, but more likely on foot.[2] He was a simple cobbler, and he was broke. All the money he had invested in Colorado silver mines was gone, and he made his way to the first person who could help him, Albert S. Whitaker. He brought with him a letter of introduction from Marcus M. "Brick" Pomeroy, Whitaker's boss and the president of the Atlantic-Pacific Railway Tunnel Company.[3]

Pomeroy, a wealthy New York newspaper owner turned mining speculator, was the first entrepreneur to attempt digging a railroad tunnel through the Rocky Mountains. The proposed twenty-five thousand–foot tunnel, forty feet wide and twenty feet high, would allow standard-gauge trains to take passengers directly through the Rockies, while at the same time opening up rich silver veins deep inside Gray's Peak west of Denver. For nearly twelve years the company had been selling stocks and buying up mining properties for cash to support the tunnel's excavation. By the time Francis Schlatter invested his savings in Pomeroy's project, only a fifth of the five-mile-long tunnel had been completed, and its bore was no bigger than eight to ten feet.

All construction ceased with the silver crash of 1893, and "Pomeroy's folly," as the tunnel was known, ended with his death in 1896. But though he had offered false hope to Francis Schlatter and thousands of investors like him, he was a central figure in the cobbler's decision to come west—and not simply to gain wealth and fortune. Pomeroy gave Schlatter another reason to head for Denver in par-

ticular, for the city was the center of spiritualist activity throughout
the Rocky Mountain West.

The belief in spiritualism, which both Francis Schlatter, a modest
tradesman, and the wealthy mining magnate Brick Pomeroy discussed and shared, had its American origins in a series of mysterious
rappings that occurred on March 31, 1848, in Hydesville, New York.[4]
Sisters Kate and Margaret Fox heard strange noises in their upstairs
bedroom that turned out to be messages from the spirit of a murdered peddler. That's what they claimed, at any rate, and further
rappings led to a wildfire of interest in the Fox girls and in "spirit-
ism," or spiritualism.

In spite of accusations of fraud throughout its formative years,
the spiritualist movement expanded rapidly over the next few decades and evolved beyond the crude communication of rapping into
conversations with spirits of the departed through mediums, hypno-
tism, and séances. It quickly found its metaphysical underpinnings
in the work of Emanuel Swedenborg, an eighteenth-century Swedish
thinker who proposed an afterlife consisting of stages of spiritual development rather than a static vision of heaven and hell, and in the
American thinker Alexander Jackson Davis. By the time Schlatter
came to it, spiritualism had begun to generate considerable speculation about the human personality, spirit, and soul after death.

How and why—or when—Schlatter took an interest in spiritualism is unknown. But how he came to meet Brick Pomeroy is less
problematic. As a highly skilled cobbler, he frequently made shoes
for wealthy businessmen. Pomeroy, who kept a sixty-five thousand-
dollar mansion in Denver, established his home and main office in
New York in 1890 or 1891, and the two probably met at that time.
Besides, Pomeroy was no snob. In spite of his wealth and influence,
he was a liberal Democrat and a champion of the underdog, unpretentious, and generous to a fault. He had been a national leader in
support of the Greenback movement, a cause Schlatter supported
because it favored laborers. Pomeroy's newspaper, *Pomeroy's Advance
Thought*, championed the economic interests of the common man.

However, Francis Schlatter was no common man—as he would
later demonstrate. Coming to America in 1884, he spent a few years
in obscurity, his place of residence and activities largely unknown.[5]
But in the late 1880s he appeared in Jamesport, Long Island, and
established himself as a shoemaker in "Aunt" Sally Corbin's board-

inghouse on the main road through town.[6] Already he had gained a reputation for his work. A doctor named Lawton in New York City employed him to produce custom-made shoes from leather and soles, which the doctor sent to Jamesport, and Schlatter made about fifteen dollars a week—a healthy income that he saved through his frugality and simple lifestyle.

After a while he met William Ryan, about four years younger than he, who worked on the *Annie Wilcox* and later the *Cora P. White*, fishing boats operating out of nearby Greenport. Ryan convinced his friend to give up shoemaking and serve as a fireman's assistant on the latter boat—and Schlatter did. He also left Sally Corbin's home and began boarding with the Ryan family—including Ryan's parents, three brothers, and six sisters. The family was happy to have him—father Thomas said he always paid his board on time—and neighbors and friends liked him even if he struck them as a bit strange. For one thing, he studied to distraction, holing himself up in his room at night to pursue one subject or another—and always English grammar and pronunciation. A friend of the family said, "He knew a lot, and he talked just like a book."[7]

For a few months, life seemed idyllic. Schlatter joined the family in most of their activities. He attended the Congregationalist and Methodist churches with them in Jamesport, but sometimes walked six miles to the Catholic church in Riverhead. For relaxation, he played croquet with the Ryan girls—and Mary, the eldest, said he played "as though he was making his will."[8] The sisters delighted in teasing him. When they cheated, just for fun, he would get so upset that a denture would fall out, exposing a large gap in his upper teeth.

Aside from this flaw, he had a pleasant face and a neat, clean appearance. He had a thick mustache that narrowed at the ends, hazel blue eyes, and a long, narrow nose. He looked something like an accountant or bank teller—and, given his meticulous tidiness, he could have been one. Friends in Jamesport learned that he was engaged to a woman named Kate, who lived on Staten Island, and he received letters from her—the only ones he got, according to the postmaster. Then, after a few months, she left him. People said he took it hard, and he lost interest in women after that.

He soon received another shock—and much worse. William Ryan took ill, and his general health quickly deteriorated. Schlatter tried to help his friend, even buying a magnetic belt, a widely

FIGURE 3. Francis Schlatter as a cobbler in
Long Island, early 1890s. *Rocky Mountain News*
(Denver), November 15, 1895

advertised nostrum for various ailments. But it didn't help. William
died on June 29, 1889, and Schlatter moved out of the Ryan home.[9]
He took up lodging in a boardinghouse next to the railroad station
and returned to shoemaking. Ryan's death, and Schlatter's efforts to
stave it off, may have triggered his interest in healing—and it surely
deepened his interest in spiritualism. At the same time, he was beset
by vivid dreams of frustration and loss. "They were principally of
young women in white robes," a friend said. "His chief complaint
about the visions was that whenever he tried to touch the young
women they always vanished. This was a great discouragement to
him."[10]

    Within a few months, Schlatter abandoned Long Island alto-
gether. He moved to New York City and took up residence with
another cobbler at 96 Grove Street, near Greenwich Village. Here,
in July 1891, he petitioned for U.S. citizenship—but his petition curiously lacked entries for birth date, age, port of arrival, and date
of arrival. Furthermore, there is no record that he ever became a
naturalized citizen.[11]

At this time, too, he met Brick Pomeroy. Schlatter suddenly took an interest, his Jamesport friends said, in mining ventures out west. He had accumulated a good deal of money, and Pomeroy persuaded him to invest in various mining enterprises—and, of course, the Atlantic-Pacific Railway Tunnel Company. Schlatter leaped at the chance to invest his savings and get rich. Not one to do things half-heartedly, he also subscribed to mining journals and followed the stock market. His sudden capitalistic bent suggests that he was impulsive—and this would surely prove to be true a year later, when the loss of his savings turned him into a capitalist-hating Populist. But, for the moment, he assuaged his sense of loss with dreams of wealth, and he made plans to travel to Denver, a lively center of spiritualism, séances, and psychic experimentation in the West.

PASSENGERS EXITING Denver's Union Station in September 1892 beheld the city's prosperity like a beacon as they looked down Seventeenth Street. Straight ahead, on both the left and right sides, rose block after block of handsome, high-storied commercial buildings, all with commanding facades of sandstone, glass, brick, and terra-cotta trim. In the shadow of these stone-bound skyscrapers, pedestrians made their way along concrete sidewalks or crossed over the hard-packed earthen street watching for passing trolleys, bicycles, or horse-drawn wagons. This was Denver's Wall Street of the West, the largest business center between Chicago and San Francisco.

Schlatter walked a block or two from Union Station to Larimer Street. He stopped at the Railroad Building at 1515 Larimer, went inside, and entered the offices of the Atlantic-Pacific Railway Tunnel Company, where Albert Whitaker sat.[12] He carried a letter from Brick Pomeroy asking Whitaker to help him establish a shoemaking business in Denver. Whitaker, who was not only Pomeroy's business partner but his son-in-law, was willing to oblige. They soon found space in a home at 1845 Stout Street, a block or so from Seventeenth and not a bad place from which to cull trade from the businessmen and storekeepers in the city center.

The home belonged to two doctors, Luther J. Ingersoll and his wife, Mary, who lived next door at 1843 Stout.[13] Both were practi-

tioners of homeopathic medicine, and Luther had made a few dis-
coveries in homeopathic surgery, along with inventing several widely
used surgical instruments. Schlatter was naturally drawn toward
unconventional medicine, and he befriended the Ingersolls. Aside
from the traits that made him a good boarder—his neatness, sense
of responsibility, and industry—he was friendly and talkative, especially on the subject of healing. Before long, Mary Ingersoll became
aware of his deep belief in spiritual healing, but she didn't object to
it. After all, as a homeopathic physician she had felt the scorn of the
traditional medical establishment.

Luther, on the other hand, didn't share in their discussions, for he
was totally deaf—which somewhat curtailed his clinical and surgical practice, though not his inventiveness. As he had done with
William Ryan months earlier, Schlatter set out to correct Luther's
condition. He told Mary Ingersoll one day that he'd had a revelation
about her husband. The doctor's hearing, Schlatter said, would be
restored over time, but the healing would not begin for a year or
more—to be precise, on December 3, 1894.

If this surprised her—as it probably did—it was perhaps because
she wasn't aware that Schlatter had been reading, ruminating, and
experimenting on a theory he'd developed about the convergence of
healing and prophecy. This odd combination grew out of his spiritualist beliefs, for initially he communicated with spirits to learn about
his own future and the future of others. He soon began making
short-term predictions related to healing, complete with exact dates
on which cures would take place. When his predictions failed, as
they invariably did, he laid the blame on his own neophyte stage of
mental and spiritual development. In time, he told his disappointed
subjects, he would reach the fullness of his powers.

But while Schlatter sought to cure others by prophetic healing,
he applied more conventional methods to himself. When he first
met Mary Ingersoll, she saw how sallow and unhealthy his face
looked and noticed his hard, hacking cough. He was about 5 feet
9 inches, she estimated, but walked with a noticeable droop in his
shoulders, and he kept a heavy overcoat on all the time. In short,
he showed symptoms of tuberculosis. But after a few weeks in Denver he became stronger, healthier, and more energetic. Eventually
he discarded the overcoat. His recovery was not unusual for some
tuberculars—or "lungers," a name given the thousands who sought

a cure in Colorado's sunny climate and rarefied air. But Schlatter went even further. He bought a set of barbells to build up his strength and spent hours during his free time walking the hills west of Denver.[14]

Schlatter became well known in the spiritualist community and was a regular attendee at séances. But other believers acknowledged that he was on a much higher plane—more of a teacher and guide than a student. John W. Boucher, a spiritualist companion and fellow shoemaker, admired the depth of Schlatter's thought. "Suppose you should be standing by him and be talking on some subject," Boucher commented. "He would apparently pay no attention to what was said and then would start in with a remark showing much deeper thought and a greater command of the subject than you had dreamed."[15]

In spite of its paramount influence on his thinking, spiritualism was but one current swirling into the gathering mainstream of Schlatter's thought. As Mary Ingersoll noted, he was also deeply interested in predicting the future, and he had begun reading books on mental healing, along with general works on history, politics, and religion. But the rich assortment of contemporary ideas—spiritualism, theosophy, mental telepathy, psychic phenomena, numerology, and Christian Science—were useful to him only insofar as they complemented his abiding belief that God was directing his destiny.[16]

One formative metaphysical belief system was New Thought, a movement whose basic premise was that the mind—and its correlates, spirit and will—constituted the foundation of being. Within this huge philosophical tent, various avenues of thought flourished, from the theistic proposition that God is mind to its opposite, that mind is all. An exponent of the latter concept, and an atheist, was Helen Wilmans. Her *Blossom of the Century* appeared in 1893, shortly after Schlatter moved to Denver, and it had an enormous influence on him.

Wilmans's philosophy incorporated spiritualism into a grand scheme of the universe, but with a significant twist—for she denied the reality of death. In fact, she proposed that the real world itself was nothing but mind, and mind was the visible expression of a cosmic evolutionary principle she called the Law of Being. Matter, gravity, and death—elements and forces that inhibited the freedom-seeking human spirit—could be overcome by simply recognizing the Law of Being and how it permeated everything. Enlightened minds could thus transform matter—which was but mind—to their own ends.

Thus spiritual healing was merely a way of helping others recognize the latent power within them, and to realize that disease and death were merely chimeras.

In part, Wilmans's philosophy reflected Mary Baker Eddy's principles of Christian Science. Yet the Law of Being came with no religious overtones. It was sufficient unto itself as the engine of the universe. It could be called God, or not, as one wished. But Wilmans rejected the notion that God created man, and she held in contempt the idea that anyone would draw strength from a higher power. "No one who leans on a power outside of himself," she wrote, "can be anything but weak."[17]

In spite of its denial of God, Schlatter read and re-read *Blossom of the Century* and raved about it to almost anyone within earshot, including Mary Ingersoll, John Boucher, and a new acquaintance, former Leadville judge J. B. Stansell, who had come to the shop at 1845 Stout to have his shoes repaired. Stansell found himself drawn to Schlatter's ideas and returned often just to engage the cobbler in conversation. Several times he invited Schlatter to his room at the Albany Hotel at Seventeenth and Stout, less than two blocks from the cobbler's home, and lent him books from his library on spiritualism and faith cure. Though Schlatter was a man of "dense ignorance," Stansell thought, he had an inquiring mind and great enthusiasm for mental healing, especially within the framework of Helen Wilmans's philosophy.[18]

Schlatter's "dense ignorance"—as Stansell perceived it—might well have come from his difficulty with English and the simple, measured way in which he expressed himself. He never lost his Alsatian German accent, and his self-consciousness led to constant study of English grammar and rhetoric. But Stansell might also have been referring to the cobbler's childlike naïveté in matters of religion and faith. In the spring of 1893, shortly after the opening of the Chicago World's Fair in May, Schlatter told Stansell that he had a "deep impression"—a vision of sorts—that he must attend the World's Congress of Religions meeting there.[19]

Schlatter had no money for a railroad ticket, and Stansell naturally asked how he would make the trip. "I do not know," the cobbler replied, "but the Master tells me I must go, and he will provide a way. If I do not see you again at present, you will hear from me after a while, and I shall see you afterward under different circumstances."[20]

"But how are you going?" Stansell asked.

"The Master tells me to start on foot," Schlatter said, "and walk till I am so weary that I can go no farther, when I will fall asleep by the roadside, and during my unconsciousness I shall be wafted to Chicago without human aid or agency."

A few days later, without warning, Schlatter disappeared. Except for Stansell, no one had any idea what had happened to him. The little shop at 1845 Stout stood empty, just as he'd left it, and his friends grew increasingly puzzled and concerned over his absence. Then, about ten days later, he reappeared, telling everyone that he had gotten the urge to walk to Cheyenne. It was just one more instance of Schlatter's strange behavior that led them to call him—in spite of his likeability—the "crazy shoemaker."

When Stansell finally saw Schlatter again, the cobbler told him that he had indeed carried out his plan—walking during the day, sleeping at night, and hoping that he would be borne on nocturnal wings to Chicago. "I was so tired each night," he said, "that I could not possibly take another step."[21] Yet every morning when he woke up, he was exactly where he'd fallen asleep the night before. Discouraged, he would have abandoned the journey several times had the Master not continued to whisper words of encouragement. He managed to make it nearly to Cheyenne, then realized the effort was futile, turned around, and walked the hundred or so miles back to Denver.

Stansell asked him how he felt about the Master's betrayal of his promise.

"It must be that I am not cleansed and purified enough yet," Schlatter said, without bitterness or resentment. "I must fast some more."

What Stansell didn't know about Schlatter's aborted World's Fair trip was that he'd learned that Helen Wilmans would arrive in Chicago from her home in Sea Breeze, Florida, on July 10. She was no doubt attending the World's Congress of Religions, arriving early enough to get settled in. Schlatter was desperate to get there. Now it was May—perhaps even June—and he couldn't hope to make it except by train.[22]

A week or two after Schlatter's return from his unannounced walk to Cheyenne, he showed up at Stansell's room in the Albany Hotel.

"At last I am going to Chicago," he said.[23]

"Then you have your ticket?" Stansell asked.

"Not yet," Schlatter replied. "The Master told me to start down Seventeenth Street for the depot, and that a ticket would be provided me before I got aboard the train."

Stansell decided to follow his friend to the station. As they walked, Schlatter looked intently into every face they met, but no one noticed his pleading gaze. When they got to Union Station, a few blocks away, the cobbler stood in the large waiting room scanning the crowd in search of the one person whom the Master had appointed to hand him a ticket. "At first his face was lighted with enthusiasm," Stansell said, "but as train after train pulled out, and the crowds dwindled till only here and there a person straggled along, and no miraculous transportation was forthcoming, his face grew wistful and almost pinched and then something like despair settled over it."

They waited a while longer. Then Schlatter commented that he must have accidentally missed the person who had his ticket, and they started back up Seventeenth Street. Stansell could sense his grief and bitter disappointment—especially pronounced after a day that began with such enthusiasm—and he felt deeply sorry for him.

About this time Schlatter left 1845 Stout Street and took up residence in a boardinghouse owned by George Lamping at 1139 Eighteenth Avenue, a considerable distance from Denver's business district. He set up his cobbler's shop at 1848 Downing, a half-block away, occupying the front of the building while two cigar makers worked in back.[24] The reason for the move is unknown. But his business had fallen off considerably, and he may have needed to find a cheaper place to work—and to share expenses.

Denver's economy—and the nation's, for that matter—was sinking rapidly. The collapse of the Pennsylvania & Reading Railroad in February, along with other troubling events in the business world, led to an economic domino effect. Things got suddenly worse on May 4, when the plummeting stock market brought a crisis to Wall Street and a general panic throughout the country.[25] For a while, Schlatter managed to pay his shop rental, as well as room and board. But soon even his well-to-do clients could no longer afford to keep a skilled cobbler like him in business. The day came when he had no means to pay his eight dollar monthly rent—a situation he found intolerable. Distraught, he enlisted the Lampings' son William to help him collect whatever fees he could. But it was no use. Nobody had money, and the credit he had extended his clients went into his ledger's loss column.

For Schlatter, it was time to leave. In mid-July he turned over his cobbler's tools to the Lampings in partial payment of his debt. He also left them his clothing, possessions, and a smattering of his writings. His books and other papers went into a square valise, which he took to Albert Whitaker for safekeeping.[26] He said his good-byes—not keeping his friends in the dark this time—and left Denver, heading north to Cheyenne.[27]

Yet after three days of walking, he turned around. Something stopped him—and not the attack of mosquitoes he suffered his first night out, or the cactus bed in which he spent another terrible night. Nor was it the suspicious-looking tramps who eyed his clean clothing and pocket watch. Whatever it was, it stopped him cold—and sent him back to Denver. Here, after making himself a pair of sandals, he started out again the next day. This time, for whatever reason, he headed directly east.

NONE OF SCHLATTER's acquaintances in Denver ever spoke of his having had a religious vision while sitting at his cobbler's bench. But he mentioned it several times after returning as the healer in 1895. It was on March 25, 1893, he told Ada Morley during his three-month retreat, that the voice of God commanded him to give up his cobbler's trade and begin a mission of healing. Almost precisely three years after that vision, in March 1896, Morley explored the aura of destiny that surrounded the healer like a medieval halo.

"Do you know how often the mystic numbers 3, 7, 10 occur in your history?" she asked.[28]

"No," he said. "I never think about such things. How do you mean?"

"Well, for instance, Francis has 7 letters, Schlatter 9. You were born the 9th hour on the 29th day of April, 1856. You were fourteen years old when your father died. You see two 7's, don't you? The events then seem to run in even numbers till your spiritual birth. But after you landed in America it changes, as you will see. You reached Denver on the 19th of the 9th month. When 37 years old you had your vision in the 3d month. You started to walk on the 19th of the 7th month of 1893 . . ."

When she had finished, Francis casually changed the subject. Schlatter didn't need numbers to convince him of his destiny, for it had been shown to him long ago. He was now, he told Morley, fulfilling a recurring dream his older sister had shared with him before he left Alsace, France, where he was born in the village of Ebersheim. As a boy, he had laughed at her, but she would say, "Francis, it has a meaning."[29] Eventually he came to accept it as a prophecy.

The dream had four scenes, or acts. First, his sister said, she saw him desperately alone—"Always studying, thinking, quiet, but never associating with other young people." Then she saw him start to walk, and he seemed to walk endlessly, and always with a sad, mournful look on his face. Then, he said, she saw a curtain fall. "I was behind it and she tried to see," he said, "but no. No one could see behind that curtain." Then, finally, the curtain began to rise, and Schlatter stood happy and smiling in a beautiful field of ripe wheat, waving in the breeze, while joyous children danced around him.

"You see," he said, "I am at present in the third act. The curtain is down. I've disappeared. No one may be permitted to peer behind the curtain, but in due season the curtain will rise, and I will then be in the wheat field and ready for the harvest—and the fourth part of my sister's dream will have been completed."[30] The dream was part of a prophetic drama the cobbler-turned-healer had envisioned for himself. In it he stood in a wheat field among dancing children. It symbolized heaven on earth—the millennium to come. But its source was obscure. Few people knew the formative experiences that led Schlatter on the path to his religious pilgrimage. Assuming he was not mad—and nothing he said or did suggested insanity— his adoption of the role of messiah in midlife must have had earlier roots than William Ryan's death, or spiritualism, or mental healing.

One of Schlatter's earliest character-defining experiences came from a palm-whipping he received one day from his teacher. The six-year-old Francis thought the punishment unjust, and he decided not to go back. For the next few days, though his mother dressed him and got him ready for school, he went off and played with the older boys. When he was finally discovered, his father beat him until he was purple, but it taught him a good lesson, he said. He never missed a day of school after that, but when another teacher treated him unjustly, he rebelled again. And, that time, he told Morley, "I did it defiantly."[31]

Whether passively or directly, Schlatter grew up in defiance of authority—and perhaps birth order had something to do with it. He was the youngest son of François and Madeleine Deschamps Schlatter.[32] The eldest child, Ignace, was twenty years old when Madeleine gave birth to her ninth child, Francis (or François), on April 29, 1856. His most immediate older sibling, also named François, died early. Thus Francis had the ghost of his namesake to contend with, as well as living up to his father's name.

Aside from direct punishment, Francis also learned something of the larger consequences of rebellion. In his village, he told Morley, there was a willful young boy who refused to obey his parents. Everyone in the village believed he would come to grief, and sure enough, one day he fell into the lake and drowned. The next child born into that family turned out to be "the shyest, most shrinking, timid soul"—proof to all that the willful son had returned chastened by his experience. How widespread this belief in reincarnation was at that time is unknown, but the good Catholic villagers of Ebersheim certainly tolerated it. Schlatter believed in it throughout his life; in fact, reincarnation loomed large in his reading of the Bible, his interpretation of its prophecies, and his role in God's mission.[33]

But, in his youth at least, neither the belief in prophecy nor reincarnation shaped Schlatter's character as much as rebellion against authority. That, and events surrounding the Franco-Prussian War of 1870, when he was fourteen, dictated the course of his life to come. Shortly after the war started, his father died. Then, a few months later, he lost his mother. Before his fifteenth birthday, Schlatter found himself an orphan.

He was not an orphan exactly. There were, after all, his brothers and sisters, in addition to the family home in Ebersheim. Francis could have stayed there—in fact, his mother's deathbed wish was that he never leave the village. She feared that he would fall victim to the vice and corruption of the city. Had his mother lived, he told Morley, he would probably have remained in Ebersheim his entire life; but, after her death, circumstances forced him to leave.

Those circumstances were not hard to determine. In the wake of France's humiliating defeat at the hands of the Prussian army, Alsace-Lorraine became part of Germany's spoils of war. A French-

and German-speaking people, Alsatians naturally were divided over which side of their cultural heritage should prevail. The subsequent antagonism even split families, and this was exactly what happened to the children of François and Madeleine Schlatter. When Francis spoke of enlisting in the French army, some of his siblings warned that they would not call him brother if he did. In a sense, then, he disowned *them*, for years later he told Morley that he had only one brother, Ignace, and two sisters living in Alsace—eliminating more than half his family.

In spite of the familial threat, Francis left for Paris—there to enlist in the French army. But he was too young to sign up for himself. He wrote Ignace, his only guardian, but his brother refused to "opt" for him out of fear of Prussian reprisals. The recruitment officer added to Francis's chagrin by calling him a Prussian, which infuriated the young French patriot. "I rose in my indignation and said, 'Before I'll go in the German army I'll go to America.'"[34]

For the present, however, the fifteen-year-old outcast remained in Paris—and perhaps got a firsthand lesson in social rebellion on a large scale. He arrived in the wake of the bloody attack on the Paris Commune, the radical egalitarian order of Parisian workers that ended on May 28, 1871. He undoubtedly saw the vestiges of the workers' barricades, learned of the executions at the Luxembourg Gardens, and heard stories of the Paris Commune's short-lived experiment in revolutionary democracy. If he was not already a revolutionary, the fall of the Paris Commune probably made him one.

His experience in Paris fanned Schlatter's passionate identification with oppressed workers and his hatred of the privileged classes, a temperament instilled in him by his father. "As I sat on my father's loom," Schlatter said to Morley, "he told me stories of the French Revolution, and how our ancestors suffered, and the woes of war. Moreover, my father explained causes to me; taught me the reasons of things, and led me to see the wicked ways of the leaders; how little they care for the masses; how, for the foible of a king, because he is a ruler, the common people are massacred by thousands: how few protest or think seriously of the right or wrong of it."[35]

How long the young Schlatter stayed in Paris is unknown, or whether or not he had relatives or friends who could board and feed him.[36] An even greater mystery is how he got to London, where he lived for the next thirteen years, and how he supported himself there.

But one thing is certain. From the time of his punishment at the hands of an unjust teacher, to the moment he sailed for America in 1884, Schlatter's indignation over the abuses of power and privilege grew from personal experience, observation, and reading.

Schlatter claimed that his formal education ended at age fourteen, at the time he became an orphan and left Alsace. If so, it's remarkable that a homeless boy from rural France, using nothing but his wits and grade-school education, managed to support himself in a foreign country, learn the cobbler's trade, master the English language, and broaden his learning to become well acquainted with history, politics, religion, and a smattering of science. The years in which Schlatter grew to manhood remain some of the most intriguing, yet most obscure, of his life. They can only be known indirectly, through his brief recollections. But it's safe to say that they formed the fourth leg of his apprenticeship to an unknown mission — reincarnation, prophecy, spiritualism, and an intellectual training in social revolution.

CHAPTER TWO

Pilgrimage

My walk was the fire I went through for the world.[1]

FRANCIS SCHLATTER

CHLATTER LEFT DENVER in July 1893, again heading toward Cheyenne with the intention of reaching Chicago, where he would finally meet Helen Wilmans at the World's Congress of Religions. Twice before he had tried to make the trip through God's intercession, once hoping to be wafted spiritually through the air and once expecting a railroad ticket to be placed miraculously in his hands. Now, in midsummer, he made yet another attempt for Chicago, again on foot. It turned out to be an aborted effort that brought him back to Denver after a few miserable days of incessant rain, mosquitoes, and the fear of being beaten and robbed by railroad tramps.

After a day's respite, Schlatter decided to change course, and he set out to cross the Colorado plains at the height of the summer's heat. But why? What would have compelled him to go in that direction? Lacking any evidence that he had actually been called by God to go forth and heal through prayer, the most logical supposition is that Helen Wilmans was no longer in Chicago but back at her headquarters in Atlanta, Georgia. Perhaps he planned to travel there, or perhaps they agreed to meet part way — in Hot Springs, Arkansas. Whatever the reason, he set his course for Hot Springs, and he would not wander from it.

First, Schlatter picked up a new set of cobbler's tools and leather for making shoes along the way — spending some forty dollars Albert Whitaker gave him from the Atlantic-Pacific office cash box.[2] A streetcar line took the cobbler east along Colfax Avenue to the fringes of the city. Beyond that lay scattered farms, and then nothing but dry-grass prairie. After walking some ten or twelve miles, carrying the heavy pack filled with nails, pincers, hammer, and an iron last, he ran into an unrelenting downpour. He found shelter in an abandoned house and fell on the floor exhausted. It was the Father's way, he said, of telling him that he must get rid of everything. And soon he did—keeping only his clothing, a watch, a pair of sandals, and $3.75.

Now he was truly dependent on the will of the Father—and, as he would quickly learn, the Divine Will that sent him on this pilgrimage could often resemble a willful, spiteful, impetuous, and malicious voice. Yet behind the unreasonableness of the Father's demands lay something that reason could not fathom—and this was the hard lesson of total obedience, trust, faith, and a wholehearted surrender to Divine Will itself. If Schlatter didn't understand this at first, he did so within the next few days and weeks—for the torturous (and tortured) account of his walk in *The Life of the Harp*, filled with an overabundance of minutia and the tedium of an overlong railroad journey, is nothing if not a guidebook for understanding God's direct hand in human affairs.

By the time the pilgrim reached the Kansas state line, having crossed two hundred miles of hardscrabble prairie, the tenor of his spiritual tramp was clear. The Father had laid down laws as rigid and forbidding as in the days of Moses, especially dealing with fasting and eating, walking and resting, and when—and how—the cobbler could seek shelter and food. Schlatter husbanded his small $3.75 nest egg like a miser, but eventually ten cents for this and twenty-five cents for that left him penniless by the time he got to the High Plains town of Colby—and even then the Father dictated whether or not he could buy a loaf of bread or a bucket of water.

Even so, people offered him food—good people, that is. For in the hard times that gripped the country, even well before the silver crash of 1893, tramps and vagabonds had begun moving from place to place, some seeking work, others simply looking for a bite to eat. Sometimes the homes they passed looked prosperous enough to warrant a knock on the door. Such encounters were never predictable, as Schlatter's experience amply showed, and they could lead to anything from a sit-down meal to the business end of a broomstick. So far as Schlatter was concerned, the good people did what they could. But the bad could make a wanderer's life unbearable, not only through contempt but actual malice.

The Father, it seemed, had no interest one way or the other. Schlatter's God harkened back to the Old Testament's Yahweh, who regarded the enemies of Israel as his personal enemies. But this was the god Schlatter had chosen—or, more correctly from the cobbler's point of view, the divine Father who had chosen *him*. And the Father spared his pilgrim no more than anyone else. At times it seemed that Schlatter was the most reviled, despised, and tormented creature on earth—but he knew at every step that his suffering at the hands of the Father was the price he paid for his destiny. As his sister had envisioned, Schlatter would emerge from this punishing walk into a field of flowers and singing children.

But the journey itself was a trial, and it got worse as time went on. After his money ran out in western Kansas, he faced a quandary. He didn't hunt, and he had no utensils for cooking farm vegetables that he picked up along the way. He was forced to live off the land, and for a time he was driven to eating field corn. This made his mouth raw—and may have possibly damaged his upper palate.[3] Even when local Good Samaritans offered him a meal, the Father imposed regular periods of fasting. Thus Schlatter might sit down to a hot breakfast of pancakes and molasses one day only to be ordered to turn down a loaf of bread on another. Worse, the Father struck at the very core of the cobbler's self-esteem as a working man. He made him beg for food.

Schlatter obeyed, but not without protest. After days of living off raw crops, he spoke to the Father. "You promised to take care of me," he said. "Now, I have no money and am hungry. How shall I get something to eat?"[4] The Father told him to walk over to a nearby farmhouse and ask for a meal. Schlatter cried, "Is that the way you are going to take care of me?" The voice answered, simply, "Yes." The pilgrim felt that he had been struck by lightning—a bolt of cold indifference.

Before his money ran out, Schlatter bought six yards of bleached muslin for a tent and acquired a blanket to sleep on. He fashioned tent poles from sticks and put together a small bag of supplies, including matches. In the few weeks since he'd left Denver, his appearance had changed dramatically. He was no longer the clean-shaven cobbler who prided himself on his neatness but a ragged-looking vagabond whose long beard and hair (though probably washed and clean) set him apart from other wanderers on the road. Early in his walk, someone said derisively, "Look! Here is a fellow that looks like an apostle!"[5] Schlatter had to suffer such comments, but at the same time he reinforced his alienation from society by his dress, manner, and behavior. He lived like a hermit, avoided other travelers, and raised questions about where he was going and why.

When he did confide in people he met on the road, Schlatter made it clear that his walk was a spiritual calling, not simply an overland journey. One Sunday in early October, he stayed overnight at the home of a man named Dan Driscoll outside Courtland, Kansas. They talked, and Driscoll revealed that he was a Populist, a sworn enemy of eastern bankers, industrialists, railroad magnates, and people of wealth and privilege. Schlatter sympathized—in fact, he had long been a Populist, too, he said, until he began his walk. Only recently, while on the road, he had come to a momentous realization—that "nothing earthly could break the bonds of Hell but the Creator himself." At the time, Schlatter didn't see how God planned to destroy the nation's—and the world's—oppressive system of economic and social slavery. But he hinted strongly that, whatever the Father planned, he would play a part. "Father has always told me," he said, "'All you have to do is follow Me and I will do the rest,' and I am determined to go to the end."[6]

Where the end lay, Schlatter didn't know. For the present, he regarded Hot Springs, and whatever awaited him there, as a crucial stage in the road the Father had laid out for him, and it would be a daunting task just to reach it. A day or two after leaving Courtland, as he rested on the roadside, the county sheriff came up in a carriage drawn by a team of bays. When he learned that Schlatter was heading for Hot Springs, he said: "You have a terrible walk ahead of you."[7] He asked if Schlatter had any hope. The cobbler replied, "More than ever." But he was sure the sheriff didn't understand. His hope lay beyond Hot Springs. It lay in the as yet unseen promise of God's plan.

SCHLATTER'S JOURNEY took him eastward from Denver to Olathe, near Kansas City, then almost due south through present-day Oklahoma (then known as Indian Territory) to Tahlequah, and then southeast to the Arkansas border and the town of Fort Smith before he continued on into Hot Springs. Mostly he followed the railroad lines, for they offered a surer guide for overland travel than roads—and something of a safety net. He walked the Rock Island Line from the Colorado prairie through northern Kansas, then angled south to the Union Pacific, which took him close to Kansas City, and then followed the St. Louis & Iron Mountain Railroad to the Arkansas border. Along the way, he came to recognize the railroad engineers who traveled the lines, and he never lost his liking for railroad people—except, perhaps, for roughneck section hands, whom he avoided. Early in his journey, he sat one night by the side of the track and watched a passenger express rumble by, its gas-lit windows permitting a brief glimpse of comfort and luxury inside. Those people are much happier than I, he thought. But the Father replied, "No, you are happier than they."[8]

In fact, the greater his suffering, the more it seemed to free Schlatter from the physical and mental shackles that bound him to his own willfulness and weakness. God was forging him into a new man—sometimes reluctantly, on the cobbler's part, and sometimes willingly. But the transformation could only come through deprivation, anguish, and a testing of his will to the limits of human endurance. The worst of it came on the final leg of his journey to Hot Springs, after he passed Tahlequah. His foot began to swell, and the Father told him to throw his shoes away, for he could never wear them again.

"Yes, but it is cold," Schlatter said.[9]

"Jesus walked barefooted and bareheaded," the Father said. "You can walk also."

"But," Schlatter said, "Jesus was in a warm climate and I am in a cold one."

"That makes no difference," said the Father. "I want you to walk barefooted and bareheaded."

Schlatter replied, "Well, if you want it I will do it." He threw his shoes and hat away, and began to walk. And with each step over the cold ground, a happiness came over him that he had never known, and he began to sing hymns.

The swelling in his foot grew worse. He couldn't see his ankle bone, and the pain was so bad he couldn't walk any farther. Miles from any house, he made camp in the woods next to the road. At night he moaned aloud, but a screech owl made such a horrible sound in response that Schlatter was forced to lie quietly. A couple of days later a mixed-blood farmer came by and offered to take Schlatter back to Tahlequah where he could rest and eat. The Father allowed it, and for a time the cobbler got a respite from the weather. That night, when the farmer proposed to give Schlatter some liniment for his ankle, the Father refused. "Don't use it. You will walk tomorrow."[10]

And walk he did—for eighteen miles, back to where he had lain in agony a few days earlier. By this time, a winter chill had descended on the Ozarks, and Schlatter had no idea what further agony lay in the thick woods and rocky hills that stood between him and his destination. For a time, he traveled without serious difficulty, though his ankle remained swollen and painful. Typical of his tramp, he found homes where he was welcomed—and fed—and others where he was turned away.

Once, after Schlatter had set up a camp, and was comfortably warm, the Father told him go and ask for shelter. "Oh, but I begged Him not to make me go," the healer wrote later, "to let me sleep where I was. But I had to go or disobey."[11] He walked five miles and came to a large house with several chimneys—all with fireplaces burning brightly. The Father said, "That is the place."

"They! They will not give me shelter," Schlatter exclaimed, staring at the obvious wealth and comfort inside.

"But I want you to go."

Schlatter obeyed, opening the gate and walking up to the large porch. A middle-aged woman answered the door, holding a lamp in her hand.

"Can I have shelter for the night?" he asked.

"We never give shelter to anyone," she said.[12] Humiliated, Schlatter had to walk back to his former camp, wondering what the Father had had in mind.

Nor was that the only time the Father deliberately led Francis astray—and still the cobbler kept his faith. During the final leg of Schlatter's journey east, conditions worsened on his walk while his ankle continued to throb with pain. He no longer had a road, or trail, or even a path to mark his way, and every day he headed in whatever direction the Father told him to travel. One day, after climbing over rocks, pushing his way through thickets, and crossing bone-cold streams, he found himself exactly where he had left camp that morning. Later, after wading through another creek, he cried out: "Will this never stop?"[13]

To this complaint he received only silence—and more streams. He found himself on a tributary of the Arkansas, and in crossing it he sank to his neck in water, soaking his clothes, his pack, and his blankets.[14] He climbed out, shivering, and suddenly realized that his matches were also soaked. In despair he cried, "Surely I will freeze to death here tonight." Still no response from the Father. After climbing up the bank and finding a camping spot next to a dirt road, Schlatter nevertheless set out gathering dry leaves and wood. To his astonishment, when he struck a match, it burst into flame, and he kept the fire going all night warming himself and drying his blanket and clothes.

The next morning, at daybreak, he was packed and ready to go when the Father said: "Wait."[15] Schlatter stayed by the fire; he knew such commands had a reason. The Father had already told him he would be in Hot Springs that night, but it was twenty miles away, and the cobbler could never walk that far with his bad ankle. In time two men came by in a wagon, and seeing how laid up he was, they offered him a ride—and thereby fulfilled the Father's promise. After six months, he had arrived at his destination in the fading hours of a late November evening.

Ragged, shoeless, and bareheaded, Schlatter made his way to the post office, anxious to find something in the mail that would justify his long journey. But the post office was closed, and this small set-back triggered a full-blown anxiety attack. He wandered back to the city's outskirts and found a group of small children playing around a bonfire. They ran from him, and he stood at the bonfire, immobilized. A woman came out of a nearby house, holding a lantern, and asked him what he wanted. He replied that he was looking for someone, but when she asked who, he couldn't remember. As Schlatter recalled the episode, he said, "I could not understand what Father was doing with me."[16]

After another miserable night spent in the cold atop Hot Springs Mountain, which rose over the fine resort hotels in town, Schlatter again made his way down to the post office. What he found there —sorting through some papers and letters awaiting him—was discouraging, he later wrote. That was a mild way of describing the shock and disappointment he felt when—perhaps—he learned that Helen Wilmans would not be there, and didn't plan to come. That hope and expectation had sustained him throughout his eight hundred-mile tramp, and like a spurned lover he wanted to get away as soon as possible. "Go out of the city," the Father told him, as if to confirm Schlatter's deepest wish, and he started to leave.[17]

But as Schlatter made his way through town, a black police officer approached him from behind and placed a hand on his shoulder.

"Where are your shoes?" the officer asked.

"My feet are so swollen I can't wear any," Schlatter replied.

"Where is your hat?"

"I don't wear any."

"Come along," the policeman said. The encounter was brief, but it drew a few onlookers. Unquestionably Schlatter's appearance—shoeless, ragged, and scraggly—had attracted attention in a resort town that catered to the upper classes. The woman who observed his behavior the night before, at the children's bonfire, could have alerted the police to a possible madman wandering the streets. As he was led to the police station, a crowd of people followed.

The scene at the station, as Schlatter told it, was reminiscent of the biblical Passion Story. The sheriff wanted to know what had brought him to Hot Springs. Schlatter told him he was guided by the Father.

"Can we not see that Father?" the sheriff asked.

"You may see Him before you know it," Schlatter replied.

The sheriff uttered an obscenity—one, Schlatter wrote, that no man should use with another—and the cobbler shot back a withering look.

"Take him to the cage," the sheriff told the deputies. "He is as crazy as a bedbug."[18]

Schlatter entered the Hot Springs jail on December 1, 1893. The charges were unspecified, though someone wrote "Crazy" next to his name—spelled "Slatter"—in the police ledger.[19] He had never been in jail before. In the "cage," a single large room with two- and three-tiered bunks, he found a motley group of men and boys, black and white, staring at him. He sat for a while, then walked to a corner sink and began washing some of his handkerchiefs. In a few minutes, a black man came over to him. "They want you over here in the court," he said.[20]

Schlatter ignored him and kept on washing. The kangaroo court had already assembled, and the "judge" sent a young black boy of about eleven years old to fetch the prisoner again. The boy, frightened and sobbing, said, "They want you up there." Schlatter took his hand and walked over to the assembled prisoners. The judge spoke:

"You are charged with jail breaking—or breaking into jail—and are fined one dollar and a half." Schlatter said he had no money. The judge asked for his watch, and Schlatter refused.

"This court decides you are to have one hundred and fifty lashes with a rubber hose six feet long and an inch and a quarter in diameter," the judge said. He could avoid it by turning over the watch. Again Schlatter refused.[21]

The judge then ordered several men to hold Schlatter down and called for a fourteen-year-old boy to lash him. As soon as the boy struck him, Schlatter summoned all his energy and broke free, scattering his tormentors to the sides of the cell. He calmly returned to his washing, but the court immediately reconvened. They called him again. In spite of what had happened earlier, Schlatter walked to the defendant's chair and sat down.

A Good Samaritan named Charley Williams proposed to pay Schlatter's fine and spare the cobbler a certain beating. But after quietly consulting with the Father, Schlatter refused. "I can't see why this man should pay my fine," he said, facing his tormenters. "You have asked for my watch and you cannot have it." Dead silence filled the room.

Then, as if on signal, the inmates jumped him again, and pinned him down. This time a tall, large-boned black man named Singleton, furious because Schlatter had broken away from them the first time, began whipping him mercilessly. After fifty lashes, Charley Williams, who had been counting the strokes, told him to stop. Schlatter, beaten and broken, sat on the chair and wept. When his sobs trailed away, he looked up to see the others silently watching him. Singleton, the man who had whipped him with such fury, spoke first. "The officials," he said, "are crazier than that man."

From that moment on, Schlatter had the respect of everyone in the cage. He even began healing some of the other inmates—the first time he had done any healing work since leaving Denver. For the next five months he remained confined for nothing more than vagrancy—officially, that is. Yet from the time of Schlatter's arrest, the sheriff and his deputies acted as if they had a madman on their hands. And, in fact, his behavior reinforced their suspicions.

Once, after three weeks had passed, the sheriff came to the cage. "Have you any more sense than when you came in?" he asked.

"No more, no less," Schlatter said curtly—and realized immediately that he'd failed a test for his release. Later, taken to the sheriff's office because the deputy felt he'd been confined too long, Schlatter passed up another opportunity for freedom. When the sheriff offered to set the cobbler up in business, Schlatter replied that he'd given up his business to do God's work.

"What is that work?" the sheriff asked.[22]

"I know what it was last year, but I cannot tell you what it will be this year," the healer replied. That—he later wrote—settled that.

Schlatter was convinced that he had been kept in jail for his religious beliefs, not because a small-town sheriff considered him crazy. Yet his sense of religious persecution drew from a larger myth that had been building inside him for some time—that his journey resembled Christ's forty days in the wilderness, and that his suffering fulfilled a divine plan. He may not have grasped the grand scope of the Father's design while in the Hot Springs jail, but he would understand it well enough before his journey's end.

For the present, God foretold his immediate future by way of a dream. In the dream, Schlatter saw himself in a large house, along with several other people, when a bird flew through an open window. It disappeared into another room, then flew into a third, and returned to escape out the window it had entered. "Catch it!" everyone said, but the bird was gone.[23] On awakening, Schlatter realized what the dream meant. If his two meetings with the sheriff had gone well, he might now be a free man. But that was not God's intention. He wanted the healer to *escape*.

The opportunity came in due time. Schlatter had become a fixture at the jail, and because he was a model prisoner, the deputy made him a trusty. The Father told him to work hard, and he did— cleaning the courthouse and chopping wood and doing odd jobs. He was so prompt, energetic, and industrious that the deputy called him Cyclone. The deputy also got Schlatter to help with house and yard chores. One day, when the deputy's wife called her husband into another room to help with the baby, Schlatter heard the Father's order: "Go!"[24]

He strode out of the deputy's house and headed straight for Hot Springs Mountain, keeping a brisk pace but not running. He made it to the top, then walked down the other side, and when night fell he found an old log to sleep under. He woke up around noon the next day, then ate supper with a black family, some of whom he treated for ailments, before returning to the mountains.

Now, having gained his freedom, he faced the question of his destiny.

———————————————

LIKE SCHLATTER's false start at the beginning of his journey, his escape from Hot Springs began in confusion and vacillation. "I was surprised," he said later, "because Father had always told me to go south. I asked Him why He made me go North, but He told me to go on; it was not for me to quarrel with the Father, so I obeyed."[25] Schlatter's course of travel—left, right, north, south, and back and forth at the will of the Father—eventually took him into Indian Territory, and there he finally headed steadily southwest toward the Red River and Paris, Texas. At one point he spent an evening with a large family who took him in and fed him. They began talking about religion, and Schlatter said: "Did not Jesus say if we have faith only as large as a grain of a mustard seed we can move mountains?"

One of the listeners said, "But that man is not living."

"Yes, he is living," Schlatter replied, "and he is right before you. And some day, when Father gets ready, I will move mountains."[26]

To what must have been a roomful of dumbfounded faces, Schlatter announced his divinity for the first time. From this point on, in his own mind, he no longer followed in the footsteps of Christ; instead, he *was* the living Christ, the promised Messiah, and he was ushering in a new dispensation of God. All his dreams and visions, as well as his sister's, seemed directed to this conclusion.[27] Whether or not he knew for certain what God wanted of him, he understood that his destiny went far beyond becoming a mere healer. Healing, like other miracles, had been but the expression of Christ's divine mission, not the end. And what of Schlatter's end? If he were the reincarnation of Jesus Christ, the fulfillment of the promised Second Coming, what would the Father ultimately ask of him?

To be sure, in the meantime God wanted his servant to suffer just as Jesus had. The journey beyond Hot Springs, it turned out, was as arduous as the one that took him there. One night, exhausted, he lay down under a bush and wept like a child. "Father," he said, "the world is too heavy for me. Oh! why did you not take somebody else to do the work?"[28] Then he fell asleep, and in the morning he awoke surprisingly refreshed and strong, and traveled on.

Aside from the rain and cold, which tormented him on his westward tramp through Texas, following the line of the Texas & Pacific, Schlatter increasingly became the object of hatred, scorn, and humiliation—largely because he was a vagabond and a beggar. Women laughed at him in Paris, a man chased him away from his porch in Fort Worth, and in Weatherford two little girls urged their dog to attack him. Through all this the Father told him to keep still, bear the shame, and look to the day when he would emerge victorious.

As Schlatter well knew, he wasn't the only person to suffer such abuse. Nearly a year had passed since the silver crash brought down the nation's economy, and in the deep depression that followed thousands of jobless men wandered the roads and railroads looking for work or food. Schlatter had seen plenty of destitute people on his journey, but he identified mainly with workers who had been cast out of their homes and jobs by what he believed to be the greed and indifference of unchecked industrialism. Now these once-proud men were forced to beg for food, and it pained him to see this as much as it did to beg himself.

He was a Populist—or had been until he began his pilgrimage. Now, even though the injustices of the system still infuriated him, he knew that economic and social reform would do nothing to change conditions. The abuses of the rich and powerful, and the oppression of the masses, had reached a point beyond the power of human agency to correct or change. Now matters rested in the hands of the Father—and the Father would apply the remedy. In the meantime, he saw slights and insults doled out to the poor everywhere, and with the Father's help he looked behind the human mask to the spiritual goodness or ugliness of people he encountered.

It was a sign of his own freedom from prejudice that, even though despising authority, he did not prejudge authority figures. On his way across Texas he found himself in Throckmorton, where the Father had prophesied that he would be jailed once again.[29] Indeed, he was—for some three days, and again presumably for insanity.

But the sheriff and judge, he concluded, were good men, and they made sure that he was comfortable and ate well.

For the next five months Schlatter remained in the far Southwest, first making his way to the mission country near Los Angeles, and spending three months there, wandering from village to village healing the Indians and Hispanos of the San Jacinto Valley.[30] Here he began his first series of "pronounced healings," as he put it, working primarily with women and children. For some reason—and the only time he was ever known to do it—he took small amounts of money for his healing work. "I did not know why Father wanted me to take it," Schlatter said later, "but trusted that he would soon make it known."[31]

During his three-month stay in southern California, and in spite of his losses, Schlatter earned enough money to take a steamer from San Diego to San Francisco—again, following the Father's commandment. But he stayed only three hours, and soon he was walking down the San Joaquin Valley, heading back toward the San Jacinto villages near Los Angeles. Just why the Father had ordered this seemingly aimless loop is unknown, but for Schlatter it was no more unusual than the wandering of the Israelites during the Exodus. Every step of his journey, and every event, however minute and passing, fulfilled the Father's mysterious plan. And, as to that, the worst was yet to come. When Schlatter reached the end of the San Joaquin Valley, he turned east, walked to Barstow, and found himself entering the fabled Mojave Desert.

In spite of his experience on the road, he was ill-equipped to face such hostile country. He had a tent, tent poles, a water pail, a blanket, a frying pan, and a hatchet that had been left behind by a fellow camper who robbed him one night. With all this junk, he looked like a hobo, bearded, long-haired, and unkempt, and his effort to make a bit of money from healing faltered because people refused to put their faith in a tramp. Nevertheless, he'd earned enough to buy fifty pounds of flour, which sustained him on his long walk through central California, and now, camping outside of Barstow, he pitched his tent and rested up for the ordeal ahead.

To make things more difficult, the Father told him he couldn't beg for food. Schlatter had abhorred the humiliation of begging, and it hadn't always worked in practice—even when the Father

FIGURE 4. Frank Sauerwein, a noted southwestern artist,
depicted Francis Schlatter at midday walking through the
Mojave Desert in 1895. The artist mistakenly has the healer
heading west rather than east. Frontispiece, *The Life of the
Harp in the Hand of the Harper,* courtesy Denver Public Library,
Western History Collection, c265.8s338Li.

assured him it would. But now his very survival rested on the charity of others, or on whatever natural foods he could find in the dry, barren land through which he traveled. He had long ago realized that physical suffering strengthened his inner happiness, but now he was beset more than ever by Satan, who urged him to give up his quest. "Throw down these things you carry and go back," Satan said, taunting him incessantly; but Schlatter would not abandon his God-given destiny.[32] "On I went on that terrible walk," he wrote later, "for the sake of humanity."

Entering New Mexico, Schlatter passed Gallup and stopped at Fort Wingate. He then walked north ten miles to the Navajo reservation and spent five days with a Navajo chief and his family. Though he did not mention the episode in *The Life of the Harp*, a rumor spread that he had come across the chief's hogan in a severe windstorm. Welcomed inside, and given water to drink and splash on his face and hair, he soon saw a very sick baby lying listlessly at its mother's breast, and the woman was paralyzed with fear.[33]

"Sick?" Schlatter asked.

"Two, three day, she sick," the woman said. "We send for doctor. No come." Schlatter touched the infant's forehead and prayed, and soon the woman offered her baby daughter to the bedraggled stranger. As both parents watched intently, he gently placed his hand on her head and silently moved his lips in prayer. When Schlatter left the reservation two days later, she was well.

From there, "through the hot sands and sun," he said, "I came, in due season, to Las Lunas, New Mexico, in July, 1895."[34]

CHAPTER THREE

The Desert Messiah

He does not proclaim himself Christ from the housetops,
but when asked, he quietly but firmly says, "I am."[1]

FITZ MAC

A T SUNRISE on July 16, 1895, four men left Albuquerque in a
two-seater buckboard and headed south over a well-traveled
dirt road to Peralta, New Mexico. Will Hunter, a reporter for
the *Albuquerque Morning Democrat*, sat in front, next to the buckboard's driver. The newspaper's photographer sat in back, next to a
man they brought along as a witness. Not twelve hours earlier, they
had learned for the first time of a long-haired, barefooted healer who
was treating the sick and suffering in villages along the Rio Grande.[2]
The news came from their buckboard driver, a rancher, who entered
the *Democrat*'s office with his breathless story.

The people called the healer Saint Francisco, the rancher said.
Yesterday he was in Peralta, the man's hometown, and he had per-
formed wonders there. The healer looked just like images of the
Savior.

The newspapermen were skeptical. A faith healer imitating Christ
could mean many things—that he was a deluded crank, a fraud,
or perhaps some gifted psychic playing on the superstitions of the
faithful. But the tale their visitor told was intriguing. He had seen
the healer give sight to a blind man. He had seen him restore free
movement to a woman's long-crippled arm. These were not strangers, but neighbors and friends. He would be happy to take the men
there. But it was already late in the afternoon, so they decided to get
an early start in the morning.

Now, as the buckboard made the gradual descent from the dry
mesa into the verdant bottomlands of the Rio Grande, they could
see the scattered wood and adobe houses of Peralta warming in the

morning sun. They passed several wagons on the way and learned that the healer was not in Peralta, but they would find him, the driver said. He couldn't be far. In the meantime, he would show them the effects of the healer's work.

He took them to a small home set inside a wide adobe-walled enclosure lined with plants and flowers. When the buckboard pulled up to the gate, the driver called a greeting, and an old man emerged from the house. He held a cane in his hand but didn't use it as he walked to the buckboard. The driver spoke with him in Spanish for a few minutes. Then he told his passengers that this was Jesus Valesquez, and he'd been blind for three years.

Until a few days ago, the driver said, Señor Valesquez had not been able to see his fingers in front of his face. Then, after the healer held both his hands, taking the left in the right and the right in the left, his sight had gradually improved. First he could see the flickering light of a candle in the dark, then the candle itself, and now almost everything. The two men spoke in Spanish again, and the old man pointed to the horses and tapped his cane against the side of the wagon. The driver told them he had described everything perfectly.

Hunter wanted to know who the healer was, and where he had come from. After a short, rapid conversation with Valesquez, the driver said: "No one knows his name. His coming was strange indeed. Some boys went to the top of that black mountain there to play and there they found this man lying flat upon his back with his arms stretched up towards heaven. Beside him was a small tepee-shaped tent and outside this was a couch of blankets. They ran from him in terror and the man followed them to the village."

Next the party traveled down the road to the home of Silverio Martino, a prominent resident of Peralta. Martino invited them in and answered their questions. For a week the healer had lived at his house, he said, and perhaps would return. In the meantime, he had left his belongings there. In a back room, Martino showed them the healer's canvas tent and blankets, neatly folded and resting in a corner. They also found a long wooden shaft, sharpened at both ends, that seemed to have come from a fence board. Wrapped with leather thongs and wire, it looked like a weapon or a hunting spear. The healer had brought nothing but these items, his own clothing, and some worn-out socks.

Ever since he arrived, and even before, Martino said, the healer had been fasting. Martino's family had watched him day and night. All he had taken was a bit of water, nothing else. They made a special effort to watch, for he had accomplished a miracle. Martino's mother, Juliana—Martino pointed to the woman out in the garden behind the house—had been paralyzed in one arm for sixteen years. Now she could use both hands. Martino led them outside, and they watched the older woman work a wooden hoe on the earth between rows of bean stalks.

The day was passing quickly, and they retraced their steps, heading back north to Isleta. As they rose out of the valley, they came across a group of pilgrims the healer had touched. All testified, through the driver, that they had been greatly relieved of their pain and marveled at the healer's gifts. Some thought he had come down from the clouds.

As the group traveled on, now several hours into their search, it seemed to Hunter that the healer had returned to the clouds again. At Isleta, not ten miles from where they had started out that morning, he was gone. Nor did they find him at Los Padillas, a mile or so to the west. From there they rode another two miles to the village of Pajarito, and here they found a group of people crowding the door of an adobe home. Its owner, Juan Garcia, ushered them inside. Finally, Hunter's daylong quest had paid off.

The healer sat on a plain wooden chair, turning slightly to hold the hands of an old man sitting next to him. On the opposite wall Hunter noticed a cheap print of the Christ, and immediately he felt as if he had come across a scene out of the Bible. The spare room, the small house in the village of Pajarito, and the murmur of voices outside all reinforced the impression that something both humble and marvelous was taking place here.

The healer wore a calico shirt, a blue-jeans jumper falling to his hips, and a pair of overalls that didn't quite reach the tops of his salt-and-pepper socks. As he bent toward the man at his side, his thick brown hair, parted in the middle, curled luxuriantly around his ears and came to rest on his shoulders. Hunter could not hear the words he was mumbling but studied his delicately cut mouth, barely visible under his heavy mustache and beard.

For five minutes the healer sat with his patient, almost motionless but with an intensity that nearly shook his body. From time to time, he shuddered slightly and looked up to the ceiling, and the man seemed to sway in response. Garcia whispered to his guest that the old man was a relative, and he was blind in one eye. Even so, the old man kept both eyes fixed on the healer throughout the session. Finally, the old man sighed, withdrew his hands, and got up. As he walked out of the room, tilting his head to make his way, Hunter could see that the treatment hadn't worked.

Others, young and old, came and went. Some were helped, some not. In the meantime, Hunter asked Schlatter a few questions about himself, and the healer was remarkably talkative. He described his vision as a cobbler in Denver, and the commandment to go out and heal the sick. He spoke of this fast, now ten days old, and said that he had fasted for seventy-five days while walking the line of the Union Pacific before reaching Denver in 1892.

Before long, the wife of a prominent Hispanic official came up to Schlatter and asked him if he would come to her home. Schlatter thought about it for a moment, during which he seemed to be praying, and then said: "I will go one week from today at noon."

"Where will you be at that time?" she replied.

"Only my Master knows," Schlatter said. "But wherever I am if you send a messenger for me I will come at that time."

It was now getting dark inside the room, and Hunter asked the healer one more question. "Will you come out into the sunlight and have your picture taken?" The healer again raised his eyes, as he did in prayer. Then he replied, "My Master says I must not." It was clear that whatever the Master told him, Schlatter must do it. There was no room for argument.

As a storm crept up over the western mountains, the healer emerged from the Garcia home and started alone for Las Lunas.

WILL HUNTER's breaking news story of July 17, 1895, radically changed the healer's life. Schlatter had spent two years in obscurity, alone and avoiding crowds, and only rarely telling anyone about his mission for fear that he would be scorned or humiliated. Suddenly, he faced a daily congregation of suffering pilgrims, many of whom looked to him as a savior who could heal them. Not only that, he became an object of curiosity, speculation, and wonder, as well as a target of disapproving voices who considered him to be either a charlatan or a megalomaniac. As the news of his powers spread, both by word of mouth and by telegraph, the number of people surrounding him grew daily, and he found himself bathed in public attention.

Nothing Schlatter said or did was lost on the small crowds that gathered about him. Rumors arose almost daily, most of them illustrating the healer's Christlike character, unusual gifts, and even divine powers. In one instance, when a patient insisted on pressing money in his hand, Schlatter took it but then passed it directly to a needy bystander. "I have no use for money," he said.[3] Later, when a small party of Zuni Indians prostrated themselves at his feet, he said: "I want none to kneel to me," and helped each of them up.[4] And, early on, a fabricated story made its way around the villages suggesting that Schlatter was a man of miracles. It was said that he carried a blanket, which he placed on the ground one day while healing. When he was ready to leave, a man bent down to pick up the blanket, but couldn't make it budge. Nor did it when another man came to his aid, both men tugging at the immovable blanket. Then Schlatter, not noticing their efforts, reached down, easily took it off the ground, and went on his way.[5]

The blanket story, when published, angered a few prominent Hispanos because they thought such tales reinforced the Anglo view that Mexicans, as native-born Hispanos were universally called, tended to be superstitious and ignorant.[6] Yet, as Silverio Martino told Hunter, the family kept a close eye on their guest day and night to make sure he was true to his word. In this, Martino was following a well-practiced Catholic tradition of testing miracles and supernatural claims. And, as for Schlatter's healing powers, Martino and others relied on direct experience—they saw the cures the healer had brought about. Nevertheless, the chain of belief, as it was perceived, seemed to move upward from the uneducated villagers to the educated Anglos and Hispanos who were the community's leaders.

After some two weeks living with the Martino family in Peralta, Schlatter agreed to move his healing ministry to Albuquerque— a predictable decision because he had been getting pressure to do so from the time he came to public attention. He was invited to stay with Josefa Werner, the widow of Albuquerque pioneer Major Melchior Werner, a German immigrant who had been the city's postmaster and built the Centennial Hotel in 1876.[7] Josefa and her family lived in Albuquerque's Old Town, the original eighteenth-century settlement that grew up around the plaza whose most prominent landmark was the church of San Felipe de Neri. Inside the compound of the church, in fact, priests were abuzz with tentative opinions about the strange healer. "There has come into the plaza a man who is thought to be an Alsatian," one wrote on July 20, "and who promises to cure the people through faith. He is a Protestant fanatic, from what appears."[8] Five days later the man wrote: "The American *curandero* is (it is said!!) curing the people by touch; it is believed, or so it is said, through his mouth there comes a spirit or something to that effect."

Schlatter's move to Albuquerque coincided with the arrival of two men from Denver, one of whom had read about the healer as soon as the story broke. Edward Fox, a prosperous freighter and former Denver alderman, and Henry Hauenstein, a firefighter who had begun losing his sight, arrived in Albuquerque soon after midnight on July 19.[9] Waiting patiently at the station until sunrise, the men then went in search of the healer—and, like Hunter's party, they spent hours looking in vain. They lost a day, and a good deal of patience, until finally directed to the Werner home in Old Town. There Schlatter sat down with Hauenstein, looked in his eyes, and gave him greater attention than he had afforded anyone thus far in the Rio Grande valley.

The arrival of the two men, and their unsuccessful daylong search for Schlatter, made the front page of the *Albuquerque Morning Democrat*. Perhaps this is why Schlatter spent so much time with Hauenstein, because the man had traveled so far to find him. Over a period of five days, Schlatter sat down with him twenty-seven times. "It was a peculiar feeling I can't describe," Hauenstein said of being touched by the healer. "Every nerve in my body twitched."[10] On the first day, sitting in an adobe room in the Werner home, Hauenstein faced the healer, hands crossed, with his back to a window. "When he let loose," he said, "everything in front of me was dark. As I turned around, it seemed a little lighter." Gradually, he said, he began to distinguish objects that came between him and a source of light, and at the end of the sessions he could make out a hand moving in front of his face.

The results were modest, but they were enough to convince Edward Fox that Schlatter could do great things in Denver. He asked the healer if he would come.[11] Yes, Schlatter said, if Fox would pay his train fare. The deal was set that day, and Schlatter agreed to leave Albuquerque for Denver after he had completed his fast. Fox not only arranged for a railroad ticket but a special Pullman car. Then he and Hauenstein returned to Denver to spread the good news among their friends.

In the meantime, Schlatter continued healing at the Werner home, whose adobe walls practically burst with people crowding inside to pass under his hands. While there, he revealed another of his seemingly miraculous gifts—clairvoyance. One day, as a small, withered old woman tried to make her way to the healer, she found herself continually pushed aside by stronger, taller people who crowded the home. Soon a voice came from a back room, and it was the healer's. "There is a little woman in the hallway who desires to see me," he called. "Make way for her."[12]

In another instance, an Albuquerque cobbler, Tom Dye, offered to make a pair of shoes for the healer. After he measured Schlatter's foot size, Dye said he would begin that evening so they could be ready early the next day. The following morning, someone mentioned to Schlatter that the shoes ought to be finished. "No," the healer replied, "the man did not begin work on them last night." The cobbler had started in the morning, Schlatter said, and the shoes would be ready late that afternoon. Sure enough, when a messenger arrived at 4:30 p.m., Dye was completing the last stitch. He confirmed the truth of Schlatter's statement—that he had not begun the night before, as promised, but early that morning.

Schlatter's clairvoyance added yet another element to the aura of the holy, miraculous, and mysterious that gathered about him during his healing ministry in New Mexico. Indeed, the shoes pointed to yet another aspect of his larger-than-life character. Will Hunter, when he first saw the healer, had estimated that he stood about six feet tall—at least two inches taller than anyone else who later ventured a guess. Yet the measurements Tom Dye took of Schlatter's feet were nothing short of astounding. At 13 inches long by 4¾ inches wide, they were so big that Dye had to make a special shoe just for the healer.[13]

However, there are reasons to doubt Dye's testimony and, of course, he was a fellow cobbler. On July 26, the day Schlatter was to receive his new shoes, he had his picture taken in a local Albuquerque photo studio. He stood for a full-length portrait against a painted backdrop of trees and ferns, his right hand resting on a worn pile of plaster rocks at his side—altogether an odd setting for a messiah figure.[14] His long-sleeved shirt fell around his baggy, creased pants, and his shoes were clearly pre–Tom Dye. They looked hardly more substantial than slippers, and the leather on his right shoe had begun peeling off the sole. From a close study of this first portrait of the healer, it's abundantly clear that Schlatter didn't have thirteen-inch-long feet. They were hardly bigger than size nine or ten.

One of the few indisputable characteristics of the healer's body was the size of his hands. They were known to be large, with long fingers—and the Albuquerque studio portrait confirms it. Many people who presented themselves to his touch commented on his hands, just as they did his two missing upper teeth, his steel-blue eyes, and his wavy brown hair—which, at early middle age, was already streaked with gray.[15] Most people noticed that he stooped slightly, a characteristic that Mary Ingersoll, his Denver landlady, had noticed back in 1892.

Saturday, July 26, was a busy day for the healer. First he had his portrait made, then received his new shoes from Tom Dye, then met several prominent Albuquerque people at the home of Walter C. Hadley, a mining and business entrepreneur who helped to found the Automatic Telephone Company of Albuquerque.[16] This was an important gathering, for it mobilized the community's leaders around the healer. Already he had won the endorsement of influential Hispanos like Andres Romero, an Albuquerque grocer; Mariano Armijo,[17] who operated the Armijo House, a fine hotel; and, of course, Josefa Werner, a distinguished Albuquerque pioneer who represented the blending of Hispano and Anglo culture in the city. Now he met with some of Hadley's friends and associates—people who could pave the way for him outside of Albuquerque—and he didn't disappoint them.

The next day Schlatter left the Werner home and took up residence with James A. Summers, the deputy clerk of Bernalillo County's probate court.[18] Why the healer made this move is unknown, but he dropped out of sight for almost two weeks. During this unusual period of silence, Will Hunter took the opportunity to recapitulate the healer's story for the *Rocky Mountain News*, which eagerly pub-

FIGURE 5. Portrait of Francis Schlatter made at Albright Studio,
Albuquerque, July 26, 1895, probably by owner Emma Albright.
Albright Studio, Albuquerque, courtesy Palace of the
Governors Photo Archives (NMHM/DCA), 132505.

lished it with his byline on August 4 and followed up three days later with an extended interview with Henry Hauenstein. Denver seemed to be preparing to receive the healer. Meanwhile, all was quiet at the Summers home in Albuquerque's Old Town.

WHEN THE HEALER finally emerged from his silence, he immediately touched off a controversy. Rev. Charles L. Bovard, the New Mexico superintendent of missions for the Methodist Episcopal Church, called on Schlatter.[19] Bovard wanted to get at the bottom of rumors about the man many people regarded as the Messiah. They spoke for a few minutes. Then Bovard asked, "Do you claim to be Jesus Christ returned to earth?" Schlatter replied, "I am. Since you have asked me, sir, I say plainly I am."

Bovard took Schlatter's answer as proof that the man was insane, though harmlessly so, and wrote him off. Others did as well—particularly the editors of the *Albuquerque Citizen*, a rival to the *Democrat* and a newspaper particularly scornful of the healer. But the *Democrat*'s Will Hunter also had doubts of his own, and the next day he questioned Schlatter closely.

"Is it true," he asked, "that you claim to be the Christ?"

"Yes," Schlatter said. "I am not here to give information but I will always answer direct questions."

"Do you claim to be the Christ who died on Calvary?"[20]

"Yes."

"Do you believe in the teachings of the Bible?"

"Yes," Schlatter said. "It is the holy scripture."

"But the Bible says Christ was a Hebrew. You are not a Hebrew."

"No," Schlatter replied. "But this is my third life."

Hunter was astounded at Schlatter's words. But, unlike Bovard, he regarded the healer as a riddle and a mystery, not a lunatic. He had seen too much of Schlatter's kindness and candor—and the results of the healer's work—to doubt his sanity. But the next day his puzzlement only deepened. He asked Schlatter if the *Democrat*'s account of their conversation had been correct. Yes, the healer said, with one exception. The paper had mistakenly quoted him about his third incarnation as Christ. "It is only my second appearance," he said, "and I would be glad if you would make this correction." He added: "It may mean more than you know."[21]

Hunter probably never guessed what lay behind Schlatter's earlier statement—that, when he misspoke the evening before, he was anticipating his *next* life, not his current one. The broad field of flowers, sunshine, and joyous children—his sister's vision of his destiny—had not yet materialized. *That* would be the healer's third incarnation, when he returned as the resurrected Messiah. His current life was nothing more than a preparation for the next. When Hunter asked him why, if he *were* the Messiah, he needed the Master to help him in his work, Schlatter replied, "I have not yet reached perfection."[22]

On August 15, the day he ended his fast, Schlatter sat down in the Summers home with Fitzjames McCarthy, a columnist for the *Denver Post* whose nom de plume was Fitz Mac. The healer looked gaunt and worn—much changed from the lean but robust man who appeared in New Mexico in early July. But he was dressed in a suit and tie, the gift of a local retailer, perhaps sent in honor of the occasion.[23]

For several hours, while the two men huddled together and held hands in a gesture of intimacy and confidence, Schlatter told Fitz Mac of his vision, his two-year pilgrimage, and his divine mission. Meanwhile, in another room a table was spread with fine linen and adorned with flowers, and in the kitchen cooks prepared the extraordinarily large meal that awaited the healer in the late afternoon.

Fitz Mac believed it would be the day of Schlatter's death. He later wrote: "I was so sure that it would kill him that I could not remain. I said to myself: 'He is now tackling a purely physical proposition—the rest of it has been largely psychical—he will be a dead man in six hours or less.' "[24] So sure was he of that, Fitz Mac left the house. He didn't want to see the healer, his newfound friend, eat his last meal.

Schlatter entered the dining room at exactly five o'clock, said the Lord's Prayer, blessed himself, and sat down to eat. On the table sat a dish of fried eggs, salt pork with gravy, cheese, chili con carne, pickled apples, a loaf of rye bread, roast chicken, and cake. The healer took major helpings of everything, and washed it all down with four glasses of port wine and a cup of coffee. He ate slowly and methodically, savoring everything. Throughout the meal a doctor sat by his side taking his pulse—100 beats per minute at the start, 80 beats at 5:30 p.m., 92 beats at 6:00 p.m., 90 at 6:15 p.m., and 96 at 6:30 p.m., when the meal ended. Effectively, his heart rate remained unchanged.[25]

When Schlatter was done, he excused himself and retired to his room—and remained virtually out of the public eye for nearly a week. Outsiders became so alarmed that Summers had to assure them the healer hadn't died and that his health was fine. Indeed, Schlatter met with Will Hunter in the parlor of the Summers home. "I am first rate," he said. "During my long fast everyone remarked how cold and lifeless my hands felt, but you see they are warm now. I feel remarkably well."[26] He went on to say that all he needed was a rest from public healing.

But, in spite of his facade, Schlatter's health had taken a serious blow, not only from the fast but the shock to his metabolic system. Nothing he said could hide how pale, lethargic, and ill he had become. In essence, he had returned to a state of fasting, for he was reduced to oatmeal and milk once a day. Ever since the fast, he told Hunter, "I have eaten regularly and can readily digest my food," but he was clearly lying.[27] A few days later he admitted his condition: "The Father is preparing me for my trip to Denver," he told Hunter, "and He has some good reasons for making me sick."[28]

Meanwhile, crowds waited daily in front of the Summers home —in vain. Too weak and sick to conduct healing sessions as he had done before, Schlatter allowed only a few people into his room for treatment. One of them was a nine-year-old boy from Pajarito who had been lame from birth.[29] The day after his treatment, it was reported, the boy was running and playing with his friends—as if the physical cure had also spontaneously given him balance, coordination, and confidence. But witnesses who knew the boy insisted that he had undergone a remarkable transformation, and the episode turned out to be Schlatter's last miracle in Albuquerque.

Another miracle, however, was in the making—and in practice it would have far-reaching consequences. Deprived of the opportunity to receive Schlatter's touch, some people who stood outside the Summers home sent in handkerchiefs, scarves, and jewelry for the healer to bless and return to them. The idea of using handkerchiefs struck Schlatter as novel, and he immediately adopted this new talismanic method of healing.[30] In fact, that afternoon he sat with an

Indian from Isleta who knelt down and kissed his hands and feet. Normally contact with the healer in itself was enough to effect a cure, but Schlatter got a handkerchief for the Isletan and told him to place it where he suffered pain. The man, who did not speak English, must have been somewhat baffled by the substitution.

In any case, there was no better time for Schlatter to heal vicariously through handkerchiefs, for he could hardly lift himself off the bed, and the crowds of needy sufferers had not diminished in the least. He did try to assuage them the day before his departure by agreeing to come out and sit on the porch, but only on condition that no one come near him — and that lasted but a few minutes. The healer's last day in Albuquerque, in fact, testifies to a kind of hero worship usually considered modern. The carriage that took him to the depot from the Summers home could hardly get through the throng, and at the depot a police officer had to keep people away from him. In the end, it was impossible to hold the crowd back, and while some caring souls used fans to cool him from the evening heat, men reached out to touch him and women took turns stroking his luxurious hair.[31]

With help, Schlatter managed to climb up into the waiting Pullman car, which contained a private section that Edward Fox had secured for him. He shook hands and said good-bye to his Albuquerque friends, including his host, James Summers, and his public voice, Will Hunter. As the Atchison, Topeka & Santa Fe train pulled away from the station, and the crush of people near the Pullman dissolved into the growing darkness, Hunter returned to the office of the *Albuquerque Morning Democrat* to write his final story about the man he'd known for barely six weeks. Skeptical of Schlatter in the beginning, and generally reserved and neutral in his pieces, Hunter concluded with his admiration for "this strange, remarkable person who lives for everyone but himself."[32]

THE RAILROAD TRIP north took almost twenty-four hours, from early dark on Wednesday, August 21, to sunset the next day.[33] All along the route, groups of people would gather to see the healer, often slowing the train down or bringing it to an unscheduled stop. In Cerillos, a few miles south of Santa Fe, three hundred people waited to see the healer; in Lamy, where the train arrived at 2:00 a.m., another three hundred stood in pouring rain; and in Trinidad, Colorado, another large crowd was waiting for him early the next morning. Once or twice he stepped to the loading platform and spoke. The Father, he told the crowd, would cure them simply for expressing their faith in the healer. But many wanted more assurance than that—and they handed him their handkerchiefs to be blessed and returned. Eventually the healer merely looked out the window, waved, and blessed handkerchiefs from his Pullman drawing room. He was still extremely ill and exhausted.

Since the Atchison, Topeka & Santa Fe train didn't go to Denver, Schlatter had to switch at La Junta—probably to a Rio Grande train. In Colorado Springs he sought some rest but instead encountered a group of Denver newsmen competing to get a scoop on his story. One of them was Joseph Emerson Smith, a young reporter whose *Denver Post* editor had ordered him to do his best to expose the healer. "See if you can pick a flaw," the editor told him. "If there's fakery there, it will make a better story than the truth."[34]

A porter helped the healer down from the train and to a high-backed bench in the Colorado Springs depot. Schlatter, looking weak and ashen, asked the man for a handkerchief. The porter gave it to him, and Schlatter held it between his palms and silently prayed.

"This'll bring me good luck, yes?" the porter said. He called him Mr. Messiah.[35]

"It will bring you health," Schlatter replied. "It will comfort you, as long as you are a good Christian."

The train whistle blew, and the porter ran back to the boarding platform, leaving Schlatter with the Denver reporters in the terminal.

One of them ventured a question.

"Did you actually fast forty days and forty nights?"[36]

"Yes," Schlatter said. "You can see. Open my coat."

The *Denver Republican* reporter unbuttoned the healer's jumper, and the others stared at the man's prominent ribs. Schlatter had them place their fingers along the intervening grooves, and Joseph Emerson Smith felt how cold and clammy his skin was. The healer sat back, smiled faintly, and closed his eyes. Smith had already noticed Schlatter's eyes—"as blue and deep," he later remembered, "as Chesapeake bay was blue and deep under gray clouds."[37]

"Do they call you the Messiah?" Smith asked, remembering that the porter had used the word.[38]

"No, I am not," Schlatter replied. "I have never said so. Some call me that, but they are mistaken."

"Do you believe you can heal sick people?" another reporter asked.

"I am," Schlatter replied.

"What?"

"I am."

"What do you mean?" the baffled reporter answered.

But the healer had already fallen asleep, his tunic open, on the bench.

Colorado's nascent telephone service was among the best. Within three years of the first long-distance line from New York to Chicago in 1892, Denver was connected to Colorado Springs. Smith found a hotel near the depot, and he called his boss from a wall phone.

Before he could explain, the editor said, "Didn't get much of a story, did you?"

"As much as the other boys."

"Get back to him," his boss said, "buy him a meal, and get the *story*."

But by the time Smith arrived at the depot, Schlatter was gone. Friends had put him on a Colorado Midland train to Denver, and the cub reporter barely caught it. He never did manage to expose the healer, as his editor wanted; but as the *Post*'s religion reporter, standing with the healer on a daily basis for the next two months, Smith brought in exceptional stories. In spite of his youth, he was perhaps the finest reporter there — but he would never quite understand what the healer meant by "I am."[39]

CHAPTER FOUR

Healer of the Multitudes

To look at the expectant multitude one
would think that all the world was sick.[1]

JOSEPH WOLFF

THE HEALER'S arrival in Denver was anything but notable.[2] Edward Fox expected him on a Rio Grande train, as did scores of other people who pushed and shoved to get a place on the boarding platform at the Union station. When Schlatter didn't show up, they left disappointed and disconsolate, including Fox. Schlatter came in a few hours later on the Colorado Midland, along with a small retinue of reporters and a trainload of Denverites returning from a flower carnival in Colorado Springs, unmindful of the holy man in their midst. Somewhere along the way, Schlatter had befriended a man named Ryan, who knew of a cheap hotel nearby, and the little group walked up Seventeenth Street in search of it.[3] If the healer had any thoughts about his arrival in Denver three years past, he didn't mention it.

This event, in any case, made one reporter think of William T. Stead's *If Christ Came to Chicago,* a best seller that appeared a few months earlier. Stead was a social reformer who highlighted the corruption and venality of society by imagining its response to the return of the Messiah. Here, now, was someone in the flesh whom people called the Messiah—and without doubt, the reporter thought, Schlatter had the bearing and confidence of one. His clothes were cheap but clean, his oversized shoes broad and flat, and his cheeks sunken from near starvation. Yet when he spoke in his thickly accented but clear voice, he exuded authority.

At the hotel, the reporters watched him sign the guest register, and one of them asked him for his signature. He wrote it on a card and handed it over. "That name will heal any pain that you may have," he said.[4] Then someone asked if he had ever been married. He turned his gaze on the questioner. "No, I never was married," he said. "I have no family, no relatives."[5] For that matter, he remained silent about his old friends and associates in Denver, including the Ingersolls, Albert Whitaker, and John Boucher, and said nothing about his interest in spiritualism or preparation to become a healer. For all practical purposes, he arrived in Denver a man without a past.

Early the next morning Edward Fox found him at the Union Hotel — probably by calling several. Fox, a coal and grain merchant and former Denver alderman, lived in a small two-bedroom home at 725 Witter Street in north Denver. He was struggling in the wake of the silver crash, but he was still able to own a telephone. Fox was more than ready to open his home to Schlatter — as was his wife, Mary, who hadn't yet seen the healer. At best, it would be a sacrifice, since Fox's daughter, Anna, occupied the second bedroom, and a nephew, Leonard Kern, also lived with the family while working in his uncle's business.[6]

In fact, the number of people who showed up to see Schlatter at the depot may have given Fox pause about his readiness to host the healer. The next morning, instead of taking Schlatter home, Fox drove him to Henry Hauenstein's place just a few blocks away. There the healer could rest and recuperate while Fox made the necessary preparations to handle the onslaught of pilgrims. L. E. Ryan, with whom Schlatter slept for two nights as a curative treatment, found someplace else to board — but remained near the healer for several weeks.[7]

Within hours rumor passed through the city that Schlatter was at Hauenstein's, and people soon crowded in front of the home to see the healer. Hauenstein, ever respectful of his guest's wishes, refused to let anyone inside — but listened to the plea of one woman, Mrs. Richard Webber, whose young son Harry suffered from hip disease. He stood at her side, supported by a crutch. One of his feet was shrunken and useless. Hauenstein told the woman to wait, disappeared inside, and returned shortly. Did she have a handkerchief? he asked. She found one, and Hauenstein returned again with a small covered basket. As she looked inside, Hauenstein told her to apply the handkerchief to her son's hip every night. She walked away, her face lit with joy, exclaiming, "It's in here, in here! Here is my boy's cure. God be praised!"[8]

Schlatter was canny. He knew that, in effect, if he saw and treated the boy, he'd have to treat everyone else. Since the beginning of his ministry in July, he'd given special attention to a few people now and then, Henry Hauenstein being the most notable example. But now that Schlatter could heal through the agency of a handkerchief, or a letter, or any other object, he could maintain a semblance of fairness without placing himself at the multitude's beck and call. The boy's mother could not say that Schlatter had touched her son's hip, only that he had blessed a handkerchief—which the healer could do easily for anyone else while he stayed out of the public eye.

Schlatter well knew that he needed plenty of rest after his nearly disastrous meal of August 15, barely a week past. During that time he had eaten a daily portion of boiled eggs, toast, and coffee—and that was all, except for cracked ice and some peaches and grapes that Hauenstein had placed in a bowl for him. He spent most of his days lying on Hauenstein's parlor couch in darkness and quiet, and he seemed to enjoy the attention he received from his host. "Fill this, please," he said to Hauenstein, handing him a glass. "Water is the best thing after all."[9] For himself, Hauenstein was perfectly happy to meet the healer's needs. "Mr. Schlatter can stay here a month or a year, if he wants to," he said.[10]

In point of fact, Schlatter had already determined how long he would stay in Denver. Back in Albuquerque, when questioned about his plans, he said his Denver ministry would not last more than two months.[11] A few days later, speaking to a reporter en route, he was even more pointed: he would stay in Denver for sixty days, "and then disappear for an indefinite period of time."[12] He repeated his intentions several times—and though not consistent as to the timing, he made it clear that Denver was only the first large city to which he planned to take his healing ministry. Chicago would be next. He stated, in fact, that "in all probability" he would also visit England and France. Once, when asked if he considered establishing a church or gathering disciples, he said all that would come later.[13]

Schlatter remained in seclusion during his entire stay at Hauenstein's. But he did meet with a few people who visited quietly, and he performed a handful of healings that were kept secret, among them that of a woman who survived after doctors had given up hope for her recovery.[14] One of Schlatter's most influential visitors was Clarence Clark, a wealthy investor and real estate man who became fascinated with his story—and image—in the *Rocky Mountain News*. Clark introduced himself to Schlatter with a bottle of port wine and some fruit, and on a second visit they entered into a deep discussion.[15] As he was leaving, Clark asked if Schlatter would agree to meet with some of the city's intellectual and social leaders. Yes, the healer said, as long as they didn't include traditional preachers of the Gospel, whom he knew would be prejudiced against him.

Clark invited some forty or fifty people, among them a U.S. senator, judges, teachers, and "students of mental and spiritual questions," including Rev. Myron Reed, a liberal minister who championed social and religious reform.[16] The gathering, which took place in Clark's home on September 15, did much to ensure the success of Schlatter's healing ministry and solidified his reputation as an honest man of God. One of the few ministers present, probably Reed, said: "I never talked with a man who answered questions on such a spiritual basis or so truthfully."[17]

The meeting lasted about two hours. "Yet, what do you suppose he did after that reception closed?" Clark said. "He went out in the back yard and played marbles with the small boys."

The next day the healer—a Christ figure who could discuss spiritual matters with elders and play marbles with children in equal measure—began one of most phenomenal healing ministries of modern times.

———————————

THE FOX HOME STOOD on the west side of Witter Street in a quiet residential neighborhood graced with oak and elm trees. The dirt street, as yet unimproved with gutters or sidewalks, sloped gently south to Fairview Avenue, which itself descended gradually eastward to the banks of the South Platte. Across the river lay Denver proper, accessible from the Fifteenth Street Bridge a quarter mile away. Cable cars from the city stopped at Fairview and Cass, a mere two blocks from the Fox home, on their way into the Highlands neighborhood.

The block on which the home sat was nearly bare of other structures, except for the family's horse barn. In front of the house, bordering the street, Fox had thrown up a plain board fence—part of his preparation, no doubt—which offered some protection for his lawn, shrubs, and flowers. A few trees along the street kept the yard shaded during the morning hours. All in all, the neighborhood could not have been better suited for the unprecedented event that was to take place. There were plenty of open fields and empty lots surrounding the Fox home where vendors' tents, wagons, and stalls could serve the crowds.

By seven o'clock on September 16 some three hundred people—and growing—had gathered in the street along Fox's makeshift fence.[18] Mary Fox came out from time to time, reassuring them that the healer would make his appearance, but primarily keeping them off her lawn. Edward Fox had seen firsthand how the crowds in Albuquerque had ruined James Summers's lovely flower-filled adobe patio. It was enough that reporters had already taken a position in the yard, along with L. E. Ryan and a couple of other friends and assistants.

As nine o'clock approached, all eyes were locked on the Foxes' front door, and some of the curious strained to see inside the windows. So it was with disappointment that Schlatter appeared quietly from the rear of the house that morning and took his place behind the picket fence. The day was already warm, and as the sun climbed higher in a pale blue sky, a few watchers and waiters opened up their umbrellas to shield themselves from the heat.

Schlatter wore gray pants, a vest, a black cotton shirt, and a plain necktie—a simple suit of clothing described as cheap but not shabby. His hair was carefully oiled, brushed, and parted in the middle, and his beard had been trimmed back a bit. He began his work without fanfare, taking the hands of the first person in line and holding them for half a minute or so, tightly, and saying a short prayer. When he released the pilgrim, he said, "Thank you, Father." Then he took the hands of the next person, and the next, in the same way. Meanwhile, the reporters looked closely to see if they could find a story in any of the people he had touched. (Joseph Emerson Smith was not among them, for he had barely escaped death after a fall from a cliff over the weekend. But when his editor learned that Smith had skipped the healer's first day, he berated him for not testing Schlatter's curative powers on his bruised and battered body.)[19]

Schlatter's first day healing set the tone for all the rest. He treated the crowds for three hours in the morning, took an hour's break for lunch, and worked again from one to three o'clock in the afternoon, then spent some time treating the lame or disabled in carriages. One of the first people in line was an Italian woman who began listing her complaints. "I do not want to know what is the matter with you," Schlatter interrupted.[20] "The Father knows all about it. All that is required of you is faith." He had to correct several others in the same way; but, after a while, the message filtered down the line, and thereafter sufferers approached him silently about their condition. In one instance, an old woman whom he had treated moved back a few paces and held her hands in prayer. "By and by it will be all right," Schlatter told her. "In seven months it will be all right."[21] She seemed immensely relieved.

Word of Schlatter's use of letters and handkerchiefs as healing agents had already become common knowledge. Nearly everyone who arrived the first day carried a handkerchief. At first, Fox had sufferers mark or initial the handkerchiefs, then placed them in a wicker basket to be retrieved later. But the practice of dropping off and returning several hundred handkerchiefs a day grew to be extremely cumbersome, let alone distracting, and before long the healer simply blessed them as part of each supplicant's treatment. On the first day Harry Webber, the boy whom Schlatter had treated by handkerchief three weeks earlier, appeared with his mother. She testified that her son's hip pain was gone and his leg was improving, but it was clear she still sought the assurance of Schlatter's direct touch.[22]

While Schlatter's first day of healing went well, the second bordered on disaster. Nearly four times as many people showed up—reports said two thousand—and the crushing mass of humanity overwhelmed Fox's fledgling operation. He found himself chasing away people who tried to climb over his fence, and several times Schlatter had to admonish the crowd to behave. "Get into line!" he shouted. "Get into line or I will not treat you at all. I mean what I say."[23]

The shoving and jostling was so bad that pilgrims in line had to hold on to each other or to Fox's fence. One woman lost her cape; another her pocketbook. Still another, holding a baby, was pushed to the ground by a pair of jittery carriage horses. Neither the woman nor the baby was hurt, but her attention was so focused on Schlatter that she hardly noticed when another woman dusted off her crying baby and placed it back in her arms.

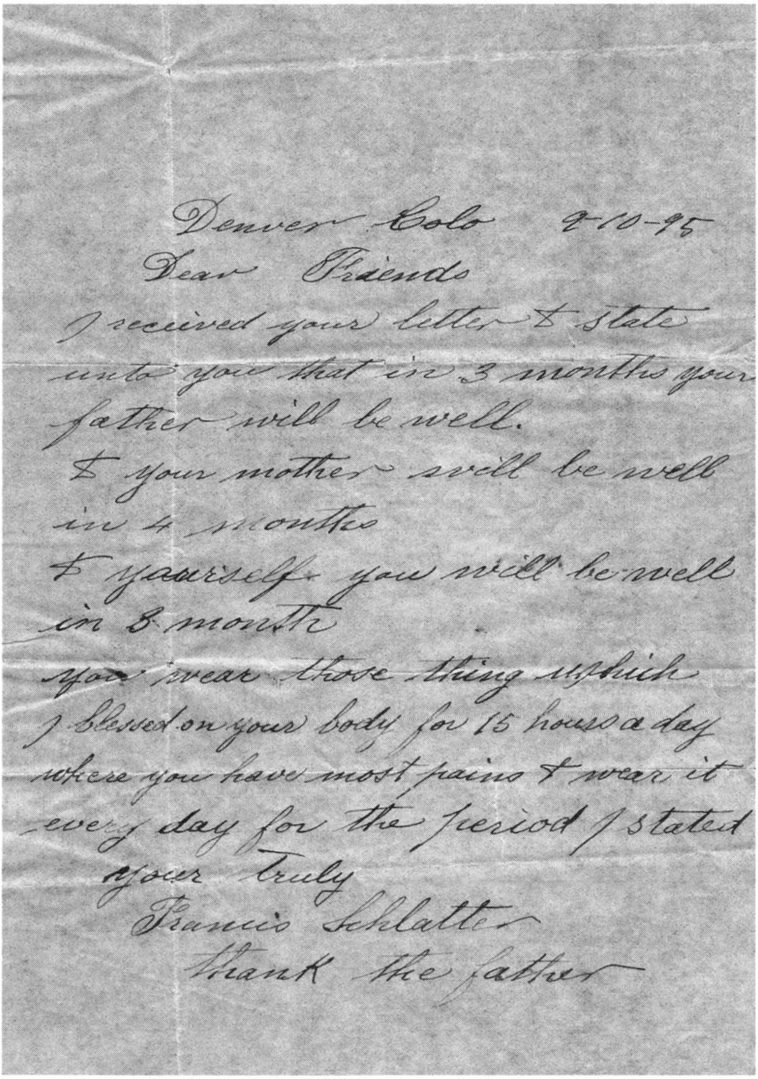

Denver Colo 9-10-95

Dear Friends

I received your letter & state unto you that in 3 months your father will be well.

& your mother will be well in 4 months

& yourself you will be well in 8 month

you wear those thing which I blessed on your body for 15 hours a day where you have most pains & wear it every day for the period I stated

your truly

Francis Schlatter

thank the father

FIGURE 6. Schlatter wrote a healing letter dated October 9, 1895, to the Kansas family of Alonzo A. and Nancy Jane Goff, parents of an ailing daughter, Melissa Goff, containing handkerchiefs they had sent to be blessed. Of the many hundreds of healing letters Schlatter wrote before he disappeared, this is the first to have come to light. Courtesy Kathryn Goff Kent, High Bridge, New Jersey.

Many who showed up that day were irreverent. Fox had put out a barrel of water, and chained a few tin cups to it, for thirsty observers. It became the scene of a typical encounter. One young wit saw a weary, gray-haired woman leaning on a tree next to the barrel, looking as though she'd never make it to the end of the long line. "Imagine this barrel is the pool of Siloam, auntie," he said, "and you touch the waters when I stir them. You won't then have to—"

"Remember whose presence you are in," she snapped. The boy went away laughing. But he and other scoffers, while getting their laughs, failed to seriously dampen the overwhelming spirit of hope and expectation that filled the air—and that kept emotions high. One man held his infant son in one hand and kept an arm around his six-year-old daughter, who sat on the fence. They were near Schlatter, and the healer turned and smiled at the little girl.

"See, Helen," her father said, "Mr. Schlatter is smiling at you."

"It's just as good for me to see her as to touch her," the healer said. "She is all right."

The father broke down in tears.

Most people who passed by the healer wept as well, and some were so overcome by the moment they regarded it as holy. One Italian woman, after grasping the healer's hands, did not move ahead but backed slowly and reverently into the street, as if from Jesus on the cross. Another young woman brought a letter from her blind sister in Holland, and Schlatter held it in his hands. Those living far away, he said, are healed as easily as those who are near. It didn't matter whether those with faith lived in China or Denver. "Your sister will recover her sight in seven months," he promised. The young woman left him, crying in sadness and joy at once.

The disorder of the second day ended on the third. Fox had found an excellent way to control the jostling crowds. Overnight he worked with several men to build a waist-high railing that paralleled his property fence all the way back to Fairview Avenue. Now only one person at a time could pass by the healer, and the onlookers milling in the street couldn't easily vault the fence into his yard. Fox also laid down some wooden panels on the ground behind the fence, and eventually Schlatter stood on a low platform to raise him slightly above the supplicants. This allowed him to grasp their hands more easily.

Standing in the unmerciful September sun, Schlatter wore nothing on his head and had only one or two sips of water during the day. His hands became badly sunburned, both on the back and front, and his hour-by-hour skin contact with the public had created a kind of stigmata in the middle of his palms. "A vivid red spot," wrote Joseph Emerson Smith, "burned in the center, and radiating from it in all directions was a pinkish tinge, fading from a bright shade to the natural color of his flesh." Smith asked Schlatter how he felt.[24]

"Feel?" the healer asked. "I feel all right. This sun doesn't affect me at all. I'm strong now. Two weeks ago I could take my fingers and span my wrist. Now I can't." To prove it, he wrapped his left thumb and forefinger around his right wrist, and Smith noted a good inch of space between their tips. The healer's wrists were normally large—and his hands, and especially fingers, exceptionally large and long.

Everything about Schlatter struck people as Christlike—and not only his looks. He combined modesty with authority, kindness with toughness, patience with decisiveness. Just as he had related equally to the august leaders of Denver and the small boys in Clarence Clark's backyard, he took full control of the hypnotic religious event that was unfolding around him. Someone cried, "Jesus, save me, save me!" and he reached out his hand.[25] But he just as quickly turned away a woman who tried to kiss his feet. When people thanked him unduly, he reminded them that it was God, not himself, who healed them. To a man who addressed him as "doctor," he said: "I am no doctor. The Doctor is above."[26] He was the epitome of tenderness to most of the supplicants, but he rebuked a woman for holding her bareheaded baby too long in the hot sun. "Take that child home," he shouted—but he made sure that the woman took a handkerchief he had blessed to lay on the child's scabby face.

Even ministers who saw him—unlike those who criticized him from their pulpits—came away impressed. One admirer, a clergyman with gold-rimmed glasses, said: "I seem to see a vision of the actual Christ receiving the multitudes by the lake of Galilee. Somehow, I can't shake off the thought."[27] Many sufferers envisioned the same thing. But, in the end, they didn't consider Schlatter, literally, to be the second coming of Christ—or at least they didn't say so to reporters. Schlatter held to his rule of answering "I am" or "I am Christ" only to direct questions—and he became testy when told that it was undermining the public's confidence in him. "Then they ought not to ask me," he said.[28]

Nevertheless, the more acceptable image of the healer, not as Christ reincarnate but as a spiritually transcendent man of God, prevailed. "He is not looked upon as Christ, as he says he is," said the *Denver Times*, "in a serious way, but he is considered to have a gift not given to ordinary mortals."[29] Rev. Myron Reed argued that people misinterpreted Schlatter. "He does not assume that he is Jesus Christ," Reed said. "He is the Christ spirit and the Christ method."[30] Edward Fox also said that Schlatter never claimed to be Christ, or ever did. "To me," he said, "he avers that he is nothing but a poor, ignorant man."[31] The impression Schlatter made of an uneducated holy man might have been false, but it reinforced the miracle of God's grace in modern times. God had raised up a simple cobbler to give comfort to the suffering, and had instilled in him a Christlike purity of spirit. Nothing could attest to this more than Reed's wonderment at Schlatter's wisdom. When he asked the healer to define self-sacrifice, Schlatter answered: "It is an act for which you want nothing and for which you won't have anything." That, said Reed, "is out of sight."[32]

The scene in front of the Fox home took on the character of a holy shrine—and it soon became known as the New Mount. But instead of Christ's dividing loaves and fishes among the multitude, modern-day vendors sold sandwiches, popcorn, peanuts, and watermelon, and one lemonade stand operator sent "bare-legged urchins" with tin buckets and cups into the crowd. Some Denverites brought their own food, like one German family that unwrapped a picnic basket of cheese sandwiches and beer to the envy of those around them.

Each day's line of pilgrims brought some new affliction or disability—a child's blindness, a legless man propped on a wooden cane, a woman with an ulcerous mouth, or some kind of horrendous injury. But the majority of pilgrims had no visible sign of disease or illness, and those who did usually suffered mainly from rheumatism or arthritic paralysis. Most of them, as well, were older people whose aches and pains simply came with aging.[33] They spoke of immediate relief, and they were the first to demonstrate how their fingers and limbs could suddenly move with miraculous ease. For the seriously afflicted, the healing came more slowly, if at all—but

FIGURE 7. Perhaps the most widely used photograph of
Francis Schlatter in 1895, this portrait from the Albright Studio
in Albuquerque was made on July 26. The *Denver Post* later printed
it on a special flyer. Albright Studio, Albuquerque, courtesy
Palace of the Governors Photo Archives (NMHM/DCA), 051264.

reporters, ever watchful for dramatic results, described instances of spontaneous healing. And who could explain the healer's power to quiet a screaming child, especially when Schlatter gripped small hands—even those of infants—as tightly as those of adults?

Schlatter treated all people who came to him equally. Not only did he ignore race, class, and nationality, but he also refused to follow a widespread practice of the day—to judge others by their physical appearance. To many of the observers at the Fox home, including some reporters, afflictions of the flesh were the marks of moral depravity. A *Times* reporter commented openly on a baby's blotched and reddened face—"signs," he wrote, that the infant was bearing "the sins of its father's or its mother's carnality and lust."[34] He went on to speculate on the motives of pregnant women who stood in line to see the healer. "For what?" he asked. "To be relieved of the unwelcome life that depends upon their own? Or for a blessing on a life dearer than their own?"[35]

Yet Schlatter's incredible empathy—some called it clairvoyance—kept observers at his healing sessions wondering. Once, in the middle of October, a well-dressed young woman came to him, and he took her hands. For the next two hours they stood together in silence as nearly fifteen hundred other cure-seekers waited. Schlatter held the woman up by the force of his grasp, and the two seemed to be joined together in wordless communion. At the end of the unprecedented healing session, the woman fainted, and Schlatter braced himself on the fence while he recovered. He refused to talk to reporters about the episode, and when asked about the unusual length of the treatment—most sessions were only two to three minutes—he said: "Be it unto them according to their faith."[36]

The second episode occurred a month later. Schlatter was performing his blessing on a man when he suddenly stopped and removed his hands.

"I cannot treat you," he said. The man, refusing to move on, demanded to know why.[37]

"Shall I tell you," Schlatter said, "right here, before all these people?"

"Yes," the man said.

"I cannot treat you," Schlatter repeated. "You are a murderer!" In a moment the man was gone, losing himself in the crowd. By itself, Schlatter's accusation hardly amounted to proof. But to those nearby, the man's hasty disappearance betrayed his guilt—and Schlatter's psychic powers.

The next day the healer again rejected a supplicant, this time even more violently. He took the man's hands reluctantly, for the feverish and shaking patient looked like he was drunk. Before the healing session had fairly started, however, Schlatter exclaimed "Nein!" and pushed the man away. Like the suspected murderer of the day before, this man also fled. Asked why he had reacted so violently, Schlatter replied: "The man hath a devil!"[38]

An embarrassed silence followed. Then a little girl spoke. "Couldn't you do anything for the poor man, Mister?"

"No, my child," Schlatter said. "In these latter days devils are cast out by the power of Beelzebub. I have only the power of my father."[39]

The little girl looked at him blankly, and the people nearby stood in silent embarrassment for several minutes. Few in this modern age really believed in possession by devils. But for Schlatter, the ethos of the Bible—both Old and New Testaments—was alive and present in the latter days of the nineteenth century. Devils, miracles, curses, and wondrous signs may have been bygone ideas for most people, spoken about in sermons and Sunday school, but for him they were as real as the dust of old Jerusalem's streets. From the time of his vision as a cobbler, he saw the world through different eyes. They were the eyes of the prophets, of visionaries, and of religious charismatics down through the ages. Occasionally he even fell into using the archaic pronoun forms "thee," "thou," and "thy," the sonorous language of the King James Bible. If anyone had argued that Jesus spoke a much different language than seventeenth-century English, Schlatter would have undoubtedly countered that first-century Aramaic, the language of Jesus, would not be understandable to modern ears.

He was Christlike, to be sure. But did he cure? And if he did so, how long did his cures last? These questions swirled around the healer's ministry in Denver. It was exactly what the reporters were looking to find out directly at the Fox home. All kinds of opinions made their way into the popular press. Most attributed the healer's more dramatic effects to the power of suggestion, others to animal magnetism, or a kind of human energy, "life force," or vitality that could pass from one person to another. Christian Scientists and advocates of mental healing saw nothing unusual in the power of the human will to effect one's own healing, especially when motivated by faith. And one Denver doctor, J. H. Tilden, advanced his own theory that disease was the result of moral transgression, and only the excitement of the moment led the moral degenerates who passed by Schlatter to pronounce themselves cured.[40]

Tilden's position, though extreme, fell within the prevailing medical view that Schlatter's "cures" came about through the power of suggestion. Its corollary was that some people were more susceptible to suggestion than others—for whatever reason. In fact, most doctors interviewed by the *Denver Times* in the first week of Schlatter's ministry attributed the cures to superstition, imagination, and the mental susceptibilities of certain classes of people—all suggesting that his power to heal rested on various degrees of human weakness in his subjects.[41] Real diseases—cancer, insanity, or degenerative afflictions—he couldn't possibly cure, they said. One doctor pointed out that he had recently performed an autopsy on a patient who died of a brain lesion while wearing a handkerchief Schlatter had blessed.

Perhaps the most unusual contemporary voice on the issue belonged to Rev. Edward Southworth. His sermon "In the Messianic Shadow" challenged the idea that Schlatter only healed imaginary ailments. Not only had Southworth witnessed dramatic cures, including relief from rheumatism, sciatica, kidney disease, and Bright's disease, but he argued that health and disease, like life and death, are interconnected aspects of the natural world. "For all healing is accomplished only by nature, moving her potencies along the avenues of vitality," he said.[42] "Now, if Schlatter really starts these hidden energies, even though they do not continue as long nor extend as far as we may wish, he is thereby entitled to be called a healer." Not even Christ, Southworth argued, manifested permanent cures: "Lazarus certainly died after having been raised from the dead."[43]

Whatever position one took, religious or secular, on the effectiveness of Schlatter's cures, no one believed him to be a charlatan or fraud. *Something* was happening, and it could only be explained as the work of God, the mysterious forces of nature, or the psychology of suggestion. Even today, the camps are the same, with perhaps greater weight given to the insights of psychology and mass behavior. But a large body of modern Evangelical Christians accepts and practices healing by the holy spirit, and a sizable number of New Age believers attribute healing to natural powers harnessed through modern-day mediums, incantations, or restorative objects like crystals. As Southworth so effectively argued, "Did Schlatter heal?" depends on what one assumes healing to be.[44]

SCHLATTER TREATED from fifteen hundred to two thousand people a day during his Denver ministry, and generally some five hundred awaited him at nine o'clock each morning. That number jumped considerably in the middle of October, as Denver inaugurated its first Festival of Mountain and Plain, a Mardi Gras–style celebration meant to counter the economic pall that hung over the city after the silver panic of 1893. Thousands of people traveled to Denver for the three-day festival, and many would not leave until they had taken the trolley to the Fox home in Denver's Highlands. The Denver Tramway Company, in fact, set aside several cars for that purpose, complete with signs stating "This Car for the Healer." During one two-day period in the middle of the festival, the daily number jumped to five thousand, and at its peak the *Rocky Mountain News* guessed that between seven thousand and twenty thousand people crowded around the Fox home.[45]

What *did* increase steadily was the number of people who arrived extremely early in the morning to find a place in line. At one point in mid-October, 430 people stood waiting at five o'clock in the morning.[46] Some of them wrapped themselves in blankets or fur robes and stayed all night, and a few huddled around small fires to stay warm. The fields that lay in and around the homes on Witter Street, in fact, eventually filled up with vendors' tents and squatters' shelters—to the consternation of Fox's neighbors. At one point, Schlatter refused to begin one morning until a "landlord" removed a tent in which he charged people two dollars to sleep.[47] The healer called it "robbing unfortunates."

Several money-making enterprises blossomed in the fertile ground of Schlatter's ministry. Not only did vendors' booths line the street—one of them a broken-down soup kitchen—but a few people

FIGURE 8. Hundreds of people gathered daily at the Fox home in
Highlands, northwest Denver, during Francis Schlatter's phenomenal
two-month ministry there in 1895. Emerging from the New Mexico
desert in July, he rose to national, even worldwide, fame before suddenly
disappearing on November 13, 1895. This image by William A. White,
looking southwest, captures the crowds in late September or early
October. William A. White, Library of Congress, LC-USZ62-105407.

tried to satisfy the crowd's curiosity about the healer. One of them
was Charlie R. Stedman, a resident of Highlands who got the idea of
writing a pamphlet on Schlatter after reading an article on the healer's life in the *Denver Times*. In fact, Stedman appropriated the *Times*
article wholesale, borrowed heavily from other newspaper articles,
and put together a pamphlet called *Life of Francis Schlatter, the Great
Healer or New Mexico Messiah*. He hawked the eighteen-page pamphlet
to the crowds for twenty cents on Witter Street from early October
to the time of Schlatter' s disappearance, and he made about $350
in sales.[48]

But, barring Stedman's plagiarism—a common practice—not
all entrepreneurs were as honest as he. In mid-October three men
purchased a bundle of handkerchiefs and had them steel-engraved
with Schlatter's likeness. They rented a storefront on Seventeenth
Street, set up a crude sign bearing his picture, and mailed out circulars headlined "Believe in Father."[49] The circulars, posted in towns
throughout Colorado, offered handkerchiefs for a dollar apiece that

presumably had received Schlatter's blessing. When applied to any part of the body affected with any disease, the circular stated, "the same effect will be produced as would be by a personal contact with the Great Healer."

One of the trio began peddling the "blessed" handkerchiefs at the Fox home, and at Schlatter's urging Edward Fox called the police.[50] The handkerchief vendor was sent away, and the next day the police ordered removal of the sign in front of the "miraculous picture and handkerchief emporium" on Seventeenth Street.[51] The confidence men complained that Fox was running his own handkerchief scam, but no one believed it. Instead, federal marshals soon arrested the handkerchief dealers and charged them with mail fraud. The U.S. magistrate set a date for the hearing and ordered Schlatter to testify—as a prosecution witness, not a defendant. The hearing was twice postponed and rescheduled for November 14.

The furor over the handkerchief scam brought attention to all the vendors hawking goods, food, and shelter at the Fox home—their tents and lean-tos forming the camp city that had come to be called "Schlattertown." Soon the fire marshal visited the site, and looking over the hodgepodge assemblage of wood and canvas, he ordered the squatters to decamp within twenty-four hours. As the healer carried out his work the next day, oblivious to the commotion around him, Witter Street slowly recovered its suburban landscape. At the end of the day, little remained of Schlattertown except some bedroom furniture and kitchen utensils and a glowing stove around which a family cooked its last meal. "The disappearance of the tents," stated the *Denver Republican*, "is regarded as a severe blow to the army of fakirs who are making money out of the crowds."[52]

As November arrived, vastly greater numbers made their way to the Fox home—but they were visitors, not locals. Most Denverites had seen Schlatter at least once, and many had returned two or three times. The healer's stated day of departure, November 16, had filtered through the media of the day—newspapers—and the pilgrims he now attracted came from rural parts of the West and Midwest. They had no hope of getting through the crowds in Chicago, and even a few Chicagoans arrived for the same reason.[53]

In the meantime, Schlatter had all but given up responding to the volume of mail that came daily to 725 Witter Street. A mountain of letters lay piled against the corner of the dining room, and many

were simply addressed "The Messiah, Denver, Colorado." Schlatter
told a reporter: "If I should try to answer every one of these, there
would be a year's work before me. All I can hope to do is to handle
the handkerchiefs and return them by mail."[54] He also began preparing for his departure, cutting down on his food intake, especially
meat. His meals were simple, sometimes nothing but a slice of but-
tered bread and a glass of wine.[55] One reporter noted, as well, that he
had a faraway look in his eyes and was less communicative. "While
he is evidently preparing for greater works than he has ever yet un-
dertaken," the reporter wrote, "he faces the future with absolute
faith in the divine assistance which he believes accompanies him
every moment of his life and directs every action."[56]

Schlatter was indeed planning for his departure, but not in a way
the public expected. He remained extremely vague about his visit to
Chicago, and he became annoyed when hearing that people there
were finding a hall in which he could do his public healing. "They
made a mistake," he said. "I have not been consulted in the matter
and it is not at all probable that I will go to any hall."[57] In any case,
only God knew what lay in store for him.

But, as it turned out, so did a few close friends. Clarence Clark,
for one, knew that Schlatter was not going to Chicago. About three
weeks before his scheduled departure, Schlatter asked Clark to visit
him. "The Father told me last night that I would not have to go to
Chicago," he said, "but that he wanted me to go to Old Mexico—to
the mountains far to the south, and I am going to do what he tells
me." Schlatter then made a request—of a sort. "The Father says
that you will fit me out for the trip, and I want you to get me a white
horse to travel on."[58]

Clark was happy to oblige his friend. He looked around the city
and found a white horse at Kuykendall's Livery Stable. Its name
was Old Butte because it had come from Butte City, Montana, and
it was one of the gentlest horses in the stable.[59] Before its retirement
just two days earlier, Butte had carried a blonde woman advertising
cigarettes at the Festival of Mountain and Plain. But as Clark told
Thomas Dawson years later, "he was the worst looking specimen of
horse-flesh you ever saw—a mere skeleton with sore back and so
weak and crippled that he stumbled along like a hobby horse."

Clark returned to Schlatter and told him he couldn't find a white horse anywhere. "Oh, yes, you did. You found one," Schlatter said. "The Father tells me that you found one but did not like him." The healer told Clark to go back and buy the horse, and the Father would make him sound again. Clark did what he was told and paid twenty-five dollars for the horse. Sure enough, within two or three weeks Butte was looking well, strong, and fit for the journey. Edward Fox had a large stable behind his house, primarily for his wagon animals, and it was a perfect hiding place for Butte until the time for the healer's departure arrived.[60]

Part of the surge in the final week of Schlatter's Denver ministry came from an unusual source—the Union Pacific Railroad. One of the people the healer treated was the wife of the railroad's general superintendent, Edward Dickinson, who traveled from Omaha to see him. Schlatter gave her special attention, probably at Fox's urging, and his treatment seemed to improve her deafness. When she told her husband, he posted an order that any Union Pacific employee who had suffered injury or illness, and their family members, could ride to Denver free of charge to see the healer. Almost immediately Union Pacific trains began filling up with employees, averaging 150 to 200 a day.[61]

Having spent the better part of two years walking along railroad tracks, Schlatter had a special fondness for railroad people—not necessarily the section workers but the engineers, conductors, and porters whom he came to know by sight. One engineer, William Norris, first saw Schlatter on the last part of the healer's pilgrimage, as he walked across the New Mexico desert. Soon after, Norris's leg was crushed in a train wreck, and he went to see Schlatter in Albuquerque. Later he came to Denver just to thank the healer. "Oh," Schlatter exclaimed, in spite of the myriad faces he had seen, "you are the engineer!"[62]

As the Union Pacific, the Denver & Rio Grande, and the Texas & Gulf railroads disgorged their sick, afflicted, or disabled passengers, Denver's Union Station began to look like the crowded emergency room of a modern hospital. "They were in all sorts and conditions," stated the *Republican*. "Crutches were everywhere, paralyzed arms hung helplessly downward, bandages were common."[63] There were sick children, schizophrenics, arthritics with bent fingers, and crippled people who lined Union Station's long benches. But there were also nurses, family members, and helpers. "Able-bodied men tenderly carried in their arms the invalids of the family and tottering steps were supported by strong hands," wrote one reporter. "Others were supported on crutches and many were so weak from the long journey by rail that they were obliged to rest in the depot before proceeding to a lodging place."[64]

As the crowds increased, Schlatter's timing quickened. Back in September he would spend twenty to thirty seconds with each person; now he spent five.

"Is a quick treatment as efficacious as a long one?" a reporter asked him.

"Oh yes," Schlatter replied. "All that is really necessary is for me to touch them, but the people would not be satisfied."[65] Schlatter had consistently maintained that his mere touch, either directly or through the medium of a handkerchief or letter, would achieve the desired effect if the patient had faith. He even argued that cure-seekers who merely *wanted* to see him, if their faith was unwavering, would be healed. In short, faith in the Father was the one and only condition necessary for healing—and Schlatter's adoption of such a simple and universal principle infuriated conservative ministers.

E. B. Jordan, a Methodist minister and follower of Rev. A. B. Simpson of the Christian Alliance, came to Denver specifically to investigate Schlatter's healing methods and to prove them false.[66] For nearly half a century, divine healing within the Protestant tradition had been associated with the holiness movement, a precursor to twentieth-century Pentecostalism, which emphasized the "supernatural intervention of God" in the lives of Christians.[67] This event, often referred to as the Baptism of the Holy Spirit, closely resembled God's transcendent grace in the immediacy of divine healing, and the association between the two became stronger as the century progressed—through religious healing sessions, healing homes, and influential serial publications like John Alexander Dowie's *Leaves of Healing* and books like A. B. Simpson's *The Gospel of Healing* (1896).

Although Schlatter probably read Simpson's *Gospel of Healing*, his inspiration as a healer drew from spiritualism and New Thought, both of which had little in common with the holiness movement. In fact, Simpson disdained any healing activity that did not require faith in Jesus Christ.[68] When Reverend Jordan investigated Schlatter, he was appalled that so many people at the Fox home were not

Christians—and he appealed to those who were deluded by Schlatter. "Do not become discouraged and give up," he advised them, "but shut yourself in with God, and hold on to him, until you know him as your Savior and sanctifier." Only then would they receive God's healing grace.[69] Schlatter would not have condoned Jordan's narrowness, for in part his understanding of healing had its roots in Catholic tradition, which took in *all* of suffering humanity.

NOVEMBER 13, 1895—a Wednesday—dawned cold and clear at the Fox home. The gathering light fell on a line of people three abreast that steadily lengthened block by block. Downtown, groups of people crowded the trolley stops to take the next car to Highlands. As they got off the cars and made their way to the end of the line, Fox's assistants gave them numbered tickets.[70] For many, it must have been disheartening to realize that they held a number in the six or seven hundreds at nine o'clock in the morning or in the fifteen hundreds at noon. But the line moved steadily. The healer had abandoned the blessing of handkerchiefs, and he was seeing 450 to 600 people an hour. The total number of pilgrims who passed by him exceeded that of any other day of his ministry. It was five thousand.

A sense of urgency prevailed now. The healer's expressed date of departure was Saturday the sixteenth, so only two full days remained of his ministry. Furthermore, he had been subpoenaed to testify the next day in the fraudulent handkerchief case, and the hearing would surely take up at least a half-day of his precious time. Thus the hours he could spend on the sick and suffering were limited, and quickly winding down. Acutely aware of the healer's fast-approaching departure, people of means and good income paid young boys—kids who got up early and stood for hours—up to seven dollars apiece for a place near the front of the line. Honest folk who stood nearby might despise these interlopers, as well as the rough-and-tumble boys who were their shills, but things were getting desperate.[71]

In spite of the pressing crowd and the healer's quickened pace, there were one or two outstanding examples of his miraculous healing powers on this day. The first was that of J. P. Handy of Ellsworth, Kansas, who suffered from severe rheumatism. Assisted by his wife, Handy made his way on crutches to the healer. As soon as Schlatter touched him, Handy felt his limbs relax, "like a hand opening," he said.[72] Then, instead of dramatically throwing his crutches aside, he tucked them under one arm and walked around amiably, as if he were a messenger of goodwill. But the real story didn't come out until a day later. Handy had developed hard, painful swellings or nodes on his palms from using crutches for many months. As the *Rocky Mountain News* described it, "they were gone twenty minutes after he touched the healer's hand."[73]

The second healing, which aroused considerable acclaim that day, also didn't reach the larger public until later. Colonel Frank M. Foote, a leader of the Wyoming National Guard, arrived that morning with his twelve-year-old daughter from Evanston, and she barely managed to see Schlatter that afternoon before the healing session ended.[74] She had been blind in her left eye since birth. Fifteen seconds with the healer, her father claimed, restored her sight. Once it had been determined that she could see again, he hastily scribbled a note, then held his hand over her good eye while she read the words that described her miraculous cure. They were: "Daughter—12 yrs age. Blind from birth in left eye. Sight restored fully instantly."[75] Later that evening a *Post* reporter again tested her in Colonel Foote's hotel room, and he found her sight in the left eye to be nearly as good as in the right.

Colonel Foote's daughter became the last celebrated case of Schlatter's healing ministry in Denver—or anywhere, as the world knew it. He left hundreds waiting in line at four o'clock that afternoon, and after treating a few in carriages he disappeared inside the Fox home. A large crowd lingered for more than an hour, straining to catch a glimpse of the healer through the windows. Then, as the vendors began shutting down their stalls, the last holdouts drifted away. Some, in fact, may have been attracted by an animated conversation Fox had with a man in a business suit.

"You might just as well offer him $5,000,000 as $5,000," Fox was saying. "If he decided to go you wouldn't have to pay him anything. The very quickest way to keep him away from your city is to offer him money for going there."[76] As it turned out, the man was a St. Louis speculator sent on a mission to attract the healer away from Chicago. The more they argued, the more baffled and frustrated he became—and the more Fox seemed to relish the exchange.

"What sort of a man is he, anyway?" the businessman said. "Does he think he's too good to take money? You can get pretty near any minister you want for $5,000."

"But Schlatter isn't a minister, you see," said Fox. "He doesn't need any money. He has no use for it, and you can't bribe him or buy him — and I would advise you not to try it."

Later, when Fox informed Schlatter of the offer, the healer said: "I don't want his dollars." He seemed much more interested in telling a *Rocky Mountain News* reporter about the power he'd felt that day, and how tired his neck had become.

"Why is that?" the reporter asked.

"Why," Schlatter replied, "you know the power comes through here" — he touched his forehead — "and passes down through my neck."[77] It was a clue to the habit Schlatter had of raising his head, as if in prayer, whenever he treated the next person in line. In these last days, the healer said, he had more power than ever before. He took hold of Fox's hand, and his friend reacted visibly to what he felt to be an electric shock.

As the evening passed, a man named Scott arrived at Fox's front door, along with some friends. Scott had seen the healer that day, and Schlatter remembered him as a man who had lent him fifty cents in the Mojave Desert. They sat and talked for a while, but were interrupted when a man from the state asylum came to the door asking that the healer step outside and treat a patient suffering from insanity. They could hear moans coming from a carriage parked in front. Schlatter immediately went out to help the stricken man, for he was particularly sensitive to victims of insanity and mental distress.

After Scott and his friends departed, Schlatter spent time talking with Fox and his family. Normally he would sit down and answer letters, but not tonight. In one corner of the dining room, a mountain of mail rose so high that it was difficult to pass around the large dining room table. Letters continued arriving daily in bundles of some fifteen hundred, and the *Rocky Mountain News* reporter estimated that the pile contained thirty to fifty thousand pieces of mail. Schlatter admitted that it was now beyond all human power to answer them in the time he had left. Instead, he brought out his Bible and read a few Old Testament prophecies. Afterward, he told the reporter, he did nothing that was not "inspired by a higher power, even to the selection of a chapter in the Bible from which he read."[78]

The reporter left the home about 9:30 p.m., when Schlatter generally began preparing for bed. But this night would be different. There was much to be done—and quickly. The first thing was a note that Schlatter wrote, probably with Edward and Mary Fox standing nearby, that read: "Mr. Fox. My mission is finished. Father takes me away. Good-bye."

CHAPTER FIVE

"Father takes me away"

Mr. Fox. My mission is finished.
Father takes me away. Good-bye.[1]
FRANCIS SCHLATTER

EDWARD FOX WAITED until ten o'clock at night before setting in motion the plan to steal his friend Schlatter out of the city and on his long journey south. About thirty minutes later, he told his nephew Leonard Kern—who likely knew nothing of the plan—to hitch two good driving horses to a rig in the carriage house behind the Fox home. Kern was to ride the white horse, Butte, which had only recently become part of Fox's stable. At 11:00 p.m., concealed in a slicker and hood, Schlatter entered the rig, which sat in readiness in front of the Fox home. With Fox holding the reins, the two men rode slowly down Witter Street, Kern following behind. A young coffee vendor, William McDermott, witnessed the hushed activity and thought it suspicious, but he had no idea what it meant.[2]

The party turned left at Fairview and headed for the Nineteenth Street viaduct. Once across the South Platte River they made their way through the semidark downtown streets to the brooding stone spire of Trinity Methodist Episcopal Church, where they turned south to follow Broadway Avenue to Cherry Creek. The creek, which ambled into Denver from the southeast, had its origins about fifty miles away in a pine-covered spur of the Rocky Mountains called the Black Forest. This would be Schlatter's escape route. Setting out, the small party crossed neighborhood streets that bridged the creek—Grant, Washington, Downing, and Corona—passing by houses large and small that slowly thinned out as they approached the city's outskirts. Then there was nothing but farmhouses, barns, and pasture land—and beyond that they passed along the creek's untamed banks thick with chokecherries and cottonwoods.

After about ten miles, they stopped. Kern dismounted, and the men packed the white horse, Butte, solidly with the healer's gear and possessions. To the west, under a clear, star-bright sky, the men could see the dark line of the Rocky Mountains and the hint of storm clouds moving in. They shook hands and said a few words of good-bye. Then Fox and Kern turned the carriage back toward Denver, and Schlatter pointed his fine new horse toward the Black Forest. He was on the first leg of his journey back to New Mexico.[3]

By dawn on November 14 the sky above the Fox home had be-come dark and foreboding. Sometimes cloud cover like this dispelled winter's cold in Denver, but not today. Lately a group of small-time entrepreneurs had come up with the idea of selling heated bricks. On this morning they were doing a good business in spite of the ban on fires in the neighborhood. By seven o'clock the line had again gone around the corner, and people stamped their feet and bundled up their young for a two-hour wait before the healer was to begin.

One of Fox's helpers, Harry Driscoll, arrived at the Fox home about half past seven.[4] When he entered, Fox showed him the note the healer had written, now pinned to the pillow on Schlatter's bed. Driscoll was shocked, but there was no time to lose. They had to do something right away. Driscoll offered to break the news to the crowd. He removed Schlatter's note from the pillow and stepped outside, to the front of the line of pilgrims. He didn't make an announcement—simply showed the note to those nearest the door and let the news travel down the line. It was electrifying. The an-guished cries, angry shouts, and general commotion rippled down the street like a moving train that had suddenly come to a stop, its couplings reverberating in the distance.

The line broke up, and people surged toward the Fox home in a frightening wave of anger and distress. The healer was gone! They had been waiting for hours in the cold, and some had traveled hun-dreds of miles to see him. Streetcars were still bringing hopeful pil-grims to the neighborhood—and for the next two or three hours, the shock of disappointment and grief played out again and again as new pilgrims arrived. In the meantime, confusion reigned. Fox emerged from the house and tried to explain. "Yes, he's gone," he said, "and that's all I know."[5] An old man on crutches shouted that Schlatter was a fraud, and the U.S. marshals should take him to jail.

Immediately word passed along that the healer *had* been arrested by federal agents.

Some of the pilgrims coalesced into an angry mob and began attacking a portion of the fence, pushing it over and stomping into Fox's yard. But enough of the crowd held them back to prevent much actual damage, and in time the prevailing mood became one of overwhelming sadness, grief, and resignation. Righted again, the fence soon became a shrine for handkerchiefs, pocketbooks, and trinkets—mementos of thanks and loss. But also, as everyone knew, anything Schlatter had touched was infused with his healing powers. "Even by placing things here," one man said, "we obtain some good."[6] Many people who made their way to the spot where Schlatter stood the day before held their handkerchiefs on the fence posts or cross planks, hoping that they might carry away some of his healing power. Others picked up handfuls of dirt from under the fence, or pulled out bunches of grass. Some merely thrust their hands through the fence planks as if to draw power from the space that surrounded the healer.

For weeks a sign had been tacked to Fox's porch: "No treatment after 4 p.m.—keep out." Now he replaced it with another that read: "The healer has disappeared—where, we don't know," followed by the words of Schlatter's farewell note.[7] The organized line of pilgrims that had been a distinguishing sight at the Fox home now became a disorganized cluster of groups filling the street and fields, along with aimless wanderers moving here and there. Some left, others stayed—and wept, railed, speculated, or philosophized. The street vendors still hawked coffee, rolls, and warming bricks, but very quickly the sense of a dissipating throng led some of them to dismantle their canvas tents and dampen their fires.

When the *Denver Post*'s Joseph Emerson Smith arrived on the scene, he was amazed to see the transformation that had taken place since yesterday. "You could hear the low buzz of talk," he said, "of questions asked, and the frequent moans and cries of women. Some were weeping quietly."[8] He pushed his way through the crowd and entered the house, where he found Fox explaining things to his neighbors, who were curious about the sudden quiet. "It's all a mystery," Fox said. "For the life of me, I can't say where he's gone or when."[9] Fox explained that he had tapped on the healer's bedroom

FIGURE 9. Artist's rendering of the empty bed reporters saw on the morning of November 14, 1895, following Schlatter's disappearance. The Fox family gave up the master bedroom in the rear of the house for the healer. *Rocky Mountain News* (Denver), November 15, 1895.

door at seven o'clock, as was his custom, for Schlatter was a light sleeper. Hearing nothing, Fox tapped again, then went inside to find the room empty and the bed unmade. He then saw the note pinned to the pillow.

"Was that all he wrote?" Smith asked.

"Just those eleven words," Fox replied. "Nothing else."[10]

Smith ran to Fox's wall telephone next to the parlor, beating the *Denver Times* reporter by seconds. By late afternoon both papers had broken the story, and the *Times* sent it out on the Associated Press wires. In the meantime, Smith and other reporters surveyed the littered waste and devastation outside the Fox home—finding in it a poignant analogy to the bitter disappointment of the abandoned pilgrims. "The dismantled and deserted look of everything in the entire block," the *Rocky Mountain News* reporter wrote, "struck a chill to the hearts of thousands who had come long distances expecting a scene of life and healing come to be regarded almost as miraculous."[11]

Yet the scene's pathos merely served as a backdrop to two burning questions: why had Schlatter disappeared, and where had he gone? To the first, nearly all of the healer's friends offered the same answer—his revulsion over the greed and profiteering that had grown up around his healing sessions. No doubt Schlatter hated the commercialism that pervaded his healing sessions, and had condemned it. Nevertheless, had the selling of ham sandwiches and watermelons, or the hawking of pamphlets and hot bricks, or even the scalping of line tickets been able to drive Schlatter out of Denver, he would have been gone in less than a week. He stayed for nearly two months, and he disappeared secretly overnight—because, *and only because*, he was following what he believed to be God's plan.

His disciples understood this well, and that's why they met with him at noon the day before, on November 13, to finalize the details of his disappearance and to develop a consistent, reasonable explanation for it.[12] When the meeting ended, they all understood their part in fulfilling the mission—which was to establish a blanket of false rumor, confusion, and deception that allowed the healer a decent opportunity to escape the city and its reporters.

And perhaps to escape the federal marshals, too, for some people believed that Schlatter vanished to avoid testifying at the hearing Thursday morning in the case of the "blessed handkerchief" sellers. A few, like the angry old man at the Fox home, even thought he was implicated in the scheme. The ringleader, Daniel Hanley, testified to Commissioner Adolphus B. Capron that Schlatter had blessed several bales of handkerchiefs that Hanley and his partners brought to him, suggesting that Schlatter and Edward Fox would have shared in the enterprise. He expressed confidence that Schlatter's testimony would vindicate them. But Hanley—a small-time, lying schemer if there ever was one—undoubtedly felt relief Thursday morning when he learned of Schlatter's disappearance. The absent healer, he knew, now couldn't testify against him. What Hanley *didn't* know was that Schlatter, the day before, had turned down five thousand dollars simply to take his ministry to St. Louis—and that this fact *alone*, in the eyes of the court, would have cleared the healer of any complicity in the handkerchief scam.

However, the prospect of testifying at a hearing on Thursday morning probably did convince Schlatter to carry out his plan sooner than he intended. He had everything to lose and nothing to gain by going to court the next morning. He was not on trial. He had no obligation to the court, the law, or the federal government, except for the verbal summons he had received a week earlier. And his mission—God's mission—superseded anything the courts of the land, or the jails, could administer. As his disciples knew, he was moving in accordance with the dictates of the Father, carrying out a divine plan that transcended the bonds of law, custom, tradition, or any other earthly limitation.

THE FIRST "HEALER" sighting took place that very morning. The conductor of the Denver, Lakewood & Golden Railway spotted a man with long hair, a thick beard, and a heavy corduroy coat walking west along the railroad tracks toward the foothills of the Rockies. Others on the train did too. Some waved to him; he waved back. He could have been anyone. On the other hand, if Schlatter's friends had wanted to steer public attention away from the healer, who was riding a white horse to the southeast, what better way than to have a Schlatter look-alike walking due west.

If that was the case, it succeeded beyond all expectation. In the foothills south of Golden lay a fifteen hundred–acre ranch established in 1860 by Alexander Rooney and his wife, Emaline, which featured a ranch house of Dakota sandstone that Rooney had quarried and built.[13] Now an old man, he had brought one of his daughters to Schlatter the week before to be treated for "dull hearing." As he approached, the two men recognized each other—for Rooney had been a frequent visitor to Schlatter's cobbler shop on Downing Street in 1893.[14] After their greeting, Rooney handed Schlatter a note. It was an invitation for the healer to stay at his ranch any time.[15]

In the wake of Schlatter's disappearance, the sighting of a Schlatter-like figure walking along the railroad to Golden meshed with the story of Rooney's invitation to convince the public that the healer lay in hiding on the Golden-area ranch. In spite of the family's many denials, it proved to be a difficult perception to dislodge. A couple of *Rocky Mountain News* reporters knocked on the door of

Rooney's stone house late Thursday night, and a detective came the next day.[16] Rooney graciously invited them inside but ultimately could not satisfy them.

Meanwhile, the *Rocky Mountain News* hit Denver's streets on Saturday with the headline "Schlatter Mounted on a White Horse." The story, unlike many others at the time, contained specific detail and reliable witnesses. Schlatter, it said, had passed through Elizabeth, Colorado, at 8:30 the previous morning—Friday—riding a large gray horse loaded with gear. Elizabeth lay some forty miles to the southeast of the Rooney ranch.[17] The rider wore a bright woolen hat and a canvaslike coat, and shoes without heels. His hair was tied up in a white handkerchief. A canvas-covered bedroll lay behind his brand-new saddle, and, the reporter noticed, hanging from a saddle strap, a long leather scabbard that he assumed held a rifle.

But was it Schlatter? Everything about the man—including his well-packed gear, fine travel clothing, and unseen rifle—argued against the conventional image of a bedraggled, long-haired healer plodding with a bundle on a stick across the high plains. No, the Elizabeth sighting was an aberration, everyone thought, just like another report that the healer had entered a hotel in Beatrice, Nebraska. "Schlatter in the window of a hotel and Schlatter on a white horse," the *Denver Times* editorialized that very afternoon, "are two halftones of the imagination that are well worked up, but the negatives will not wash in the acid of veracity."[18] More prosaic was the *Denver Post*, which merely called the Elizabeth sighting "improbable."[19] But the *Post*—like most everyone else—had it wrong.

Only one other reliable eyewitness sighting occurred—and this was near Manitou, Colorado, the day after the Elizabeth sighting.[20] That afternoon, section hands repairing the cog railway leading to the summit of Pikes Peak chatted with a man who was walking slowly up the track. He was hatless and had long hair, and his soiled corduroy trousers and leather jacket resembled the clothing Schlatter wore at the Fox home. On his back he carried a blanket roll tied with thongs, a shawl, and a pair of boots. The man was affable and seemed pleased that they recognized him as the healer.

If this *was* Schlatter—and no one will likely ever know—why would he have boarded his horse somewhere and taken a leisurely hike up the mountain? The only logical reason would have been to visit a long-established community of spiritualists who had settled on the slopes of Pikes Peak in the early 1870s.[21] Crystola, developed by a former Illinois congressman, Henry Clay Childs, was also a utopian labor experiment—something Schlatter might have heard about in Denver. He could easily have ridden there in two days from Elizabeth and spent time in the community before moving on.

———————

BY THE TIME the healer was discovered just north of Pueblo, the residents of Denver had resumed life as usual. Only the healer's conspirators remained to congratulate themselves silently on the job they had done, and to think about the great work he would accomplish. The core at the center consisted of Edward Fox and his wife, Mary; Joseph Wolff; Clarence Clark; and cattle baron Charles N. Whitman, who shared half the cost of outfitting the healer for his journey.[22] As a group, they represented considerable wealth and influence. They could easily have paid a couple of long-haired veterans of Coxey's Army of the Unemployed to walk along the track to Golden or register as Francis Schlatter at the hotel in Beatrice, Nebraska.

Feeling safe well beyond Denver, Schlatter admitted his identity, answered questions about himself, and openly treated people who came to him for healing. To Charles Gatza, who invited him to dinner at his home near Overton, about eight miles north of Pueblo, he revealed even more.[23] He showed Gatza and his wife his copper rod, which they incorrectly thought was polished brass. He told them it was his walking stick—though this must have struck them as odd since it looked more like a baseball bat. Where he got it he didn't say; but since the reporter in Elizabeth mistakenly thought Schlatter had a rifle in a scabbard, the likelihood is that the healer set out from Denver with the copper rod in its custom-made leather holster. It would later be determined that Clarence Clark had ordered it cast for him, every detail of it made to Schlatter's specifications.[24]

By the time Schlatter met the Gatza family, he was confident that nothing would interrupt his journey south. More than likely he'd received word that the handkerchief case had been dropped—and this, along with other information, came through a chain of friends and sympathizers that stretched well into New Mexico. Just as Clarence Clark and others had helped Schlatter plot his route of travel, they also identified islands of retreat, warmth, and comfort. For instance, George Sears, a store proprietor in Greenhorn, thirty miles west of Pueblo, was looking for Schlatter four days before the healer arrived there.[25]

From Greenhorn, Schlatter rode across the western edge of the Arkansas River valley to Walsenburg, a mining town. Inexplicably, he went straight down its main street without stopping, gathering in his wake a large assembly of people on horseback, on bicycles, and in carriages, who followed him up a rise to the tiny mining camp of Rouse. As he emerged on the hill, a small boy shouted, "Here he comes! Here's Schlatter!"[26] There Schlatter stopped and began healing for the first time in two weeks.[27]

The whole tenor of the healing session at Rouse was different than Schlatter's last days in Denver. There were far fewer people, the scene was a spacious hilltop, and the healer was unhurried and at ease. At one point he entered the home of a Rouse miner who had an ailing child and spent nearly twenty minutes holding the child's small hands in his giant grasp. Women surrounded him and kissed their babies after he blessed them, and a black woman he'd treated walked away weeping.

The scene would repeat itself in a handful of villages and ranches Schlatter passed through on his way south. He avoided large towns like Pueblo and Trinidad—and it was just as well, for hundreds of people could detain him from time to time at village or ranch stops along his journey. Denver's reporters covered his reappearance at Walsenburg and Rouse, but news coverage slackened off sharply once he left the small mining camp.

For the next two weeks, no word of Schlatter's whereabouts appeared in print. During this time he crossed over Raton Pass, hugging the line of the railroad, and skirted the eastern side of the Sangre de Cristo Range, heading south to Springer. From there he went to Cimarron and followed Cimarron Canyon (now traversed by U.S. Highway 64) to Moreno Valley, a high mountain park.[28] After visiting the mining camp of Elizabethtown, he descended Taos Canyon to the western side of the Sangre de Cristos, emerging just south of Taos. From there he began a walking trek down the Rio Grande valley.

News of his presence traveled ahead of him, and it drew hundreds as he made his way along the road, a veritable tableau lifted from scenes memorialized in the Bible. People surrounded him, traveling on foot, on horseback, in wagons and carriages—adults shouting to neighbors, children running to keep up, animals chasing the throng down the dirt road to the next place the healer might stop to bless and heal the crowd.

In the village of La Joya (today's Velarde), he stayed overnight at the home of Don Mariano Larragoite. So many pilgrims surrounded the home, quietly moving forward to receive his touch, that he didn't finish his healing work until well after midnight. So many others were waiting at eight o'clock the next morning, when he'd planned to depart, that he stayed until noon treating them. Yet he seemed perfectly content, unhurried, and at one with *la gente*—the people.[29]

Don Larragoite insisted Schlatter take an hour or two for dinner, and the two men talked at length. Having learned something of Schlatter's private beliefs from Denver associates, Larragoite asked him how the world would end. By fire, Schlatter replied—but the flames would wipe out only the Pharisees, leaving a new generation to take their place. When would this happen? Only the Father knew, Schlatter said. But he would have a significant role to play. "I will soon disappear," he said. "No one will know my whereabouts."[30] After a few years, however, he would reemerge, "and then I will preach to the people."

When they parted, Larragoite asked Schlatter where he was headed. The healer said south, and he planned to visit San Felipe pueblo, which lay near Santa Fe. But he wouldn't commit to Santa Fe itself, which Larragoite had urged him to do, probably since the rancher's friends and business acquaintances lived there. Then, beyond that, Arizona—all vague. And with an urging of his horse Butte, laden like a Spanish galleon, the healer departed.

As he made his way down the valley, rumors continued to fly that he was returning to Albuquerque, the birthplace of his fame. Will Hunter, the reporter who had first discovered the healer five months earlier, again set out to find him. Hunter and a small party traveled to Peña Blanca, where they discovered Schlatter at the home of the local priest a few days after he left Larragoite's ranchero. As they entered, Schlatter rose from the dinner table and greeted them. "How is the *Democrat*?" he asked. "How are all the old friends in Albuquerque?"[31] He looked stronger and healthier than ever before, Hunter noted, yet still wore simple clothing and the flat-heeled shoes Tom Dye had made for him. The men sat down in front of a cheerful fire in the priest's parlor.

"When will you reach Albuquerque?" Hunter asked.

"I can't tell," Schlatter replied. "If the Father says go to Albuquerque, I will." But, he added, "I am going on a long retreat, where or for how long only the Father can tell." To other questions about his immediate future, he gave the same answer. He would only say that he was heading southwest. In that direction, Hunter knew, lay a good deal of rugged, forbidding country—and it was the dead of winter. Did Schlatter fear for his safety? "No," the healer replied, "the Father will protect me and no harm can possibly come." He then showed them a compass he'd picked up in Flagstaff, a miraculous gift of the Father—unaware, it seemed, of the contradiction between the compass and God's providential guidance.

As Hunter and his party left the priest's home, they passed through a crowd of pilgrims waiting to be touched. But even as the healer grasped each person's hands, a boy was bringing Butte out from a stable. As the reporter's stagecoach arrived, Schlatter called out to him. "I wish to go. The Father wills it." Then: "Will see you soon."

But he didn't. He never made it to Albuquerque.

<hr />

EXCEPT FOR A SMATTERING of newspaper reports, Schlatter had disappeared into time and space. Time—because these few reports were all over the chronological map. Space—because they located him here and there within a large triangle encompassing 6,700 square miles. The only certainty, in spite of contradictory information, was that he arrived at Ada Morley's ranch on the night of January 7, 1896. The date was significant. For Morley, it was a night never to be forgotten, and for Schlatter, it resonated—as did every step of his journey—with divine providence.[32]

But divine providence didn't guide him to Morley's ranch. A chain of human events did. First, Ada Morley wrote to James Summers and his wife, inviting the healer to her ranch.[33] Next, Summers probably met with Schlatter in Peña Blanca, or perhaps in Bernalillo, which was a bit closer to Albuquerque.[34] There Summers may have convinced Schlatter that Ada Morley would be a perfect host. She was intelligent, sympathetic to his ideas, and completely trust-worthy. And her ranch was virtually isolated from the outside world.

After their talk, only one question remained—how to get there. The easiest way to reach Morley's ranch was to follow the Rio Grande south, past Albuquerque to Socorro, then follow the railroad tracks west to Magdalena and cross the Plains of San Augustin to Datil. At the rate he was traveling, the entire trip would have taken him little more than six days. But that meant passing once again through Isleta, Pajarito, Peralta, and Las Lunas—all the stepping-stones of his miraculous rise to fame. But now those stones would only burden him, weigh him down. He had healed those people; he was done.

Instead, he headed west—into a formidable desert wilderness. The healer had already told Don Mariano Larragoite, and oth-ers, that he was bound for Arizona. Then, he said, he'd go south, into Mexico, and then to Central America.[35] That seemed to be his plan—and it might well have been his plan before he met with Sum-mers. Now he had a new destination, the Datil Mountains, which lay more than a hundred miles due southwest, and no easy way to get there.

Abandoning his original plan to enter Arizona through Fort Win-gate and Gallup, he took a different, and much more dangerous, route.[36] Just southwest of Cabezon rises the formidable San Mateo mountain range, topped by 11,300-foot Mount Taylor. There Schlat-ter turned south, and ended up, a few days after Christmas, near the Acoma pueblo on the Atlantic & Pacific Railroad line.[37] Joseph Saint, a former mayor of Albuquerque, saw him on December 31, as Schlatter was leaving the Acoma pueblo, and learned that he was heading toward the "American valley," which lay in the vicinity of the Datil Mountains.[38] Accompanying Schlatter were about two hundred Acoma Indians. In the short time he stayed with them, the healer had won them over. Their leaders, stated the *Rocky Mountain News*, "declared that Schlatter is their Montezuma, and have decided to capture him."[39]

Before he disappeared entirely, however, he ran across Sol Block, a merchant from Grant's station (now Grants), outside Acoma. Block recognized the healer, and they traveled together along a serpentine Indian trail that followed the eastern edge of the *malpais*—miles of black lava rock spreading southwest from Mount Taylor's volcanic summit. Block tried to convince Schlatter to turn back. The trail, he said, was barely passable in winter. But Schlatter replied that the Father told him to follow it, and he must, "regardless of the consequences."[40]

Block asked the question so many had posed to Schlatter. "Yes, Sir," the healer said. "I am Christ."[41] Then, free to speak in the solitude of the desert, as he hadn't in the city, he told of the transformation to come. "I will soon disappear," he said, "to return in another form." Block was curious about this modern-day messiah, and their conversation became deeper as they walked along the trail, leading their horses. The healer opened up even more, offering a judgment he'd never publicly revealed before. "When I am gone those who have not believed in me will regret it," he said, "and they will shed bitter tears and will call for me even in the desert, but they shall not find me."

They spoke for a while of heaven, hell, and purgatory.[42] Then, by and by, they came to a large ruin, and Block asked Schlatter if he knew why the ancient pueblo people had disappeared. Without hesitation, the healer pointed to the miles of lava stretching off into the distance. "Fifteen hundred years ago this country was thickly settled," he said. "It was occupied by a happy, gentle race. They cultivated the soil and lived mainly from the immense herds of deer and antelope that roamed at will over the country. Then an eruption took place and all the lava beds you see around us were red hot." People died by the thousands, and the game disappeared. Some of the settlers escaped to the mountains, but savage tribes invaded the country and slaughtered them.[43]

After walking for two hours, Block turned back. As the two men parted, he urged the healer to return with him, afraid he would die in that hostile country. Schlatter replied that there was no death in him. Then he said good-bye, urged his horse forward, and let the curtain fall on the last vestige of his former life.

CHAPTER SIX

Winter Retreat

I told him one day he reminded me of a musical
instrument, being played upon by some unseen force.
The idea pleased him. and he laughingly answered,
"I've been wanting a title for my book. Now I have it."[1]

ADA MORLEY

O
N THE NIGHT Schlatter appeared at Ada Morley's front door,
she missed his knocking—on two separate occasions. She was
intent on helping Karl, a German boy who lived on the ranch,
to read English.[2] A ranch hand saw Francis bedding down in
the barn, brought him back to the house, and ushered him inside.
When Ada looked into the dim entrance hall, and recognized him,
she rose in complete silence, unable to move or speak. "Unalloyed
joy filled my being," she later wrote.[3] It was perhaps the greatest
moment of her life.

When she recovered from her shock, she asked Karl if he recognized the visitor. The boy pointed to the mantelpiece over the
crackling fire. Yes, he said, "I know him by his picture."[4] Ada had
purchased the healer's photograph in Denver, framed it, and carried
it back to the ranch. She'd also made a pledge, after standing in line
and receiving his touch, that if she could come to know him in some
way, perhaps serve him, she would give up her incessant quest for
religious truth.[5] Ever since her husband died thirteen years earlier,
she'd struggled to find comfort—and an answer—in New Thought
philosophy. Now, in one instant, the healer had wiped all that away.
"Like a tidal wave," she wrote, "the memory of the Via Dolorosa
swept over the soul, but I knew inwardly it was finished. Intuitively I
saw a vast and happier future and knew I was free."[6]

She likened her situation to Paul's conversion on the road to
Damascus—a profound shift in her view of the world. In accepting

Schlatter as divine, perhaps even as the promised Messiah, she was turning her back on years of deliberate thought and study. The very book she was helping young Karl read, Henry Wood's *Ideal Suggestion through Mental Photography*, expressed her religious belief—until Schlatter arrived. It contained a series of meditations summed up in simple declarations: "God Is Here," "Christ Is Within," "I Am Soul," "I Am Not Body," "Spirit Is the Only Substance," and "There Is No Death."[7] These and other concepts, nearly all of which she would be forced to abandon in the coming weeks, evoked an abstract deity that was as remote from Schlatter's "Father" as Zeus was from the Old Testament's Yahweh.

Ada had met the healer only once before, briefly, in the company of thousands of others. When he placed his hand on her head, she told her daughter, she experienced an "immense illumination."[8] Now he was in her home, and the language he spoke—not his curious accent, but his disarming familiarity with God—disturbed her. It was as if she were to believe the creator of the universe was right there, in the room, with them. At the end of the first evening, filled with scores of questions and the healer's detailed account of riding seven hundred miles to her front door, she began to see that God surrounded Francis Schlatter like an invisible aura. "Father says" was his natural way of speaking—"his own individuality," she wrote with wonder, "submerged in the Unseen Presence."[9]

In spite of her long-ago abandonment of Methodism, Ada still had it deep in her spirit—not only in her strict morality and honesty, but in her acceptance of personal sin. Suddenly, with Schlatter's arrival, the old Methodist fire of soul-searching and self-criticism returned. But instead of leading to repentance and forgiveness, Ada's awareness of her pride and vanity turned into something truly remarkable. She made herself the crucible of Schlatter's faith. Their discussions, which she carefully noted, consistently favored his ideas over her own—as if she were the imperfect foil for his divine truth.

It happened often. When she condemned brutality toward animals, especially horses, Schlatter replied: "I do not believe in cruelty, but I was glad I had a quirt when Butte would not go down that abandoned Indian trail" descending Putney Mesa.[10] When she spoke of cruelty to children, he told the story of how his father had beaten him for truancy, and what a boon it was to his character.[11] When she expressed her hope that women's suffrage would reduce political corruption, he replied: "Women vote in several states, and what have they accomplished? Have they changed things? Of course they have a right to vote but what good has it done up to date?"[12] Ada did not repudiate her own beliefs, but slowly and by degrees she came to see the wisdom of Schlatter's. Beyond that, she came to believe that he spoke directly to God—the God of the Bible she had abandoned so long ago.

During the first day or two, Ada sent Schlatter's meals up to his room, thinking that he wanted to be alone with his thoughts—and with the Father. When he asked her why, she said: "Because I thought even such association with ordinary mortals would interrupt the necessary quiet of your life. I thought you were of the order of the Asiatic Adepts, and had to be alone as much as possible."[13]

"Oh, no," he replied. "If you will, I prefer to eat with the family."[14]

From that time on, their relationship changed. Ada's outward reverence for her messiah-like guest deepened into a more human appreciation of his strengths and weaknesses. For his part, Schlatter enjoyed the freedom to mix with the family or retreat to his room as he wished. At the same time, their conversations became free-ranging and mutually exploratory. Ada saw immediately that Schlatter was anything but a simple peasant healer. He'd spent years reading and studying history, economics, and political thought; he seemed familiar with most of the journals that lay scattered about Ada's parlor; and he knew the social issues of the day. Moreover, he could easily surprise her with a fresh, unexpected point of view—especially for someone as thoroughly steeped in the Bible as he was. Once, when she read him something by Robert G. Ingersoll, the free-thinking critic of Christianity, Schlatter said: "Father says he is a man of great faith; only the professing Christians have given him too much material to use against religion by their hypocrisy and mouth worship."[15]

Free of his demanding burdens as a healer and relieved of the hardships of his journey, Francis revealed a side to his character that people rarely saw. He laughed, joked, and sang; he spoiled his horse, Butte; and he became friendly with everyone on the ranch. To be sure, these folks numbered only a few—and all were duly sworn to keep his presence a secret—but the healer trusted his hostess completely. One day, when an old friend, Billie Swingle, showed up at the door, she quickly removed Schlatter to the girls' room in another wing of the house. "That is Mr. Swingle," she said. "He has ever

FIGURE 10. Frank Sauerwein's 1897 drawing of Ada Morley's Hermosillo ranch house near Datil, New Mexico. Schlatter stayed in retreat for three months here in early 1896, revealing to Morley his spiritual destiny. *The Life of the Harp in the Hand of the Harper,* courtesy Denver Public Library, Western History Collection, c265.8s338Li.

been kind to us." Francis stopped her gently with a raised hand. "Let him come in," he said. "Father says he can keep still."[16]

Ada did her best to make sure Francis had all the comforts of home. She learned about his mother's methods of cooking, sent away for special meat and produce, and had the cook prepare it in the Alsatian way.[17] She encouraged him to go outside, weather permitting, and practically gave Butte the run of the ranch. At one point they puzzled over a broken sugar jar in the kitchen and laughed when they discovered that Butte was the mysterious intruder.[18] Ada sometimes saw Schlatter spending long, tender moments in the corral with his arm across the horse's back. At his happiest, the healer would sing the Marseillaise.[19] He was a far more sensitive and emotional man than she had been led to believe.

After much prodding, Francis agreed to put into writing the narrative of his two-year journey, a tale he recounted in detail over several evenings in front of the fireplace. His audience included Ada, young Karl, possibly Mr. Swingle, and a small group of winter ranch hands. It was a riveting story in the telling—at least as Ada described it. They sat, she said, listening at times to joyous aspects of his life, especially his youth, but particularly to "that horrible tramp and its mystic meaning to mankind."[20] They learned of threats, humiliations, and physical suffering—of episodes he couldn't bear to write about later—and came to see him as a man chosen by God to endure incredible hardships for the sake of humanity.

Ada's visitor was an impassioned speaker. "Those who have not heard him talk," she wrote, "can scarcely conceive the intensity of his language and emotions."[21] Indeed, a few people in Denver's crowds had witnessed his anger, but he was careful to maintain a Christlike demeanor. Now, in the solitude of the Hermosillo ranch, he could throw off the shackles of his public role and be himself. Sometimes within the space of a day, Ada might see him run the gamut of moods, from exhilaration to deep sadness to pensiveness.

On Ada's parlor table sat Wilmans's *Blossom of the Century*, Mary Baker Eddy's *Science and Health*, and Madame Blavatsky's *Key to Theosophy*, and he was familiar with all of them. But, he told her, she must put all this reading aside if she wanted to understand the truth about the approaching kingdom.[22] So, although they spoke of current issues like women's fashions, vegetarianism, and temperance, they inevitably drew closer to the heart of his divine mission—the core teachings of the Bible, the centuries of disobedience and corruption that followed Jesus's sacrifice on the cross, and the impending final days.

IF THERE WAS ONE THING Ada Morley and Francis Schlatter had in common, it was a hatred of capitalism—a system they believed was based on greed, selfishness, competition, economic and social inequality, and parasites who benefited from misfortune. As a small, western cattle rancher, Morley saw the evils of the system in the course of her work, particularly big ranchers who swallowed up smaller outfits, and the inordinate power of the railroads—which dictated where, when, and how western produce and livestock could be sold. Then, too, she nearly lost her entire estate—which included valuable property in downtown Denver, property in Moreno Valley near Elizabethtown, and other land in New Mexico—to creditors.[23] Her son, Raymond, moreover, barely escaped losing a large head of cattle to a conniving partner.[24] But Ada believed that the evils of capitalism could be blunted through reason, moral persuasion, legislative reform, and political action.

Schlatter, on the other hand, had no hope that human effort could change the system. But capitalism alone wasn't the problem; it was just the final mask of a beast that had worn many masks over the past two thousand years. Whether it was the oligarchies of the ancient world—or medieval feudalism, Renaissance mercantilism, or modern capitalism—the economic order of the day merely served the rich and powerful, along with their retinue of politicians, clergymen, and lawyers. The failure of reform, as Schlatter saw it, was that the system always deceived or compromised the honest person who sought to change it. "If a man is too honest they get him out of the way somehow or other, either by corruption, scaring him, or, by some method, he is quietly put out of their path if he refuses to be a tool. For that dollar, of course, the self-sold slave will do dirty work—become a willing tool."[25]

To be sure, Schlatter included himself among the duped—the working slaves who were no different, in his mind, than plantation slaves. "There are classes and classes of wage workers. Ah, yes! there are the self-sold slaves; they are a different class from the industrial slaves. The former are now helpless, I know. Have I not been one? Did I not sit at the bench twenty-three years? Never forget I was a workingman. It's the devilish system!"[26] In other words, he now understood the false sense of freedom and independence that tradespeople, or small business entrepreneurs, who were self-employed, seemed to enjoy—until the silver collapse of 1893 caused a depression that stripped them of their shops, trades, and livelihoods. But behind it all, he believed, lay the manipulators of currency—the eastern and European speculators who became popularly known as the "gold bugs."

In all this, Schlatter was hardly different than many Populists of the time. They were an emerging throng of farmers and ranchers, laborers, small business owners, and mining people who had long suffered under the unprecedented growth of railroads, industry, manufacturing, and business enterprise in the post–Civil War years—all tied together by a worldwide monetary and trade system that neglected their needs. The "silver question," which basically boiled down to how much credit was available to these economic second-classers, became the primary political issue of Populism—and 1896 presidential candidate William Jennings Bryan (and Colorado's senator Henry M. Teller) championed the cause of silver over a highly restrictive gold-based economy.

But Populism went far beyond the silver question. Like many grassroots movements, it attracted — and gave a broader context to — social and political ideas that swirled around the ideological landscape of the late nineteenth century. Some of these were democratic, like the direct election of senators, referendum and recall, and women's suffrage. Others drew upon a passing anti-Semitism within Populism, which meshed perfectly with the idea of a "gold bug" conspiracy — commonly attributed to the House of Rothschild.[27] Still others postulated a class war that would pit the downtrodden against the power elite. In this respect, the labor strikes and riots of the time instilled a widespread fear of class conflict throughout the nation.

Back in September, at the beginning of his ministry, Schlatter told Rev. Myron Reed: "I was a Populist — red hot."[28] But, he added, "I know now that the evils of the world cannot be cured by politics and I am out of politics entirely." Nevertheless, Populism shaped him — as much as reincarnation, spiritualism, and the works of mental healing and New Thought. If anything, Schlatter was a provocative and unpredictable thinker.

At one point, impressed with the depth of his thought, Morley asked him why he hadn't spoken out in Denver. He replied: "It would not do that they knew I had another mission than healing. I had to be still."[29] He had, of course, met with those Morley called the "Wise Men of the West" at Clarence Clark's home.[30] But he knew how radical his ideas would appear to the general public. They would cause immediate controversy and undermine the role of healing in his mission. Yet now, as Morley knew intuitively, Schlatter's thought *must* be broadcast to the world. She had already been transcribing their winter conversations — most likely — and had in mind a biography of his life that would supplement the simple but searing account of his pilgrimage.[31] It would also contain a spiritual treatise, drawn from their talks.

If Christ's Sermon on the Mount expresses the core tenets of Christianity, Ada Morley's "Teachings in Retirement" in *The Life of the Harp* masterfully summarizes the basic principles of Francis Schlatter's radical agenda for humankind. From the beginning

of their talks, Schlatter pointed to the prophecies of Daniel, espe
cially chapter 9 of the King James Version, in which the Lord spells
out the number of days until the new dispensation. At that point,
Morley gave little credence to what she considered Old Testament
dogma—but she was to embrace Schlatter's argument that the
world, since Christ, had degenerated into materialism, greed, and
servitude to the power of money. They came back, again and again,
to Daniel—and to the wrath of God. "Jesus was the Lamb of God,"
Schlatter said, "—but this time He has sent the Lion of the tribe of
Judah."[32]

The Lion, of course, was Schlatter—meek as he seemed to be. He
was the reincarnation of Christ, called from his cobbler's bench to
undertake an extraordinary mission. The time was at hand for God
to cleanse the earth of evil and greed, and to establish an earthly
kingdom of peace, righteousness, and well-being. The kingdom, as
Schlatter explained it to Morley, looked much like a secular utopian
society of the future—with one-story houses forty feet high, heated
and cooled through pipes, and children taught by direct contact with
nature, not through books or slate boards. Schlatter waxed long and
eloquent over the physical shape of the kingdom, but he argued that
its most important characteristics fulfilled the human spirit. It would
be a thousand-year reign of freedom, democracy, and equality. Most
important, it would be an earthly kingdom living under God's direct
hand.

But it would not come about peacefully. Schlatter had not spoken of Armageddon openly before now. Of all his ideas, it would
have been the most controversial, the one most likely to brand him a
crackpot. But he believed it was coming, just as he believed the New
Jerusalem would be an earthly kingdom of peace and prosperity for
the righteous. Signs of discontent, turmoil, and class struggle were
everywhere—widespread poverty and homelessness, violent labor
strikes, protests and marches, and armed state militias ready to attack American workers at the behest of industrialists and politicians.
It was all coming to a head, the inevitable culmination of two thousand years of disobedience to the will of God.

Schlatter likened the final days to the worldwide apocalypse in
Ignatius Donnelly's *Caesar's Column*, an anti-utopian Populist novel
published in 1892. The book, Schlatter told Morley, was one he
bought and read "without food till finished."[33] He considered it to

be prophetic of events to come. The book, set in New York City in the 1980s, describes a world dominated by the moneyed elite, who hold at their command large military forces on land, on the sea, and in the air. Eventually, however, the Brotherhood of Destruction prevails and spreads death and havoc across the land. The final monument to the triumph of democracy over greed and oppression is, in fact, a symbol of horror rising above New York City's Union Square—a gigantic concrete monolith packed with the corpses of the oppressors.

Ada protested against the healer's dire view of things to come. She offered Edward Bellamy's *Looking Backward*, a benign socialist utopia published in 1888, as a possible alternative. But, as with everything else, Francis steered her gently toward his perspective. "Have patience and faith," he said.[34] "Father will help us out. But *Caesar's Column* is nearer the truth than *Looking Backward*." Then he added an important lesson he'd learned as a cobbler in Denver. "Give up all books. Turn to your Bible. Go back to your Bible and learn there the truth. We are living in Revelations and are soon to enter a new dispensation."[35] And that time was coming soon. "According to Daniel," he said, "I will return in 1899, probably, though with Father time is nothing."[36]

Thus far Schlatter had proposed a message of warning, one that had been issued hundreds of times down through the centuries. In the end, it was no different than that of the prophets of the Old Testament, or of Revelation. But then he introduced something totally new. The fundamental principle of the Bible, he said, was reincarnation. "It is the only solution to conditions and apparent inequalities, and it is the one eternal, invariable law," he said. "No chance, no accidents, no variableness. Father told me in the beginning of my walk that this is the one great truth, the vital supplement to come to the Christian world at this time."[37]

Everyone, he told Morley, has had the opportunity of advancing through human life many times. Up to the end of the nineteenth century, no one on earth had lived less than three lives or more than three hundred—the latter, he said, attributed to the "innumerable deaths of infants."[38] Where he got these numbers is unknown, perhaps from theosophy, perhaps from his abundant imagination. But, as in most theories of reincarnation, Schlatter's incorporated a moral component. Of the many possible lives available to each person, at least ten had to be "good lives" to fulfill the promise of individual salvation.

Ada misunderstood. "That is the lowest degree," she asked, "ten lives?"[39]

"No." Francis replied. "I said ten *good* lives; for some have come here and been so lukewarm that incarnation doesn't count. They are born, vegetate, marry and die; and what have they done? A life must be active, helpful, good, to count when the sifting time comes for the Kingdom. There must be growth, and there can be none in selfishness."[40] Those who had lived ten good lives he called the "faithful," the others the prejudiced.[41] Once, when Ada leafed through a special edition of the *Arena* containing portraits of prominent Americans, Francis easily picked out the faithful from the others. "It was startling," Morley wrote, "and rather upset my preconceived notions of certain celebrities to have him say, 'prejudiced, full of it,' about a noted woman leader, though he did not recognize the face; then, again, 'ambitious, has not had ten good lives.' "[42]

Schlatter took no credit for such apparent clairvoyance. "I of myself could never tell a faithful from a prejudiced," he said, "except I ask Father and He tells me; then I always know the hidden character."[43] Above the faithful, in the hierarchy of beings that inhabited Schlatter's world, were people he called the chosen ones. "Ah! how few, how few of them!" he said. "Father says He can hold them all in the hollow of His hand. But the chosen will help to straighten out this world and its false standards and wicked conditions." Among them were the prophets and disciples of old, all reincarnated and living unrecognized in the present day.[44] "How glorious to think they are all here!" he exclaimed. "All the Bible characters." He had met the disciple John, and he knew that John the Baptist was soon to be killed in London. "Paul is here today," he said, "but not in the leading class, as the world goes. Aaron, too, is here."

Not only were the reincarnated prophets walking the earth, Schlatter said, but he would soon be reunited with his mother. "My mother is now reincarnate in Mexico," he said, "and some day I shall see her. She died twenty-five years ago, but I know she is in Mexico."[45] In fact, the challenges to belief that Schlatter put before Morley were enormous, and she had precious little time to absorb them. But he had no interest in converting her, none at all. His eye was always on the kingdom—and on the sequence of events, foretold by Daniel and enacted in the Book of Revelation, that would bring it about.

No, it was up to Ada Morley to face and overcome any rational obstacles posed by the healer's thought. They were greater than she had supposed in the beginning, no question about that. But by the time of his departure, she had resolved all doubts in favor of a belief that he was truly divine, spoke to God, and had a God-given calling to fulfill the prophecies of scripture. As a result, she looked to the number of days allotted in Daniel 9:26 until the onset of the apocalypse in 1899. Thereafter, a new world order would begin, she believed, and Francis Schlatter would return to Datil as the Messiah of New Jerusalem.

THE DAYS OF Schlatter's retreat were coming to an end. Ada could tell from the healer's restlessness that he expected to hear the Father's summons, "the order to move on withersoever the Voice directed, to the place where the Spirit led."[46] Day by day, Francis's behavior changed, and he became more removed from the others around him. "He ate little," Morley wrote, "talked less, slept more and lost interest in the topics he had so frequently discussed with vivacity. He gazed for hours into the fire. The face had lost its cheer, the manner was tense, and he answered in monosyllables. It was clear that he was listening to the Voice, much of the time, receiving instructions as to his future movements."[47]

He told her he was heading south, into Mexico. She knew the country around the border, for she had lived for three years in Mexico while her husband pioneered the Nogales-to-Guaymas railroad route.[48] The border guards were corrupt, and dangers both human and natural lay everywhere in the wastelands of the north and the jungles to the south. "How will your friends know what has been your fate?" she asked. "How can they tell whether you are dead or not? You will surely die!"[49]

"Have patience and faith," he said calmly. "Look within, and by the faith that's in you, you will know that I cannot die. I was not born to die but to live — to do the Father's work. In His time He will bring me back."[50]

She pleaded with him to stay on her ranch until the appointed

FIGURE 11. Ada McPherson Morley as a young woman,
before she abandoned Methodism for New Thought
and other unorthodox religious ideas. Morley became
Francis Schlatter's most devoted disciple. Courtesy
New Mexico State University Library, Archives
and Special Collections, MS00250004.

time of Daniel, but he had already sensed that the outside world
was closing in. "When I came I told you that Father said I must go
as soon as the people found out I was here. They have been talking
about it quietly for a long time, though no one knows it positively. But
when they know I shall start."[51]

In truth, the world came in on horseback in the person of William K. Martin, a deputy sheriff sent out from Socorro to look
for escaped prisoners. He stopped at the Hermosillo ranch about
March 10—snooped around, asked questions, and little by little
gained the truth about Ada's guest. She pleaded with Martin to give
the healer time to depart unnoticed, and he obliged her—for when
he first reported finding Schlatter, a day or two later, he placed the

encounter in Sierra County, well to the south of Datil. For a while, at least, nobody knew the exact whereabouts of the healer.[52]

Thus Schlatter and Morley had some time to prepare for his departure—getting supplies, finishing up the story of his sacred journey, and arranging for Billie Swingle to guide the healer through the Mogollon Mountains to the border. Ada got the healer's promise to write her so that she could be reassured he was well, and she gave him a Spanish-English dictionary to assist him in Mexico. As the day of his departure approached, Schlatter seemed to pace more than ever—to the distraction of everyone in the household—and worried over every detail of the journey to come. "He would arrange and rearrange his saddle," Ada wrote.[53] He also assembled far more gear than Butte could carry in addition to his rider.

Ada offered Francis an extra horse. "Three hundred pounds is too much for Butte," she said. "Moreover, you say you are going to make forty miles a day. Butte can't make it. No horse can. If you make twenty, day in and day out, it will be a marvel."[54]

"But Father will give Butte the strength the same as He does me," Francis replied. "He has got to make more than twenty miles a day, Father says."

On Friday, March 27, Ada picked up the mail in Datil, a mile or two from the ranch. She saw an article in the *Albuquerque Daily Citizen* announcing sheriff Martin's discovery of the healer. This time Martin gave details of Schlatter's location—on the Datil ranch owned by "a woman of advanced religious tendencies"—and added mangled information taken from his interview.[55] The article was inaccurate and demeaning—and, it appears, unworthy of their agreement with Martin. When she returned by wagon to the ranch, Schlatter was sitting on the porch. She kept silent. Later that night, as they sat quietly staring into the fire, she handed him the newspaper.

He read it, and she could see he was resentful of its lies, especially the faint suggestion of a love affair between them. He was silent for a while, and she thought he was "listening to the Voice out of the Silence."[56] Then he said: "Father says Sunday, day after tomorrow, I must go."[57] They went their separate ways to bed, and the next morning Schlatter began to restrict Butte's typical freedom around the ranch, keeping him tied up in the barn. Ada noticed the look in Butte's eyes. "Even the horse felt the impending change," she wrote, "and I was afraid."[58]

On Sunday they ate breakfast in silence, then Morley said: "This is your last breakfast."[59]

"It is better not to mention it," he replied, and got up from the table. He spent a long while in the barn with Butte, then silently read the Bible. "He wanted to go," Morley wrote, "was ready, and had been for ten days, but would rather not start if by any possibility he could gain consent to remain a little longer."[60] He was waiting for Billie Swingle to arrive, but by four o'clock Ada could no longer bear the tension.

"I will speed the parting guest," she said.[61]

"What did you say?"

She repeated the statement slowly, then said: "Do you want your horse? If so, I will go myself and bring him here so you can saddle and pack him."

"Yes, go get him."

As she led Butte back to the house, the healer waited with his gear—saddle, blankets, a sack of clothing, a large canteen, and his copper rod. She suggested Francis forego filling the canteen since it would add considerable weight and he could find water along the San Francisco River, his planned route of travel. But he disagreed. "I drink a great deal of water when I have no food."[62]

She followed him to the spring, then asked if she could accompany him partway down the trail. They walked over a hill and into a valley, she carrying the canteen and he leading Butte. Presently he said: "You have gone far enough. It will soon be dark."[63]

She gave him the canteen, and he slung it over a shoulder. Then, in perhaps their only intimate moment, she took his hand in a long farewell—one she believed might be their last. Without thinking, she said: "Please say the Lord's Prayer."[64] He repeated it, just the same as he'd done so often in his idiosyncratic way, saying "Thy will, *will* be done."[65] Then he mounted Butte and rode down the canyon and out of sight.

INTERREGNUM

Into Mexico

—1896—

THE COWBOY ON THE Chase and McCabe ranch, south of Lordsburg, New Mexico, immediately noticed something wrong with the healer's white horse.[1] Removing the saddle and all the attached gear—far too heavy in his opinion—he saw a large swelling on the animal's withers, where the pommel of the saddle rested. He called to Schlatter and scolded him for placing so much weight on the horse. Schlatter said nothing in response. He merely stood next to Butte and passed his hands over the tender spot. In a few minutes the swelling had subsided.

Schlatter stayed overnight as a guest of John McCabe. He ate a hearty meal. As he told McCabe, he'd been fasting for six days. It had been two weeks since he left Ada Morley's ranch, and he'd spent much of that time resting in the Mogollon Mountains. The next morning, he showed McCabe and the ranch hands how he used his copper rod. Taking it in one hand, he spun around and let it fly. Where it pointed was the direction in which Father wished him to go. It landed pointing toward the south.

The cowboys were amazed at the healer's strength—and fascinated by his heavy copper rod. It had already become famous up and down the Rockies. Everyone speculated on its mysterious properties, and some compared it to the biblical rods of Aaron and Moses. No doubt it served as a sort of divine compass, just as he had demonstrated to McCabe's ranch hands. But what was its larger purpose? No one would ever know—at least from Schlatter's lips. And in time, of course, it became forgotten altogether.

After he crossed the border, everything went silent. No reports made their way back to the United States. No newspapers in Mexico mentioned him. No messages passed along the telegraph lines that paralleled the railroad tracks. No train passengers brought back stories of the healer. Consular letters and dispatches said nothing about him.[2] In short, one of the most charismatic healers of the nineteenth century, and a Christ figure, rode a white horse into a country where crucifixes and religious statues adorned every small home and field, and where word of *el sanador* must have passed along the Correlitos Road and its byways. And yet—nothing.

Nevertheless, a year later, with the announcement of his death in June 1897, everyone seemed to have heard a story—or claimed a connection to the healer. Thomas Bulmer, an English physician living in Casas Grandes, wrote to ranchman Charles Whitman with a tale that the previous December—a month after the Mormon cowboy presumably saw him resting—Schlatter begged for food at one household and was turned away.[3] Bulmer claimed that after the healer died, his horse fell into the hands of rustlers, who used it to round up stock. "Its body lies twelve miles up the river," he wrote.

In fact, the entire episode was rife with rumor, in spite of the compelling circumstantial evidence in Tinaja Canyon. Some newspapers pointed out that the skeleton hadn't actually been examined, others that the wilderness death was simply too convenient. "It does not appear that the human remains were actually identified as Schlatter's," stated the *New York Times*, "or that any identification was possible. The copper rod, the inscribed Bible, the marked saddle would have been thought of by any novelist devising such a situation. The story of Schlatter's self-imposed starvation, circulated beforehand, might have been merely what the playwrights call 'preparation'."[4] The writer concluded: "We are therefore led to believe that Schlatter revivified may soon be heard from."

In the days following the news of the healer's death, his disciples divided into skeptics of the reports from Mexico and those who believed them. Morley rose to become the voice of the first; but only a few people supported her. One by one, the inner circle of Schlatter's friends in Denver turned silent in the face of what seemed to be overwhelming evidence. Even Edward Fox, the healer's best-known champion, was in shock. When Joseph Emerson Smith interviewed him on June 6, he saw a tormented man. Why, Fox asked, hadn't the news reports mentioned the healer's wooden bead rosary, which he always carried, or the medals he pinned to the inside of his denim jacket?[5] Nevertheless, Fox didn't seem "in full possession of his senses" at the time, and in spite of his doubts his reaction showed that he believed Schlatter to be dead.[6]

Thus Ada Morley found herself alone—or nearly so. She could at least rely on one important ally, Herbert George of *The Road*, who had befriended Schlatter in his earliest days as a cobbler and believed him to be the vanguard of a new age.[7] Otherwise, nearly everyone abandoned her—even, as it turned out, her own children.[8] But Morley wasn't about to accept any claim unquestioningly, especially one that defied common sense. As a rancher, she knew the realities of the wild. "The men who found the skeleton declared to have been our friend's say it was resting as though it had never been disturbed," she told a reporter. "I know the coyotes would never have left it so if it had ever lain there bearing flesh."[9] She also warned against jumping to conclusions on the basis of little more than hearsay. She, for one, would not abandon her belief that Schlatter was alive until the skeleton had been "measured, critically examined, and reported on in detail." And if it were, she added, "evidence will be secured sufficient to prove his words true and hope return where now is doubt and fear."[10]

Morley well understood that people might contend her faith blinded her to the truth. Nevertheless, she said, Schlatter had foretold the events that were now unfolding. He had mentioned to James Summers in Albuquerque, and later to Ada in Datil, that a good deal of money would be spent searching for him. In the end, only his possessions would be found—and that would occur in 1897.[11] "They will find my clothes," he told her, "but they will not find me." She had no doubt that the healer's possessions discovered at the site were genuine, "but the skeleton I feel sure was not his."[12]

In spite of her skepticism, she harbored no thoughts of mischief on Schlatter's part. She even had a good explanation for the clothing and possessions—though less so for the presence of a skeleton. What happened, she believed, was this: "While in that lonely camp, having carefully placed his saddle on the limb of a tree and turned loose his horse, he heard the voice of God saying: 'Leave all and follow me.'" In other words, he was merely carrying out his divine mission—one that, Ada surely knew, *The Life of the Harp* foretold. "He promised to come back in three years," she said, "and I verily believe he will come back, not in the clouds but in the flesh." The world faced a terrible tribulation in the years ahead, a "fierce conflict between those in power and the downtrodden and disinherited of the earth." Then, in 1899, Schlatter would return to bring peace. Quoting Herbert George, she said Schlatter would arrive "on schedule time."[13]

Even before *The Life of the Harp* appeared, Morley was determined to investigate the healer's death in Mexico and began looking for someone to finance her trip. "It is not probable that this lady will succeed in getting to Mexico within a short time," stated the *Rocky Mountain News*, "but strenuous efforts are being made to interest enthusiasts of Schlatter all over the country in her behalf."[14] Eventually she managed to get funding, and late in the year she traveled to Mexico intent on subjecting the rumors of Schlatter's death to factual analysis.

Little is known of Ada Morley's December 1897 trip other than a statement by Herbert George. "About a month ago," he said on New Year's Day 1898, "Mrs. Morley left Denver for Old Mexico, and told me she intended to find the healer before she gave up." She didn't—but she did find the proof she needed to solidify her faith that he was alive. "I know it," she wrote a few years later, "when I can hold the skull in my own hand and examine the teeth." As she and others well knew, Schlatter had two missing upper teeth, but the skull she examined in Mexico had a full set.[15]

— 1998 —

Sitting at the marble-topped bar in the fashionable El Camino Hotel in El Paso, I studied my notes while waiting for my friend and colleague Rick Manzanares to arrive. A couple of hours earlier, I'd flown in from Denver, and Rick was arriving via Albuquerque from his home in San Luis, Colorado. We'd planned to rent a car in Ciudad Juarez and drive to Nuevo Casas Grandes the next day. Meanwhile I looked forward to spending the evening catching up with Rick. He had graciously agreed to accompany me into Mexico, and he spoke Spanish fluently—with a Chihuahuan accent to boot.

Though we had discussed the purpose of the trip, I filled him in over dinner. I was looking for any records of the official inquiry into Schlatter's death, the one Ada Morley participated in (and perhaps demanded). Then there were pieces of information I wanted to check out—odds and ends relating to Schlatter's last few months in Mexico. To be sure, I didn't think the healer had died there, but I needed to look at the evidence anyway.

In the back of my mind lay a lingering question. How did Schlatter manage to pull off a sophisticated deception in a foreign country when he didn't know the language? Or the people of the region? Or anyone he could trust? For some time I thought he might have slipped into Mexico from El Paso in the summer of 1894, scouting the area while on his two-year pilgrimage. It would have been a 150-mile detour to Casas Grandes. There was no reason he couldn't have done it, even on foot. A train trip—if he had money for the fare—would have been less than a day.

As we drove along Highway 2, called the Old Corralitos Road after the early mining district, I could see the faint peaks of the Sierra Madre above the flat, sun-bleached desert ahead of us. Those were the mountains, I guessed, where the prospectors had found the skeleton. But by the time we got to Nuevo Casas Grandes, I couldn't see them anymore. The town lies in a flat river valley along the Piedras Verde River, and the hills to the west block the mountain range beyond. But I knew we would soon see the Sierra Madre again.

We settled into our motel room about three o'clock, then went in search of the old town of Casas Grandes. It lay about five miles to the southwest across a river I assumed to be the Piedras Verde, thinking of Hewett's story. But no. In Casas Grandes I learned that this river, which lay but a mile or two away, was named after the village itself. The closest point of the Piedras Verde River, on the other hand, lay at least nine miles away—quite a distance for Hewett's Mexican guide, as a young boy, to run with news about sighting a dead man. Hewett was such a good storyteller. For the sake of dramatic unity, he had changed the setting of the story from one river to another.

In fact, the Casas Grandes River lies near the ruins of Paquimé, the original "large village" from which Casas Grandes takes its name —and Hewett was likely investigating those ruins in 1906. Rick and I were tempted to visit them, but hunger forced us to find a nearby restaurant. It actually turned out to be a bar called La Cueva— "the cave"—on the main road through town. It was nearly empty, but the young woman who tended the bar was friendly and invited us to return that night.

We did. But as we entered around 9:00 p.m., Rick detected a noticeable edge to the revelry as we made our way to a table. He instinctively took a place against the wall. A lanky young man in a running suit stood nearby. He was, we later learned, a Yaqui Indian named Wenceslas. He and a friend engaged us in conversation.

What brought us there? What did we want in Casas Grandes? The beers came freely. Rick didn't drink. But he talked to Wenceslas and told him about my research.

"Oh?" Wenceslas said, "a *curandero?*"

"Si," Rick said. Then he explained, in Spanish, that Schlatter was a Christlike healer who became famous worldwide, then came to Casas Grandes and died here. After making a short journey outside to the car, I produced a photograph of the healer for Wenceslas.

Others became interested. A man called Rudolfo sat down at our table, where much discussion was going on. He was a *charro*, a cowboy equal to—and perhaps superior to—the American cowboys, for his ancestors had ridden horses in the American Southwest long before Anglo cowboys did.

Rudolfo was a thin, wiry man of about thirty-five. His face was leathery, eyes black; he smiled easily. Rick told them that Schlatter's bones were discovered at the top of Tinaja Canyon.

"Oh! Tinaja Canon! Ya lo sé!" He would take us there, he told Rick.

But I could see Wenceslaus was troubled. Rick glanced at him, then told Rudolfo maybe another time.

"Oh, no," Rudolfo said eagerly. He could take us on horseback —tonight.

"No, no, gracias, no," said Rick.

Wenceslas said something rapidly to Rudolfo, and started to rise, along with Rick. I must have looked puzzled, for Rick said, "We've got to leave. We're taking Wenceslas home."

It was a relief to get outside, into the fresh March air. Rick was talking to Wenceslas, and Rudolfo watched from the doorway as we got into the car. A few blocks away, Rick told me to stop the car and let the young man out. He wasn't going home. He had just saved us from a very dangerous situation.

"Rudolfo hates gringos, Wenceslas says."

"You're not a gringo," I said.

"To *him* I was."

We thanked Wenceslas, saw him go into another bar, and went back to our motel in Nuevo Casas Grandes. The next morning we returned to the old town. During the evening someone had mentioned that we could get information from the Palacio Municipal. This was a single-story building of stucco and peach-colored pilasters, built in 1903, with a deep porch that featured a large mural of the town's history.[16]

Rick asked a clerk if they had any records pertaining to Francis Schlatter, and he explained the story of the healer's death. No, a death certificate and other official information that long ago, the man said, would be in Chihuahua. But, learning that the skeleton had been found in the high sierras, he mentioned that there was a small Mormon village, Colonia Juárez, about fifteen miles away, closer to the mountains. We could try finding someone there who might have information.

The fifteen-minute drive brought us almost to the foot of the Sierra Madre, which now looked old and eroded, its peaks smooth and weathered. Coming up a rise, we suddenly looked over a valley spreading out before the range, and following the valley's contours was Colonia Juárez. The town lay in a river bottom sporting lush pigments of green within the sere brown and yellow of the desert, and the highway dropped dramatically down to it like an invited guest. Before we descended, however, I saw a sign that said "Cementerio," and I quickly turned onto a dirt road leading to it.

"Where are you going?" Rick asked.

"I want to look at this cemetery," I said.

"You think the skeleton is buried here?"

"No," I said, "but I think the skeleton might have been *taken* from here."

We drove a hundred yards or so and stopped. It was an incredible spot—remote, isolated, and far above the village. It belonged to the old Mormon colony—and one of its souls, I was certain, had secretly gone missing sometime in the early 1897.

But it wasn't until we drove into Colonia Juárez that I truly understood how this could have happened. The town was a veritable confluence of Spanish and English cultures. Alongside flat-roofed, stuccoed Mexican dwellings, some with courtyards or gardens, rose two-story homes typical of the kind found in valleys throughout rural Utah—red-brick, gabled, austere, and simple. The people had become blended, too. Most were bilingual, virtually all were Mormon—isolated from the outside world—and they had made the Mexican desert bloom like a rose. No longer polygamist, their descendants remained loyal to the LDS church and proud of their heritage. A temple was being planned.

I suddenly knew how Schlatter had—or *could have*—enlisted two Mormon cowboys to his mission. First, having taken flight with other polygamists from the United States, both of these men would have spoken English. Second, they belonged to a religion that accepted miracles, direct revelation, and mysterious divine strangers. Third, at that time they were outcasts from American society—not beholden to its laws or social mores. In addition, as simple cowboys, they might well have been working for polygamist ranchers, not wealthy enough to support several wives themselves—and thus possibly isolated from the local church leadership. Finally, Schlatter might have had a way to compensate them—and, subsequently, the stigma of grave-robbing itself would have been enough to keep them quiet.

The next day we drove to Chihuahua, but I learned that the archival records were being moved from one building to another. It would be impossible to locate the official report. But it didn't matter. I was sure that it could only tell me how an unknown man, buried in the cemetery above Colonia Juarez, died—possibly years before Schlatter went into Mexico.[17]

Returning to El Paso on the freeway, I looked out over the Chihuahuan desert. The mountains of the Sierra Madre lay to our left, and miles of sagebrush and sand began to take on a ruddy glow as the sun lowered in the sky. I marveled at how similar this landscape was to the American Southwest's. Geographically, they blended together. Yet culturally they seemed to be thousands of miles apart.

Rick and I talked about that—the invisible barrier between Mexico and the United States, while above it all the landscape imposed its common beauty and desolation. Then we fell into silence. As the miles passed by, I imagined how Schlatter might have made his way out of Mexico. He would have abandoned Butte, or left him with his co-conspirators—an act that must have been extremely difficult given his affection for the horse. He shaved off his beard and cut his hair, got new clothing, and rode the train to El Paso. From there he found a place where he could remain alone and unrecognized for many months, awaiting the fulfillment of Daniel's prophecy.

Schlatter believed fully in Daniel's prophecy—as he interpreted it—of the coming apocalypse and the promised New Jerusalem. Furthermore, given his intimate relationship with the Father, I had no doubt that he believed God had *commanded* him to stage his death at the top of Tinaja Canyon. Ever since he'd been called to his divine mission as a cobbler in 1893, Schlatter's will was no longer his own. The entire story of his pilgrimage, in one respect, was a lesson in the futility of challenging God's omnipotence.

But wouldn't it have been an act of cowardice for him *not* to die as Christ had? Some of Schlatter's disciples certainly believed that he'd done just that—by starving himself to death. However, his words to Ada Morley clearly dispelled the notion that death was a necessary transition between the material and spiritual planes. She had raised the subject, asking how one got to the kingdom except through death. "You are up in that sycamore tree looking at a sky heaven," he said. "You better come down from your sky heaven, for heaven is on this earth, and I am going to live one thousand years, Father says."[18] In other words, he expected to enter New Jerusalem as the Messiah without passing through the veil of death.

Then why had the Father ordered him to create a tableau of his death? Perhaps because the Father knew that humans—even those living in the New Jerusalem—needed miracles to believe.

PART TWO

THE HAND

of

THE HARPER

A Biographical Quest

CHAPTER SEVEN

"These men were imposters"

From time to time, Francis Schlatters have appeared all over
the country, but I have run down many of them, and have satisfied
myself that without exception these men were imposters.[1]

CLARENCE CLARK

O N THE MORNING OF June 8, 1897, two men entered a boardinghouse on Huron Street in Cleveland. They signed up for rooms,
then made their way to a large table where the current boarders
were sitting at breakfast. Some of the company had finished
eating and were reading the paper.

"I see by the morning *Leader*," one boarder said, "that healer
Schlatter's body has been found in the Sierra Madre Mountains in
Mexico."[2]

One of the newcomers, a man of about sixty, spoke. "Has it indeed?" he said. "That's very queer. I was under the impression that
Schlatter is still very much alive. In fact he is here with us." He
gestured to his younger companion, who was a clean-shaven man of
about forty with languid eyes and long hair that fell to his shoulders.
"Allow me to introduce to you—Mr. Schlatter."

The long-haired stranger in the Cleveland boardinghouse was the
first person, in the wake of Schlatter's death, to assume the healer's
name and identity. But he was by no means the last. Over the next
quarter century a succession of pretenders came forward, each pro-
claiming himself to be the great healer. Their staying power was
remarkable. Years, even decades, after his disappearance, claimants
to Francis Schlatter's identity were still making headlines across the
country—and still drawing crowds of sufferers.

Why? For one thing, Schlatter was a great healer, and his flame
burned brightly. Thousands of people came to the Fox home every
day, attracted as much by his Christlike demeanor as his actual

effectiveness as a healer. For that matter, every imitator who followed him, at one time or another, bore a superficial resemblance to him—all, at one time or another, had thick beards and let their hair grow long. More difficult to imitate were the peculiarities of his character—especially his selflessness, modesty, and righteousness. But, in spite of the many thousands who came to be touched by Schlatter, millions more never saw him. Thus an imitator could easily mimic the behavior of this man of God as well as his looks.

More important, Schlatter's rise to fame occurred in the closing years of the nineteenth century, a time of economic crisis and social turmoil. The silver panic of 1893 and ensuing nationwide depression created a class of homeless men who took to the rails.[3] It also threw farmers off their land and deepened poverty in the cities. The glorious White City of the Chicago World's Fair rose that year on the shores of Lake Michigan, but everywhere else the huge fault line between rich and poor threatened to destroy a fragile middle class built largely by post–Civil War industrialism.

Political and social reform was in the air, but so too were calls for radical change and the threat of ongoing labor violence. William T. Stead's *If Christ Came to Chicago*, which sold seventy thousand copies on the first day of publication, took its idea from a poem by James Russell Lowell in which Christ returns to decry the corruption and hypocrisy of modern life. Indeed, the image of Christ as a reformer, and the Social Gospel surrounding that image, resonated with the public at the end of the nineteenth century.

Thus, while the times begged for a spiritual renewal that the Messiah represented, Schlatter epitomized the *idea* of an incarnate Christ in the last years of the nineteenth century. The news of his death in 1897 raised the stakes even higher. There was an eerie resemblance between Christ's crucifixion and Schlatter's lonely death on a mountainside—and a hint of final suffering, although without the glorious resurrection. In its place came a series of pseudo-resurrections in the rise of each succeeding Schlatter. Every new appearance generated wonder and novelty: Is this the same Schlatter? How did he survive? Where has he been all these years? News reporters added the requisite skepticism, and the various Schlatters reveled in outlandish stories and mysterious explanations. Yet the sick and suffering accepted what they were offered without question, for many of them had no choice.

One man, journalist Thomas Dawson, a former owner of the *Denver Tribune*, took an interest in Schlatter's imposters and tracked them for more than twenty years—religiously clipping and saving newspaper articles about them.[4] In 1916 Dawson interviewed Clarence Clark, who was then living in comfortable retirement in Los Angeles. Clark gave Dawson a firsthand account of the healer's disappearance. Then he told of a letter from Mexico he received sometime later stating that Schlatter and his horse had died of thirst. Personal possessions had been found at the scene that pointed to the healer's identity. "At any rate," Clark said, "no other reasonable report as to the place or manner of death ever was received."[5]

Clark believed Schlatter died in Mexico, but he wasn't sure. "If he did not," he said, "he hid himself so effectively that he never since has been heard from."[6] That tiny bit of doubt led him to "run down" the imposters who arose after Schlatter's death. It's more likely, however, that Clark conducted his investigations from an armchair, for the news coverage that exploded from time to time whenever Schlatter died and rose again reached every major daily in the nation.

———————————

THE FIRST PERSON to make a career of impersonating Francis Schlatter was August Schrader, who emerged in 1896, about the time Schlatter left Ada Morley's ranch for Mexico.[7] With his long, dark hair, full beard, and deep-set eyes, Schrader looked every bit as Christlike as Schlatter, and he exuded a similar charisma as he carried his healing campaign through the Midwest and South. The similarity of their surnames, as well, was impossible to miss.

Schrader was magnetic. As he worked, one reporter said, "the whole expression of his mild and gentle face seemed enrapt with religious fervor."[8] He drew large crowds wherever he went, and he treated all pilgrims alike, without regard to race, creed, or color. Like Schlatter, he made no demands on them, and he followed the practice Schlatter had begun of blessing handkerchiefs. He closely emulated the great healer, and in many respects seems to have learned much by observing Schlatter at work.

The similarities, however, soon gave way to deeper differences between the two men. Schrader didn't accept money or gifts for his healing work, but he gave photographs of himself to his suffering or

FIGURE 12. August Schrader, one of
Francis Schlatter's imposters, from the
Albuquerque Evening Citizen, July 9, 1907.

curious visitors, and he proposed a free will offering in return. This,
along with using a hand stamp to mark his name on supplicants'
handkerchiefs, was an innovation that would have been foreign to
Denver's healer. In fact, Schrader was the first of Schlatter's spiritual
heirs to hire a manager to handle such matters—a circular business
that, of course, necessitated asking for donations in the first place.

But what really distinguished Schrader from Schlatter was his
need to dress the part of a divine healer. He wore a long, black
robe with wide sleeves, the kind of garment he believed Jesus wore.
Across his chest fell a pink sash on which was written "Divine Healer
Schrader," and two silver crosses and a crucifix hung from a chain
around his neck. Later he took to wearing a minister's white collar
and occasionally a tunic over his robe that bore the image of the
Holy Cross. Compared to the simple clothing Schlatter wore, much
of it donated, Schrader's ecclesiastical finery seemed to be almost a
parody of the simple man of God.

Nor was that all. Soon after he had established his name as a
healer, Schrader began formulating plans for a church—though he
seemed to have no idea what its believers would profess. In 1898 he
launched the Divine Church, which had branches, he purported,

throughout the West. Then, borrowing on Schlatter's idea of New Jerusalem, Schrader claimed to have founded two colonies of worshippers in New Mexico—Jerusalem and New Jerusalem—each with hundreds of people. No doubt he had followers, but all this reflected considerable delusions of grandeur.

While Schrader was launching his church and his colonies of the faithful, another healer came forward to declare himself the true Schlatter. This pretender first appeared in Boston in 1898, a year after reports of the healer's death came out of Mexico, and held healing sessions in auditoriums and halls across the country for more than a decade. Although he attracted no great crowds, this would-be Schlatter bragged that he had traveled the world seven times and had healed seven million people.

His real name was Charles McLean, and, like Schrader, he hadn't tried to hide it.[9] Instead, he claimed that McLean had been his real name even during the height of his Denver ministry. His German friends in Denver, he said, had given him the name Schlatter, a corruption of *schläfer* (or "sleeper"), because he kept his eyes closed while he was healing. Thus, with no sense of contradiction, McLean kept his own name but advertised himself on billboards and in newspapers as SCHLATTER, THE DIVINE HEALER. Born in Scotland in 1847, McLean attended the University of Glasgow. After coming to America, he studied at the Bennett College of Eclectic Medicine in Chicago. Later he became a Presbyterian minister and set off on a career of gospel healing. He was thus ably prepared to assume Schlatter's role as a divine healer when the opportunity arose.[10]

When people asked how he happened to be walking the earth more than a year after his reported death, McLean explained that after leaving Denver in 1895, he died in the Colorado mountains and his body lay buried for forty days. "My soul went to heaven," he said, "and the Lord told me to come back and take only those who believed and had faith in God and the Bible."[11] To doubters, he offered a challenge. He proposed to be buried again for forty days and nights, during which time his soul would rise again to heaven. There he planned to write "a history of God, heaven and the angels in Hebrew, Greek and Latin, the original languages of the Bible. Then I will translate it into English and give it to the world to prove the existence of God and heaven and a future life."

No one took him up on the burial proposition—not wanting to

FIGURE 13. Charles McLean also went by
the title "Divine Healer Schlatter." *Hastings
Daily Republican*, October 21, 1909, courtesy
Nebraska State Historical Society.

be complicit, perhaps, in what they regarded as an insane man's suicide. The lunacy of McLean's scheme clashed so markedly with the
peaceful, serene godliness of the real healer that it readily discredited
him. But exaggerated and outlandish behavior became a consistent
pattern in the healer's imposters. Simply posing as Schlatter wasn't
enough; impersonators seemed driven to push the boundaries of cre-
dulity—in speech, dress, and behavior—to the farthest extremes.

McLean eventually died of natural causes in a Hastings, Nebraska, hotel room on October 21, 1909.[12] Immediately following his
death a battle ensued between witnesses in Nebraska, who claimed
that he was the authentic healer, and Denverites, who derided him
as a fake. His published picture, which became the primary evidence
for supporters and naysayers alike, showed him to be a scruffy zealot
with a glint of madness in his eye.

By the time Charles McLean passed from the scene, August
Schrader's career had taken a sharp turn. He had moved his ministry to San Francisco, renamed it the Divine Catholic Church, and
called himself pope. Schrader had also brought in an older man,
Jacob Kunze, who called himself Francis Schlatter, the King of Di-

vine Healers.[13] For holy men, Schrader and Schlatter were surprisingly active in the worldly realm. They became involved in treasure hunting in Nicaragua, real estate deals in Cuba, and other activities that kept them living on the run under various aliases.[14] For a time they appeared as Pope Schrader and James Alexander Dowie, the so-called brother of the well-known Chicago preacher and healer John Alexander Dowie, who had founded Zion City, Illinois.[15]

Eventually the healers set out for the South Pacific, where they established the kingdom of New Jerusalem on an island they called the Port of Missing Men, six hundred miles south of Tahiti.[16] When they returned several years later, Schrader went to Los Angeles, overseeing what had now been renamed the Divine Baptist Church, while the "King of Divine Healers" took their evangelistic message and healing gifts around the country.

In 1916 Kunze aka Schlatter established a healing mission in New York City and announced that he was heading for the battlefields of France, there to heal the sick and wounded in the war. But on May 27, before he could implement his plans, two U.S. postal inspectors raided his headquarters and arrested him on charges of mail fraud. Simultaneously, federal authorities arrested August Schrader in California. The two healers were accused of soliciting handkerchiefs in the mail, asking for donations, and promising that the handkerchiefs, once blessed, would cure the aches and ailments of their owners. Since the charges had been lodged in Los Angeles, Kunze was hauled before a federal commissioner for a hearing on whether he should be extradited to California.[17]

The hearing was a charade, and Kunze took every opportunity to frustrate the district attorney, Frank Roosa. Asked to identify himself, he said "I am the reincarnation of Moses."

"How do you accomplish healings?" Roosa asked.[18]

"By the laying on of hands and prayer," Kunze replied.

"What sort of prayer do you make?"

"That is a secret that must not be given to the people."

To the commissioner, the humbuggery of divine curses and reincarnated prophets had little to do with an actual intent to defraud. After two weeks' consideration, he vacated the extradition warrant. "I feel satisfied," he said, "that Schlatter had an honest belief that he possessed divine power of healing." Furthermore, divine or mental healing in themselves "were not offenders against the law."[19]

The commissioner's opinion was unusual. With the mushrooming growth of psychics, soothsayers, and healers in the late nineteenth century—animated in part by spiritualism and kindred beliefs—law officers, city officials, and courts increasingly sought to protect the public from fraud. In the age of Progressive reform, during the early twentieth century, legislators expanded the concept of fraud to include almost any unconventional medical treatment or device— protecting, at the same time, the hegemony of the medical system.

In this regard, U.S Attorney Frank Roosa was a crusader. A few months after the hearing he traced Kunze and Schrader to Chicago. They were hiding under new aliases, one of which was "Billy Sunday." Forewarned of an impending arrest, they escaped to Toronto, Canada—but it was no use. Exploiting fears of German espionage in the early years of World War I, Roosa claimed that pro-German literature had been found in their Chicago rooms, and Toronto police jailed the two men on a charge of vagrancy. The American consul in Montreal acted quickly to have them returned to the United States, and within days they were back in custody in Los Angeles.[20]

Over the next four months, as the two healers awaited trial, Schrader's health began to decline, then took a sharp downturn when he developed pneumonia. Kunze was allowed to visit his partner in the hospital and came away convinced that he would die. "He has been poisoned," he said. "It is too late to save him. They have killed my best friend."[21] When he learned a few hours later of Schrader's death, he wept in his cell. The next week he was convicted of mail fraud and sent to McNeil Island federal penitentiary outside Tacoma, Washington, where he served for fifteen months.[22]

Thereafter Kunze gave up life as a healer and lived hand-to-mouth in Los Angeles. Four years later, in October 1922, he again made headlines when yet another Francis Schlatter—a man who had remained primarily out of the national limelight—died in St. Louis. Outraged that anyone else would share his fame, Kunze marched to the offices of the *Los Angeles Times* and announced that *he*, not the St. Louis claimant, was the real healer. "The papers say I am dead," he said. "This is not true. I am merely in poor circumstances."[23] It was the last time the public at large heard from Francis Schlatter, or about him, for nearly another quarter century. Then, in 1945, the body of the forgotten Schlatter, whose death in 1922

FIGURE 14. Jacob Kunze, also known as the
"King of Divine Healers," served prison time for
mail fraud. McNeil Island Federal Penitentiary,
Inmate Case Files (1899–1920), Record Group
129, Box 42, National Archives and Records
Commission, Pacific-Alaska Division.

had stirred Kunze to leave his park bench for momentary fame, was
discovered unburied in the basement of a St. Louis funeral home. It
was one of several bodies that St. Louis health officials found, well
preserved and orphaned, throughout the city.[24]

LIKE THOMAS DAWSON, I was drawn to Francis Schlatter's imposters
—and to this man in particular. All of them played out their dubious
notoriety in newspaper clippings that Dawson had collected from
1903 to 1922. They constituted a tiny fraction of the newspaper and
magazine articles Dawson assembled on all manner of subjects to
satisfy his encyclopedic interests.[25] Of the nearly one hundred vol-
umes in the Dawson scrapbooks at the Colorado Historical Society,

these slowly disintegrating, yellowed clippings had been pasted into Volume 88, "Oddities and Freaks." It took me a while to sort out one imposter from another, and when I had once identified Charles McLean, August Schrader, and Jacob Kunze, I was left with a man whose real name was like refractory ore — so buried in the surrounding historical rock that it defied easy extraction.

It would have remained there, too, if I hadn't accidentally run across a long-forgotten book in the Library of Congress while I was in Washington, D.C., researching Helen Wilmans and her influence on Schlatter. The book, published in 1903, was entitled *Modern Miracles of Healing: A True Account of the Life, Works, and Wanderings of Francis Schlatter, the Healer.* It was not a biography but an *autobiography.* As such, it not only asserted that Francis Schlatter was alive but provided a reliable touchstone for determining its author's truthfulness. His career, it turned out, spanned the era of Schlatter's imposters, from his first appearance in a Cleveland boardinghouse in 1897 to his death in St. Louis in 1922. Except for briefly rising to national attention in 1903, when he announced that he would return to Denver and prove himself to be the genuine healer, he remained elusive.

Modern Miracles of Healing borrowed its main title from the sermon "Modern Miracles" given by Rev. Myron Reed in 1895, when Schlatter was in Denver, and its subtitle from a popular biography of Francis Schlatter published by Harry B. Magill in 1896. The title page of *Modern Miracles* listed its authorship:

By FRANCIS SCHLATTER,

THE ALSACIAN.

and a saying:

I come not to bring a sword
but peace to mankind.
—Schlatter

Nearly everything about it, alas, was a lie. But it was a lie of such magnitude that I could not dismiss it. From the time I read its first chapter in the cavernous learning sanctuary of the Library of Congress, I *had* to know who its author really was, and why he had written such a book.

And what a book it was. The story of the "Alsacian's" boyhood, by itself, was extraordinary:

When he was two years old his parents moved to London, England, and the child attended school in that city on the East India Road, Paplar, E. C. [Poplar, East Central]. He had an own sister and brother who died in Ebersheim. His parents came to America in 1860, stopping at Columbia, Tennessee, where his father purchased a plantation on the Pulaski Pike. Being of a roving disposition, he [Francis's father] did not remain very long on the plantation, but returned to England. He came to this country again at the close of the civil war, settling on his plantation, where he soon died, and was buried at McCain [McCain's Cemetery], seven miles from Columbia, in 1868. His mother married a man by the name of Edward Martin, who was a contractor by occupation, and one son was born to them. He was named Thomas.[26]

Aside from the considerable stretch of imagination this passage required, I knew that Francis Schlatter had eight siblings, only one of whom died in childbirth, and that both his father and mother lived, respectively, until 1870 and 1871, and died in Ebersheim. But I had to accept the author's story, even if a fabrication, in order to understand his motive behind the lie. At the time of his father's death, he continued, Francis

discovered his power to heal. His mother had chronic neuralgia and he healed her by his touch. This was when he was twelve years old. It being known that the boy could do such strange things, the boys in that neighborhood would not have anything to do with him. They thought he was possessed of some mysterious power. This drove him away from home. He went to the old country and traveled about all the time, his parents furnishing him with money.[27]

Francis, wandering around Europe, then loses track of his parents. "He thought his mother had died," he wrote, "and he was determined to find out if it was true and sailed back to America, landing in New York in May 1884."[28] Yet strangely, the young man abandons his quest to find his mother and pursues work on Long Island. At this point, his narrative merges with that of Francis Schlatter's known story.

In most respects, I found, the story of the healer's rise to fame in

Modern Miracles of Healing was consistent with other accounts—not unusual considering its author would have had both Magill's *Biography of Francis Schlatter* and Ada Morley's *The Life of the Harp* to rely on as guides. But there was one glaring exception. His pilgrimage as recounted in *Modern Miracles* differed dramatically from the one Schlatter described in *The Life of the Harp*. As the original healer told his story to Ada Morley, every step of his journey followed a course dictated by the Father—and so the very route itself was sacred. Yet the author of *Modern Miracles* distorts the holy tramp of his predecessor, describing a journey that looks more like a tortured figure 8 than the simple loop taken by Schlatter.

I couldn't fathom why he would do this. One might suppose he had no knowledge of Schlatter's route, but he clearly did. Several significant places that the healer visited on his pilgrimage—Hot Springs, Flagstaff, Throckmorton, San Diego, San Francisco, Yuma, and Paris, Texas—the healer of *Modern Miracles* did too. But he did so at different times on his journey, and following a different path. It was a great mystery, but not one I could solve at the time—if ever.

Finally, I got to the part of the book in which Schlatter departs Ada Morley's ranch for Mexico. Four days later, he writes, "my pony drank some alkali water through the night and died." Grief-stricken, the healer walks to the nearest railroad station, then makes his way by train to the upper Ohio River valley. There he begins a new pilgrimage, walking down the Ohio River to the Mississippi, then down the Mississippi River to Memphis, where he reappears as Francis Schlatter in a public auditorium in March 1897. In the meantime, he is jailed twice, once on suspicion of blowing up a church in Portsmouth, Ohio, and hospitalized twice, once in Wheeling, West Virginia, from a railroad accident, and the second time in Cincinnati's Good Samaritan Hospital.[29]

I knew too much about the real Schlatter's life to accept *Modern Miracles of Healing* as a true account. Too many of the details didn't fit or were obvious lies. Yet I couldn't dismiss the book out of hand. The author clearly knew much about the real Schlatter and had studied him closely. Though clearly an imposter, he seemed to offer the last reasonable opportunity to learn whether Schlatter walked out of Mexico and into a posthumous life. Thus in May 1992 I drove east from Denver to Chicago, Cincinnati, Nashville, and into the South on a two-week journey to follow the clues left by the mysterious author of *Modern Miracles of Healing*—Francis Schlatter, "The Alsacian."

At the midpoint of the trip, having received permission from Cincinnati's Good Samaritan Hospital, I sat down at a table in the hospital's records department looking at a folio-sized book about two inches thick—the patient record book for 1896. As it lay in front of me, I hadn't any idea *when* the wayfarer in *Modern Miracles* was hospitalized. The church bombing he'd mentioned, which took place in Portsmouth, Ohio, had occurred on July 18, 1896.[30] So I started on that date and began looking forward. Each page had about three individual records, and each patient record included name, age, occupation, birthplace, residence, next of kin, diagnosis, and date of discharge.

I had been at it for about fifteen minutes when I stopped. Before me, halfway down the page, was the man who wrote *Modern Miracles of Healing.*

Name	Jno. E. Martin
Age	34
Occupation	Sculptor
Nativity	Tennessee
Residence	Columbia, Tennessee
Next of kin	Mrs. Louisa Martin
Discharged	August 11
Diagnosis	Optitis [*otitis media;* ear infection][31]

So here was the author of *Modern Miracles of Healing.* The man hospitalized in Good Samaritan in August 1896 was John Martin—perhaps a sculptor, perhaps even in that a liar—who soon undertook a life of deception as an imposter of Francis Schlatter. His own autobiography had led me into the recesses of his past and to the refractory ore that was his secret identity.

At that point, in spite of the time and effort I'd taken researching him, I could have consigned John Martin to the rogues' gallery of Schlatter imposters along with McLean, Schrader, and Kunze—and then been done with it. But he was a far more clever and intriguing personality than any of them, and there were many questions about him I wanted to pursue. Why had he written an autobiography? Why had it been filled with deliberate lies—and tantalizing suggestions of the truth? Where had he actually been born, and what was

FIGURE 15. In *The Life of the Harp*, Ada Morley included a map of the American West on which was superimposed a gigantic cross suggesting Schlatter's sacred journey from 1893 to 1895. Entitled "Symbolic Outline of Pilgrimages," Morley's map represented the extent of Schlatter's past and future travels. The precise route of Schlatter's pilgrimage, based on his account, has here been added to her 1897 map. In 1903 the author of *Modern Miracles of Healing*, one of several men claiming to be Francis Schlatter, described a very different—and highly

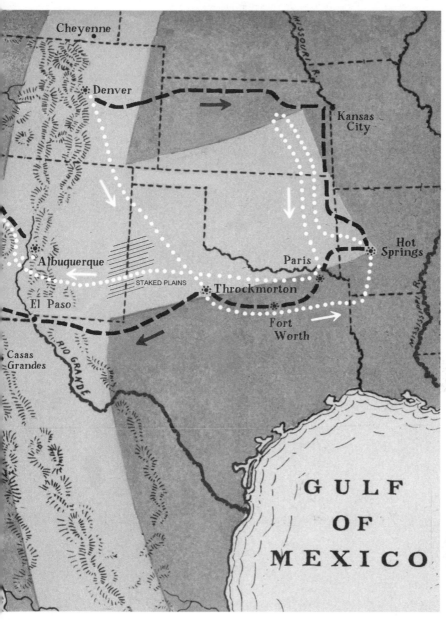

imaginative—journey shadowing the first but in some cases actually reversing the direction of the original. Both routes, as described in the two books, are shown here for the first time. Adapted from *The Life of the Harp*; original map courtesy Western History Department, Denver Public Library. *The Life of the Harp in the Hand of the Harper,* courtesy of the Denver Public Library, Western History Collection, c265.8s338Li.

his relationship to Louisa Martin, whom he called his mother? And why had he begun a career impersonating Francis Schlatter at the age of thirty-four—if that, indeed, was his true age?

Modern Miracles followed the healer's life in minute detail as he wandered across the Midwest, East, and into the South from 1897 to its publication in 1903.

"Look at my face"

"Look at my face. No other man
on earth has a face like it."[1]
FRANCIS SCHLATTER, 1897

THE AUTHOR OF *Modern Miracles*—Francis Schlatter, née John Martin—made his appearance unheralded in Canton, Ohio, at the end of July 1897, just over a month after news of the healer's death in Mexico reached the United States. He stood in the public square at the corner of Tuscarawas and Market, beneath the city hall with its high tower emblazoned with angels trumpeting the Lord's justice. He took a position on the brick-paved street, beneath a maple tree, and waited for sufferers to discover him. They did. Some of them knew he'd been treating the afflicted in Minerva, about fifteen miles away. There he had held two meetings in the opera house, and when he touched a man with eczema, the blisters scaled away, leaving his skin smooth and without a blemish.[2] Later he did the same thing with a baby; he held it for some time, and the eruptions on the infant's back disappeared.[3]

Schlatter had a manager—Ed Lengle, a man he'd met in Memphis. Aside from guiding people to the healer on the square, it wasn't clear what Lengle's duties were. But one of them was to advise sufferers to bring their handkerchiefs to the healer for blessing, and many of them placed nickels, dimes, and quarters inside. Schlatter didn't return the money—perhaps because managers had to be compensated, however small the amount. Within days, another manager, E. R. Kidd, joined them.

The most striking instance of Schlatter's abilities was the healing of ex–state senator Thomas C. Snyder, who owned the Canton Steel Roofing Company. Snyder hadn't been able to walk without crutches for fourteen years, and his family urged him to see the healer. Later, he said, "Schlatter did not say a word. He sat there with his head uncovered, and took my right hand in his left and my left hand in his right. He then put his right hand on the back of my neck."[4] Then the healer took away his crutches, and Snyder was able to walk. "Of course I limp," he told reporters, "owing to the unequal length of my limbs, but it is a relief to have such strength that I can walk this way"—and with that he made his way a hundred feet to his carriage.[5]

Others testified to improved vision, hearing, and mobility. One man said, "I have had bad eyes for twenty-five years. For the last eight years I have been quite blind. During that time I could tell old friends only by the sound of their voices. I have been treated twice by Schlatter and I can now see quite well."[6] But the *Repository* also interviewed people who had not benefited from the treatments, though some would try again. For the most part, the sufferers who came to the new Schlatter believed they had been healed completely, or very much relieved of their symptoms.

And they were ready to pay. It amounted to nothing more than small change—but *this* Schlatter didn't refuse it, as Denver's healer had done. The coins came to him folded in handkerchiefs, and his managers collected them while the healer performed his blessing. The handkerchiefs, one reporter said, ranged from the "lace embroidered cambric of the lady, to the coarse bandana of the laborer and the grimy wipe of the street boy."[7] A week after his arrival, he blessed some three hundred handkerchiefs in one afternoon, and many contained quarters. "Although quite a sum was collected," stated the *Repository*, "it is safe to say that Schlatter is not making a fortune."[8] One of the key differences, in this respect, between the Denver healer and Canton's was that the former had free room and board at the Fox home, and supporters offered their help in half-day shifts to control the crowd, handle mail, and perform other tasks.[9] Canton's healer had no such support system.

In any case, the new healer made no apology for taking money —in fact, he wasn't about to apologize for *anything* he said or did. "I have been arrested a number of times," he said, "and have been driven out of town. That does not bother me, neither does the want of money. I have no hesitation in going away and leaving my bills unpaid. Somebody will always pay them." Then he said: "I need a pair of shoes and a shoemaker has already taken my measure without my asking him."[10]

As for money, he said, he didn't need it. Before arriving in Canton, he left a Minerva boardinghouse with another man's shirt. When someone followed him to Canton and asked about it, Schlatter asked, "How much is it worth?"[11] The answer was seventy-five cents, and Schlatter threw down a few bills in payment. The gesture was arrogant—as was the presumption that he could walk off with a man's shirt. But Schlatter argued that he wasn't like other men. He'd been sent to the world for a purpose. He told of an incident while traveling through the woods, heading toward Memphis, when a deer stepped out of a thicket and licked his hand. He patted its neck and it bounded away.[12] True or not, the story reflected his belief that he was different than other men. "You know how some people say I am the second Messiah," he commented. "What do I think about it? Well, I believe with all my heart that I am the second Messiah. My life has been so peculiar in many respects that I cannot help but think so."[13]

What was even more peculiar, however, was the Canton healer's unapologetic admission that he drank whiskey—and this at a time when the temperance movement was gaining broad public recognition and demonizing drinkers of alcohol. "I am compelled to drink whiskey to keep up my strength," he said. "The Master made wine, and whiskey is only a modern modification of wine. It is a foolish prejudice that condemns the use of liquor."[14] But the idea of a godly man drinking liquor struck people as incongruous. "Now I don't like that," one woman said. "I know the Bible says take a little wine, but it did not say drink whiskey."[15]

───────────

ON SATURDAY, AUGUST 7, about a week after Schlatter's arrival in Canton, he announced that he'd been invited to spend Sunday at Brady Lake, a resort town near Kent, about twenty-five miles to the north. Though he didn't mention it, the invitation came from spiritualists who had established a camp on the shores of the lake a year or so earlier, near a popular lakeside hotel.[16] They were eager to meet the renowned Francis Schlatter not only because he was a healer but because they knew him to be a gifted psychic.

On Sunday morning, Schlatter climbed aboard an excursion train to the lake. He rode in the same car as Margaret Ferris, the widow of the Ferris wheel's inventor, George Washington Gale Ferris Jr.[17] Ferris's great invention, introduced to the public at the 1893 Chicago World's Fair, was considered to be the American answer to the Eiffel Tower, and it promised to make him a millionaire. Yet when he died in November 1896, a victim of typhoid fever, his estate had been decimated by patent infringement lawsuits and poor business decisions. He was only thirty-seven years old.

Margaret Ferris had left her husband several months before his death, abandoning their Pittsburgh home to take up residence with her mother in Canton. She had nothing to do with the funeral arrangements or disposition of her husband's ashes. Furthermore, by mid-1897 she was suffering from severe depression, and remained in seclusion. Her friends, urged by her doctor, proposed an excursion to Brady Lake to cheer her up, or at least get her out of doors. They joined her on the trip, bringing their bicycles. At the station in Kent, they wheeled to the lake while she rode there in a carriage. Francis Schlatter was one of the passengers, and they were introduced to each other along the way.[18]

Ferris soon saw Schlatter again — and more intimately. After arriving at the lake, she complained of weakness to her longtime friend Maggie Gaul, a psychic medium. Gaul ordered a room for Ferris at the lakeside hotel, then sought out the healer and brought him there. In spite of their brief acquaintance, a certain chemistry had already begun to coalesce. After her private treatment, Ferris felt well enough to join other sufferers who passed by the healer at the spiritualist camp, and the two later went boating on the lake. They spent a few more hours talking in the hotel, and they were inseparable on the trip back to Canton. By the end of the day, a courtship that would normally take weeks had telescoped down into several hours.

Monday evening Schlatter called on Ferris, and they went to nearby Meyer's Lake for another boat ride. The next morning he saw her again — and that afternoon, when he finished his healing work in the town square, he went to the probate office and took out a marriage license.[19] He asked the clerk to keep the license a secret for thirty days, but a crowd had already started to gather outside — as they did wherever he went. Among them was a reporter from the *Canton Repository* who asked him about the official-looking paper sticking out of his pocket. Schlatter admitted it was a license but replied, "The marriage may not take place for some time yet."[20]

The reporter quickly got to Margaret Ferris and told her of the license. She was surprised—and gave a guarded response. No, she said, they hadn't made any marriage plans, and she knew nothing about the license. The healer had obtained it without her consent. Yet even as they spoke, her luggage lay packed in her room awaiting the moment when she would escape to meet him in Massilon, a few miles away, to get married. She knew very well that he'd gotten a marriage license—and they had to act quickly. Ferris's family had learned of her relationship with the healer and were fiercely opposed to it.

Schlatter arrived in Massilon at the appointed hour, but Ferris wasn't there. She—along with her luggage—had been discovered by her relatives. "They reasoned with her," the *Repository* stated, and she changed her mind.[21] They convinced her that the Canton healer had exerted an undue influence over her, and in her weakened condition she couldn't resist him. They intended to protect her in the future.

Ferris merely bided her time. She was determined to marry Schlatter even though skeptics accused him of fraud and in spite of gossip about the kind of woman who would be attracted to such a man.[22] She took pains to stay out of sight and met with him surreptitiously, one day asking him to treat her younger sister, Maud, who had a lump on her neck.[23]

On Monday, back at his station on the square, Schlatter announced that he would take three days off to visit New York. Instead, he left the next afternoon for the Victoria Hotel in Pittsburgh, where Ferris had already arrived with Maud earlier in the day. The couple couldn't have chosen a worse time, or place, to elope—for Pittsburgh was then hosting the International League of Press Clubs.[24] Reporters quickly picked up the rumor of scandal, and one of them went so far as to climb through the transom above the door of Schlatter's room.

Ferris kept herself removed and aloof, if only for appearances. She didn't respond to the healer's calling card, sent earlier in the day, and she told reporters that his proposal to her was an "advertising dodge."[25] The fact that they appeared together in the same hotel was purely an accident. She was there, she said, only to counter the nefarious suggestion made by some Ohio newspapers that she'd been committed to a mental hospital in Toledo.[26] She had not seen the healer for more than a week.[27] "He is a bright man," she said, "and I have always found him a gentleman. If I should meet him here I would not hesitate to shake hands with him and thank him again for the good he has done my health."[28]

The next day Schlatter gave the Victoria Hotel desk clerk twenty dollars to keep reporters away from the two lovers. He then tried to locate a minister, and found Rev. J. W. Sproul of the Central Reformed Presbyterian Church. Reverend Sproul accompanied him to the hotel, and all three sat down in a private room. "When there," Sproul later told the press, "I had a talk with Mrs. Ferris and I must admit that she seemed perfectly willing to enter into the bonds of marriage with Schlatter. There did not seem to be any coercion upon his part and they both appeared to be in their normal mental condition."[29]

But he could not marry them. For all the excitement over the marriage license back in Canton, it was not valid in Pennsylvania. Schlatter was willing to get another one, but when Sproul came to learn who the couple were he refused to perform the service, license or no. They had gained too much notoriety for the staid Presbyterian clergyman. He gave them his blessing and left. But they were not deterred. Later that day the couple went to Rev. Edward H. Ward of St. Peter's Episcopal Church—and he, too, turned them down. Nevertheless, the rumor of their marriage spread quickly; within a day or two it was in local newspapers and on the wires.[30]

In spite of these claims, the relationship came to an abrupt end the day after the couple failed to find a willing minister. Their disappointment was surely acute, and whatever happened later that evening is unknown. But the next morning Schlatter was on a train heading toward Beaver Run, on his way back to Canton, and Margaret Ferris was on her way to Butler, a few miles north of Pittsburgh, where she stayed with a friend. She telegraphed her family in Canton: "Not married. The freak has gone to Canton and is giving me a rest."[31] Schlatter got drunk that night in Beaver Run, and was so hung over when he arrived in Canton that he quit treating patients after fifteen minutes.

For all the shenanigans in Pittsburgh, the breakup was genuine —and irrevocable. In the meantime, Schlatter had been absent from his place under the maple tree on the square for more than three days. The Canton healing ministry had clearly lost its momentum. To make matters worse, Mayor James A. Rice decreed that

the healer must pay a licensing fee of five dollars a day if he wanted
to continue healing.[32] The scale of the ministry, the mayor argued,
and the need to support two managers, had transformed the healing
sessions into a profit-making business. The healer should be charged
"the same as any other transient." Given the elopement scandal,
Mayor Rice's language suggests that he had been prompted by the
Ferris family to get rid of the healer — and it worked.

BRADY LAKE LIES NESTLED in what could be called a hollow —
a geological depression among low-lying hills on the edge of Kent,
Ohio. One could easily miss the sign marking it on the highway
between Kent and Ravenna — as I did. On top of that, the lowering
clouds and drizzling rain had turned everything on that darkening
May afternoon into a wash of green and gray. Having gone too far,
I turned back and, in spite of the rush-hour traffic urging me from
behind, slowed to look for the Brady Lake sign. Seeing it, I gratefully
turned onto a quiet road that led to an embankment of leafy trees
shading small homes. I drove on, eventually catching a glimpse of
the small lake and hoping I could find a spot to park my car, take a
picture or two — and maybe even discover the remnants of the two-
story hotel that I'd seen in old photographs.

The road led around the lake, rising and falling with the contours
of the hollow. But nowhere did it open to a lakeside park, a beach,
or even a roadside stopping place. The shore was congested with
homes and garages and boat ramps, and every eighth of a mile or so
a No Parking sign rose up. Twice I passed a squad car patrolling the
area. The message was abundantly clear: Brady Lake was a private
enclave, nearly every square foot of its shoreline claimed for personal
use. It didn't welcome the public.

When I finally got a good shot of the lake, I snapped the picture
from the car. I had to hurry, since I was in danger of blocking the
narrow two-lane road. Out of the corner of my eye I saw a woman
fishing from her yard. She regarded me suspiciously. The late afternoon drizzle morphed into rain, and I could see the haze of rainfall
on the lake's surface. It was time to leave — far sooner than I wanted.
As I drove over the hill heading back to the highway, I wondered
how Brady Lake, which had been such a public resort in the nine-

teenth century, had managed to become a private, inward-looking bedroom community in the twentieth.

Under the circumstances, I failed to make any emotional connection to Francis and Margaret's budding love affair at Brady Lake. But what *did* intrigue me was the lake's attraction for spiritualists. By the late nineteenth century, spiritualist camps were springing up everywhere—many of them in bucolic surroundings like Brady Lake. Spiritualism was one of the largest bodies of nontraditional religious thought in the nation, and it was only then becoming organized.

Francis Schlatter had been a spiritualist ever since he arrived in America in 1884—and perhaps before that. But when he began his Denver ministry in 1895, he kept his distance from his old spiritualist acquaintances. And it made sense. He had returned as a man of God, not as a mere seeker of spiritual truth. The last thing he wanted —the last thing *any* Christlike figure might want—was to lay bare the halting, inglorious, struggling lessons of the past. In Schlatter's case, they were many—from his experiments in prophetic healing to his attempts at astral projection. When he returned to Denver in 1895, some of his old spiritualist friends sought him out, but he would not recognize them. His rebirth began with his pilgrimage, and all his thoughts and ideas came directly from God. It could not be otherwise. Later, when he and Ada Morley carried on long conversations about religion, reincarnation, and prophecy on her ranch, he said nothing about spiritualism—and nothing in *The Life of the Harp* suggests that he did.

So, what was *this* Francis Schlatter doing with spiritualists at Brady Lake? Was it coincidence? In fact, it could have been. He'd been *invited*, after all. He was a successful healer, and spiritualists recognized powers in people they considered mediums. On his first visit, he met Margaret Ferris; but he returned the next week alone, to minister again to the spiritualist camp.[33] He seemed comfortable with them, and they respected his gifts. And yet in his book *Modern Miracles of Healing*, written six years later, he made no mention of them in connection to the Brady Lake episode—or in any other respect.

Perhaps there was no need, especially if it happened only once or twice. But if his ties to spiritualism were stronger, and his silence a pattern, then he shared an unusual bond with the healer of Denver. Common sense told me that an imposter must follow one principle, if nothing else—that is, to *stay in character* with his subject. It went without saying that an imposter should know his subject intimately; but if not, at least he, or she, must imitate the most *public* aspects of the role—those physical or behavioral characteristics that define their subject's identity. If the Canton healer knew of Schlatter's deep roots in spiritualism, he might well emulate it—but not when it was a virtual secret.

In fact, from the time he first made headlines nationally, emerging as Francis Schlatter in a Cleveland boardinghouse two months earlier, the Canton healer seemed oblivious to *any* guiding set of principles for imposters. For one thing, he was clean-shaven—which immediately took away a signature resemblance to Denver's healer. For another, he openly accepted donations—quite unlike his counterpart—and he had a small cadre of managers, which gave his ministry an air of venality and commercialism. In other respects, he seemed at times arrogant, willful, and opportunistic, and his defense of whiskey went counter to what people recalled of Schlatter's temperance and sobriety. Above all, his scandalous love affair with Margaret Ferris, coupled with his impetuosity and the rumored suggestion in Pittsburgh that he was after her money, tainted the Canton healer in a way that struck me as almost deliberately controversial.[34]

Or perhaps he was just being himself—character be damned. Yet along with the possible connection to spiritualism, something else bothered me. When he first made news publicly in Cleveland earlier that summer, Schlatter said something curious. "After I was compelled to leave Denver in November 1895," he told a reporter, "I went to Manitou, Colorado, to rest and recuperate, for I was thoroughly worn out."[35] Of all the places he might mention at random, Manitou was one of the least likely. Yet workers on the Pikes Peak Railway, near Manitou, *had* seen a man resembling the healer a few days after his disappearance.

Eventually, I hoped to resolve the troubling duality of Francis Schlatter vs. John Martin. In the meantime, however, I would look for aspects of their behavior and character that they privately shared, apart from their conflicting public faces. If only, I thought, the link between the two men could be something physical, something immediately apparent—but comparative photographs and drawings were either unobtainable or hopelessly imprecise.

Nevertheless, when I first studied the engraved image of Francis Schlatter in 1897, a thought occurred to me. Had anyone in Canton

FIGURE 16. Francis Schlatter (who went by the name
of John E. Martin a year earlier in Cincinnati's
Good Samaritan Hospital) in Canton, Ohio,
August 1897. *Denver Post*, August 9, 1897.

witnessed the original healer in Denver two years earlier — and perhaps returned in the meantime to observe the Canton man? When
I checked the *Canton Repository* for fall 1895, when all the excitement
was taking place in Denver, I found just what I was looking for.
Lillian Middaugh, a former resident of Canton who had moved to
Denver, gave the *Repository* a careful description the healer. She had
studied him closely at the Fox home and included a singular detail
that Denver reporters hadn't mentioned and photographs failed to
capture. The healer, she wrote, had "a slight mark on his nose."[36]
Though Middaugh hadn't returned to Canton, so far as I knew, to
compare the two men, she had provided the only physical clue that
might link them.

BY THE TIME SCHLATTER LEFT Canton, heading for Chicago, his
party had added a new member. During the previous week, when
he and Margaret Ferris went from one Pittsburgh church to another
looking for a minister, a man in his mid-thirties arrived in Canton
and made his way to the public square. There, under the maple

tree, he met Lengle and Kidd, who waited faithfully for their errant healer to return. The stranger, just in from Nashville, became upset when he learned that Schlatter was in Pittsburgh. He'd come specifically to attend the wedding, and now the couple had left without him. To the curious managers, he explained that he was Francis Schlatter's younger brother Thomas.[37] Francis had sent him a letter urging him to hurry. Now, it seemed, the couple had eloped. "He has always been peculiar and of a roving disposition," Thomas said — and Francis's sudden impulse to get married was typical of his character.[38]

Initially, Thomas tried to pass off his last name as Schlatter, but eventually abandoned the effort; he settled for calling Francis his half-brother. Thomas was Louisa Martin's second son and lived with her in Bordeaux, Tennessee, on the outskirts of Nashville. He had not seen his brother in years — until just five months earlier. That meeting, in late March 1897, was a cause for celebration all around. Schlatter had just arrived from his first public healing in Memphis, a large one but ignored by the local press. He hoped that Louisa still lived in Nashville, but he wasn't sure. "You can imagine the meeting between my mother and me after so long a separation," he wrote in *Modern Miracles.* "I was so overjoyed that I could not speak — to think that I should meet my mother again that I had mourned as dead."[39] He left Louisa after a few days to continue his healing work, but from that time forward neither Louisa nor Thomas would be absent from his life.

Thomas decided to join the healer's entourage, and within a day or two the party had departed for Cleveland and then by boat to Detroit. Their destination was Chicago, where managers Lengle and Kidd had arranged with a benefactor, G. C. McAllister, to host a healing ministry.[40]

The healer's debut in Chicago differed substantially from his solitary vigil in the Canton city square a month earlier. Now he sat in a pavilion surrounded by the shaded courtyard of the Manhattan Beach Hotel in Windsor Park overlooking Lake Michigan.[41] Here, hundreds of sufferers passed by a platform on which, like a monarch, he sat on a raised chair and leaned slightly forward to touch and bless them. He had rooms in the hotel, free meals for himself and his party, and a good manager in Ed Lengle, who consulted with a lawyer to head off a possible summons for practicing without a license.

Two years earlier, the city of Chicago had eagerly awaited the Denver healer's arrival. But not now—and *not* for Canton's Francis Schlatter. News of Schlatter's death in Mexico was still fresh in the public's mind, and the new healer's behavior in Canton hardly evoked a Christlike image. Joseph Kipley, Chicago's chief of police, went in search of witnesses who would testify that he was a fake. The *Chicago Tribune*, spearheaded by a skeptical reporter who had covered Schlatter in 1895, launched its own attack. Meanwhile, the health commissioner, Dr. Arthur Reynolds, began an investigation into the dangers posed by so many diseased people gathering together in one place. In short, the Chicago establishment officially set itself against the new Francis Schlatter.

In spite of this hostility, Chicagoans came en masse to see and be touched by the healer. People left nickels, dimes, and quarters, unconcerned about how unseemly this struck the critics, or how uncharacteristic this was of the original healer of Denver. One old Irish woman set down her entire purse after her treatment and walked tearfully away. As he had in Canton, Schlatter didn't ask for contributions, nor did he refuse them. He made no apology for accepting money—seventeen dollars or so a day—or for dressing in his Sunday best to perform his healing work. "I have to cater to the people here," he said, indicating that Chicago had wealthier classes than Denver, "and they would denounce me if I didn't dress well. I have to have money here."[42]

That sort of candor simply encouraged his attackers. One of Kipley's witnesses, J. C. Teller, a nephew of Colorado's senator Henry M. Teller, identified the healer as Rattlesnake Bill, a "patent medicine fakir" from Oklahoma who operated throughout the Midwest.[43] The accusation—probably based on a product, Rattlesnake Bill's Liniment, rather than a real person—put the healer on a par with commonplace charlatans and frauds. Rather than defend himself, Schlatter countered that he was pleased to see doubts raised about him, for Christ was also persecuted.

Except for the soft murmur of the crowd in the hotel's shaded courtyard and the chirping of birds in the overhanging trees, the scene was similar to that in Denver. As each person came to him, the healer reached out with his right hand as if to shake hands, then placed his left hand on the back of the sufferer's neck, holding it there briefly. Next he took any handkerchief offered and grasped it tightly and returned it. He said nothing, but his managers spoke softly to supplicants who were both approaching and leaving the healer. As in Denver, reporters stood nearby to describe the scene and the effects of treatment. A score of Chicago policemen ensured good order.

Unlike Denver, however, the press was anything but sympathetic. In the eyes of the *Tribune* reporter, the Chicago healer's imitation of Francis Schlatter, though it seemed practiced and studied, failed to capture the original healer's sincerity. "There is a visible attempt to act up to his role," the reporter said, "and at times the assumed dignity is dropped, the faraway look which he attempts to hold disappears, and the 'Divine Healer' becomes an unprepossessing and commonplace looking man, surveying with indifferent contempt the crowds of afflicted he is victimizing."[44]

More important, the Chicago healer's physical features convinced this reporter that he was a fake. This healer's flawed, ignoble character manifested itself in his sharp, narrow face, eyes set close together, and protruding lower lip. Francis Schlatter's face, on the other hand, had projected a look that was broad, simple, and serene. "It was a face full of compassion and belief in himself, a face which inspired confidence." In fact, to a certain extent, "it reminded one of the pictured face of the Christ."[45]

A chorus of the healer's doubters concurred, each pointing to different physical or personal characteristics that distinguished Chicago's Schlatter from the original healer of Denver. One man recalled that Schlatter had a "great flat nose" and another that his fingers were stubby, like a laborer's, while the Chicago healer's were "long, straight and tapering."[46] In contrast, Teller claimed that "Schlatter's hands were twice the size of this man's."[47]

The physical differences these men observed, however, conveyed a deeper conclusion they had made about the two healers. While Francis Schlatter, they argued, had been a coarse, uneducated, but honest man who spoke in broken English, the healer of Windsor Park spoke perfect English and seemed by all appearances to be an educated, perhaps effete, "slick." John F. Byrnes, who claimed to be deputy sheriff of Denver when Francis Schlatter was at the Fox home, summed it up. Schlatter, he said, "was just such a slob of a Dutchman, and he spoke with a strong German accent, which this man has overcome, if he ever had it. Schlatter wore corduroy or denim; he couldn't have got into that black suit and tie. This is not the man."[48]

In spite of the doubts and skepticism directed at him from every side, Schlatter succeeded in capturing the faith of the people. The baffled *Tribune* reporter commented: "And still he has his followers and is believed in and almost worshipped, and there are those who testify before his meetings that they have been cured of disease through his ministrations. It is a queer thing and it adds force to the confidence man's motto."[49]

And what was his motto? Over and over again, the healer of Windsor Park offered his critics a challenge. "Look at my face," he said. "No other man on earth has a face like it."[50] It was an assertion of supreme confidence in himself and a gauntlet thrown down to those who doubted that he was Francis Schlatter. And aside from the few witnesses Kipley had rounded up, and the manufactured aspersion that he was "Rattlesnake Bill," nobody in the crowds that filled the courtyard of the Manhattan Beach Hotel seemed to question the healer's name, his sincerity, or his power to heal. When another skeptic asked him if he were Christ, Schlatter said: "I am not a Christ; the Christ was a Schlatter."[51]

CHAPTER NINE

The Sparrow's Fall

"My friends, do you know that there is one that is
above us that marks even the sparrow's fall?"

MODERN MIRACLES OF HEALING

O N SUNDAY, SEPTEMBER 5, 1897, the same day the *Chicago Tri-bune* gave extensive coverage to Schlatter's ministry, a small, at-tractive woman in her mid-thirties stepped up to the front desk of the Manhattan Beach Hotel.[1] The lobby was strangely quiet. She proffered her card and in a soft, southern-tinged voice asked for a visit with the healer. It was late in the afternoon, and the desk clerk informed her that Schlatter, and all the hotel's other guests, had gone and wouldn't return. With certain embarrassment, he explained the situation: the hotel's management, unable to make a lease payment, had canceled all room reservations and evicted more than one hun-dred guests just as they were sitting down to lunch that day. They had all departed, along with a sea of trunks, to various other hotels around the city.[2]

Two years earlier Luverna Comer, the woman who approached the hotel's front desk, had been considered Schlatter's "female rival."[3] She was a spiritual healer in her own right, practicing in Chicago, who adopted the "Christ method" of healing as a result of her own miraculous deathbed recovery. Her career and Schlatter's had blos-somed simultaneously. While he met with sufferers in Albuquerque's Old Town, she was treating patients at the Chicago headquarters of Dr. Chester I. Thacher, a homeopathic physician who had made a national reputation selling magnetic shields to thwart illnesses and ailments.[4] Soon Dr. Thacher's factory became so packed with suffer-ers that Comer had to offer healing sessions at the Masonic Temple.

Compared to Schlatter's fame, the temporary arc of Luverna Comer's career was modest, and she soon faded from the national stage. In 1896 she left Chicago to spend a year in Washington, D.C., practicing her healing gifts but also trying to organize a nonsectarian religious movement.[5] She had recently returned to Chicago and was curious to see—and to meet—the great healer Francis Schlatter. Among her belongings was a photograph of him a friend had given her two years earlier. Maybe his voice, when she met him, would be like that of the invisible presence who had spoken to her on the night of her miraculous recovery: "Act as if I am the Christ."[6] Those words had lifted her, as if by a host of angels, to immediate health and well-being.

There was no way Luverna could determine Schlatter's whereabouts, for in the wake of the hotel's closing he didn't continue his Chicago healing ministry. But she was confident that she would meet him when the time came. After his disappearance in 1895, she had foretold that he would return and do greater works than he had ever done before. She still believed that. The long lines of sufferers whom she had read about in the courtyard of the Manhattan Beach Hotel were clear evidence that her prophecy had come true.[7]

In fact, in the six months since Francis Schlatter first appeared in Memphis, he had treated, by his own estimate, more than one hundred thousand people—forty-five thousand in Chicago alone.[8] Although those figures are questionable, it's likely that many thousands had so far felt his healing touch or watched him do his work. In any case, if Chicago taught him anything, it was that he was capable of drawing record crowds—and, as his managers knew, these could only be found in large cities. So while Luverna Comer waited on the knowledge that she would meet Francis Schlatter sometime, he launched an ambitious healing campaign that would take him throughout the Midwest, into the East, and eventually to the South.

Unlike his famous namesake, who wandered on foot or rode on horseback throughout the West, Schlatter traveled in the comfort of a railroad car. After a short stay in Canton, he made a circuit of small towns in Ohio, then headed for the Eastern Seaboard— Baltimore, Atlantic City, and Philadelphia. If he lacked for money, it didn't show; and though he refused contributions for himself, he allowed his managers to make a modest living. Their professional lives, however, were relatively short-lived. Kidd soon departed after they left Chicago, and Lengle, whose hometown was Canton, decided to stay there after Schlatter returned for a month. Half-brother

Thomas Martin, who had joined them as a lark, went back to the family home near Nashville.

Schlatter acquired another manager, Walter S. Gilbert, who happened to be the story-seeking reporter the healer had found in his Pittsburgh hotel room. They had hit it off well, and Gilbert promised to join Schlatter's ministry after he fulfilled some prior obligations.[9] Trained to be a minister, Gilbert had recently arrived in the United States from England and had been casting about for a new profession. Arranging the details of the healer's unusual ministry seemed to be the ticket, and he remained with Schlatter for a year.

Gilbert's flaming red hair added a mixture of levity to the often somber business of healing the suffering masses. In Zanesville, Ohio, eight-year-old Laura Dickson, who had been blind since birth, suddenly saw objects emerge from a haze after Schlatter touched her.[10] But she didn't recognize what the objects were. When people in the crowd, astonished at her new eyesight, asked her to identify a house, a buggy, or a lamppost, she made up anything that came to mind. People laughed in joyful relief at her wild guesses. Gilbert pointed to his hair and asked her what color it was. She said it was green.

The Dickson healing caused a sensation among the crowd, and newspaper reporters rushed to find the local eye specialist, Dr. O. T. Knapp, to confirm or deny it. With the doctor in tow, they caught up with Laura and her cousin, Callie Dickson, as the two were boarding the steamboat *Jewel*. Callie held Laura's hand tightly, and the younger girl walked with a hesitant, high-stepping gait, afraid of tripping over something in her path. They were returning to Cedar Run, a few miles down the Muskingum River, where Laura's father worked as a miner. He and his wife had approved Callie's request to bring her cousin to the healer.

When reporters questioned Laura, she affirmed that she could see better than yesterday. Callie added that Laura was not totally blind; she had always been able to get about alone — though that seemed hardly possible to those who saw them board the *Jewel*. In any case, Dr. Knapp sat the girl down on the deck and examined her eyes. She had cataracts in both, he determined, and he performed some simple visual experiments. "Testing the degree of sight," the *Zanesville Courier* said, "the doctor found that she could point accurately toward light, and she could count his spread fingers at four feet, but not at six feet."[11] Dr. Knapp had a theory about the girl's sudden improvement. It was a dark, cloudy day, and her pupils were more dilated than the day before, allowing her to see around the edges of the cataract.

Obviously the healer hadn't cured her underlying condition—the cataracts. The doctor confirmed the reporters' skepticism, but he didn't let the matter rest there. Learning that Laura's parents were very poor, he agreed to perform cataract surgery on the little girl for free if someone boarded her in Zanesville during the procedure. "Already a generous lady has offered such a place," the *Courier* stated that afternoon, and the cataracts would be removed "by the processes of modern science."

The healer's party made a few stops in small towns throughout Ohio but soon headed for the East Coast, staying for a week at Gwinn Oak Park in Baltimore before settling down for a month or so in Atlantic City. Then it was off to Philadelphia in June. Here, on July 3, Schlatter treated more people in one day that ever before —9,006 by actual count. "This was the hardest day's work I ever did," he wrote. "I was kept at it from nine in the morning until ten at night without any intermission or anything to eat. This was the only time in my life that I was tired after a healing demonstration."[12]

All during the previous spring, ever since the sinking of the U.S.S. *Maine* in February, there had been talk of armed conflict between the United States and Spain over Cuban independence. The two nations declared war on each other in April, and some residents of Atlantic City expressed concern that Spanish gunboats might shell the American coastline. By the Fourth of July, however, the Spanish-American War was all but over. On July 1 the Rough Riders took San Juan Hill, and by July 3 the Spanish fleet in the Caribbean had been destroyed. Patriotic fervor, which had been building for months, ran high and spilled over.

As Schlatter looked back on those days later, he saw that events were unfolding before him. On July 6, while staying at the Bingham Hotel, he said, "I had a presentiment that something was going to happen." Walter Gilbert was out of town—and thus unable to prevent the healer from what transpired in front of the Keystone Hotel at Sixteenth and Market. A row of small decorative American flags festooned the hotel's streetside shops, and Schlatter jumped up, grabbed one, and tore it to pieces. His action created such a stir, and such anger, that a mob quickly gathered to punish him for his

FIGURE 17. Keystone Hotel, 1524–1542 Market Street, Philadelphia. Here, on July 6, 1898, the man who had emerged as Francis Schlatter a year earlier tore down an American flag at the height of the Spanish-American War. Postcard with 1907 postmark, in author's possession.

treasonous act. Only a passing policeman saved him from a severe beating—and possibly death.

The policeman arrested Schlatter and walked him a block or so to Philadelphia's nearly completed city hall. There he was arraigned in the central police court under a newly passed state ordinance making it a felony "to insult and degrade the American flag"—a law, it seemed, almost made for him.[13] "I think this is a false charge," Schlatter told the court, unaware of the mixed blessing the officer had handed him. "The policeman didn't see me tear up the flag."[14]

The court ignored the accused's argument and set bail at six hundred dollars—a stiff fee that reflected the seriousness of the crime.[15] Unable to pay, Schlatter was sent to Moyamensing Prison in south Philadelphia to await the grand jury's bill of indictment, which came about a month later. On August 3 he appeared before Judge Charles Y. Audenried, again in Philadelphia's city hall, only a block from the crime. Schlatter's chestnut-colored hair fell to his shoulders, and he had started to grow a beard.[16] He wore a frock coat and held a large wide-brimmed hat in his hand.

The district attorney asked the accused a few questions. Did he claim to be the healer of Denver? Yes, Schlatter replied. Why had he torn down the flag? Schlatter had no memory of the episode, he said, but believed he'd been drugged or was "suffering from a temporary aberration." He couldn't explain his motives, but he "cherished no ill-feeling and meant no disrespect to the flag." A reporter listening to him in the courtroom noticed that he "spoke in a low soft tone, and his words had a peculiar twang which was somewhat pleasing to the ear."[17]

Judge Audenried accepted Schlatter's apology and warned him to avoid future trouble with the law. Then he suspended the sentence, allowed the time served to reflect adequate punishment, and discharged the prisoner. Afterward, the policeman who had arrested Schlatter scoffed at his "temporary aberration" claim. It was simply a "good, plain drunk," he said, but the arrest record and indictment had specified "malicious mischief," not drunkenness.[18] In fact, had he been visibly drunk, it's likely that he wouldn't have been charged with a felony.

———————

PHILADELPHIA'S MONUMENTAL city hall stands on land designated by William Penn as the city's Center Square—now known popularly as Penn Square. In fact, its large interior courtyard is the intersection of Market and Broad Streets, Philadelphia's historic main thoroughfares. The handsome French Second Empire building, with its complex interplay of arches, columns, stonework, and blue-tiled mansard roof, is one of the world's largest masonry structures.

I studied the building from the south, on Broad Street. Its five hundred–foot tower, topped with a huge bronze statue of William Penn, had weathered many storms and lightning strikes since it was completed in 1901. But its fiercest storm, presumably occurring in 1898, was wholly mythical—and thus never mentioned in the papers. As the Francis Schlatter of *Modern Miracles* looked back on his Philadelphia experience, he revealed how he felt about his unjust sentence with a singular lie. "During the progress of the trial," he wrote, referring to his short hearing, "the building was struck by lightning seven times."

His entire account of the arrest, as I'd come to expect of anything he wrote in *Modern Miracles*, was a mixture of truth, falsehood, and—well, mystery. His lawyer, "one of the most prominent attorneys of the city," he said, had volunteered to defend him. John R. K.

Scott, though only twenty-five years old at the time, became a U.S. congressman two years later, and so had obviously become a rising star. Yet the author of *Modern Miracles* also claims that he, the defendant, personally argued his case before the court and was "honorably discharged"—which was hardly the truth.

And what was the case the defendant had laid out before the judge? Herein—for me—lay the mystery. As he was walking along Market Street, Schlatter says, he saw a crowd of people surrounding and threatening a man accused of being a Spaniard. The healer intervened and spoke on the man's behalf. "My friends," he said, "do you know that there is one that is above us that marks even the sparrow's fall? He is the God of the Spaniard as well as of the American. We are all a people of one God and we should not be prejudiced against a foreigner. If any of you had been born in Spain you would have been a Spaniard; to oppose any man we put a barrier before us that is a stumbling block to our civilization."

The story may have been completely false, nothing more than a noble tale fabricated by Schlatter in *Modern Miracles* to justify his arrest for malicious mischief. But the Philadelphia episode—and especially Schlatter's explanation of it—immediately recalled for me Francis Schlatter's discussion about prejudice with Ada Morley. True, those words appeared for all to read in *The Life of the Harp*—as did the concepts of New Jerusalem and reincarnation, the latter of which August Schrader and Jacob Kunze appropriated for themselves. But it struck me as far-fetched to think that an imposter, acting as Francis Schlatter, would take a far less conspicuous concept from *The Life of the Harp* to explain an impulsive act of defiance so typical of the original healer. In fact, I could envision Denver's healer, angered by blind prejudice, reaching and tearing down what he saw as the symbol of patriotic jingoism—the American flag.

Then, too, I had to ask myself: why would John Martin —unless he were mad—tear down an American flag at the height of nationalistic fervor in Philadelphia? For that matter, the question raised the larger issue of madness and motive if the flag-destroyer was the imposter John Martin. His entire behavior since arriving in Canton, as mentioned, was uncharacteristic in that it didn't comport with the behavior of imposters in general—or what we might expect of an imposter. Was he playing an elaborate game? Was he out to destroy the memory of Francis Schlatter in response to some terrible slight?

Was he simply crazy? To answer yes to any of these questions would lead one into a maze of contorted argument that rivaled anything Lewis Carroll could dream up. Even the simplest question—"Was he crazy?"—suggests a victim of delusions, and one could say the very same thing about the original Francis Schlatter. Both men might have been deluded—but both were gifted, charismatic healers capable of enlisting supporters and commanding crowds.

In this respect, certain invisible lines of mutual interest, behavior, and attitude seemed to be drawing the two healers together in spite of the centrifugal pull of outward differences.

BEFORE LEAVING PHILADELPHIA, Schlatter received a handsome offer from Charles A. Bradenburg, a veteran showman who ran a dime museum at Eighth and Arch Streets in Philadelphia, to conduct his healing sessions there.[19] Bradenburg claimed to have once featured Mr. and Mrs. Tom Thumb, the dwarf couple made famous by P. T. Barnum. He eventually added vaudeville acts, including the young Jolson brothers, and the level of entertainment can justly be inferred from a statement five years later in the *New York Dramatic Mirror*: "The Arch Street Museum is presenting a better class of attractions than in former seasons, as the patronage warrants it."[20] In spite of Bradenburg's offer to be his newest attraction, Schlatter was "indignant that anyone should make such a proposition to me."[21] He wasn't lowering his healing ministry to mere entertainment no matter how much money was offered.

Stopping to conduct healing sessions in Reading, Pennsylvania, for a few days, the healer and his manager soon made their way to Ohio, then Indiana. In Evansville, as he had done so often, Schlatter began his ministry on a street corner with a simple box and an old chair, allowing the public interest to grow naturally from curiosity. Before long, an *Evansville Journal* reporter discovered him and took note of his slender frame; long, shoulder-length hair and short beard; and "a voice pleasing to the ear."[22] The comment, which could apply to any number of vocal characteristics, remains ambiguous, but the *Journal*'s rival newspaper, the *Evansville Courier*, hints at one. It remarked that the healer had a "feminine voice" and was "very polite in his manners."[23] The obvious suggestion here that the healer was

FIGURE 18. The "posthumous" Francis Schlatter
as he probably looked in Atlanta, 1898.
Courtesy of the *St. Louis Post-Dispatch.*

effeminate could be dismissed were it not for another comment the
reporter made earlier. He found the healer to be something of an
Oscar Wilde–like figure with a "strong aquiline nose," high cheek
bones, "and the air of an ascetic." Yet his worn and baggy store-
bought clothes were a drawback, as was his "red-haired, soft-voiced
manager with his feminine way."[24]

From the time he had first emerged in Memphis in 1897, witnesses who compared Schlatter with the Denver healer found him
to be smaller physically and more refined in his behavior, speech,
and manners. The same was true in Evansville. A woman named
Moakler, whom Schlatter had treated in Denver, expressed deep disappointment to find that the Evansville healer was a fake. "The real
Schlatter," she said, "is a larger man than this one. He is broader
across the shoulders and his hands are large, not the small delicate
hands this man has. Besides, his nose is crooked near the end like he
had had it broken sometime. Then, too, his features are larger and
his hair touched with gray while his eyes are blue. This man is not
at all like him."[25]

In mid-November 1898 Schlatter took his ministry to Atlanta. Once again he made a quiet appearance in the city square, but the usual flicker of interest did not catch and spread as before. His reputation, in any case, reached the city authorities, and he was asked to meet with the chief of police, William P. Manley, soon after he and Gilbert arrived. Like Lengle before him, Gilbert was adept at calming official fears about the healer, and the visit was entirely personal—Chief Manley sought Schlatter's help in getting rid of a nagging case of dyspepsia.

While they waited in the station room, under the watchful eye of an *Atlanta Constitution* reporter, Schlatter remained quiet and reserved. He ignored any questions—merely crossed his arms, sighed, and gazed at the ceiling.

"Can't he talk?" the reporter asked Gilbert.[26]

"Oh, yes, he can talk," Gilbert replied, "but he never does in public. He talks very freely to me in our private apartments sometimes."

"Why does he keep silence in public?"

"Just his way, I suppose," Gilbert said. "If he once began to answer questions there would be no end to the catechising."

Eventually called into the police chief's office, Schlatter applied treatment for about ten minutes, then left with Gilbert. "I don't know," the chief said when asked if it had done his dyspepsia any good. "I felt a warm glow over my body as soon as the healer left."

One of the problems Schlatter faced in moving from town to town—unlike having a stable "home" with the protections Fox and his supporters had provided—was that he encountered very different kinds of audiences. For the first time, in Atlanta, a group of rowdies taunted him. One came up to the healer and said: "If you are divine, throw this brick up into the air and cause it to stay there."[27] Normally, Schlatter would have given a witty rejoinder, but the threat of violence lay redolent in the challenge, and he retreated. He already knew of August Schrader, and had possibly heard of Schrader's quick escape from Fort Worth two years earlier when a group of thugs threatened to row him to the middle of a lake to see if he could walk on water.[28]

But challenges to Schlatter's divinity, or his healing power, came far less often than questions about his true identity. The issue arose again in Atlanta. "There is a difference of opinion in this city," said the *Constitution*, "whether or not this man is the one who created such a furor in Denver three years ago." As the *Chicago Tribune* had done months earlier, but with more objectivity, the *Constitution* assembled and interviewed people who had seen Schlatter in 1895. One witness, Dr. L. H. Stanley, a former Denver resident, gave his reasons why the Atlanta healer was an imposter—none having to do with his appearance but only based on the fact that Schlatter's death was well known.

Then the *Constitution*'s reporter spoke to another witness who had a much more observant eye than the doctor. The witness had studied Denver's healer closely. "Certain it is," the *Constitution* stated, based on the interview, "the original Schlatter had a small and almost imperceivable curiously shaped scar on the left side of his nose; so has this man."[29] The testimony might well have been dismissed by skeptics as nothing more than the opinion of a follower—perhaps even a plant. They could not have known that the Atlanta witness's observations had already been corroborated by Lillian Middaugh, who had also seen a "slight mark" on the healer's nose in 1895.

Walter Gilbert was well prepared for challenges to Schlatter's identity. Earlier, when confronted by skeptics who disputed the healer's claims, he said: "The birth marks of Schlatter were all recorded when he was in Denver. If there is anyone who feels he is not the real divine healer, Schlatter will roll up his sleeve and show the marks. He will expose his neck and will open his mouth and let the doubter see the marks in its roof."[30] Gilbert's ready defense, however, was not necessary in Atlanta. In fact, just the opposite. The same witness who mentioned the mark on the healer's nose reported to the *Atlanta Constitution* that Denver's healer had "a cleatrice upon his arm just above the wrist, which this man also has."[31]

THE DISCOVERY THAT eyewitnesses had confirmed the marks on Schlatter's nose and forearm raised my quest from one of hopeful speculation to something of a confident hypothesis. It constituted the first physical evidence that the healer of Canton and Chicago—and Philadelphia and Atlanta—was indeed Francis Schlatter, the healer of Denver. Yet it hardly seemed possible. The patient record book at Good Samaritan Hospital stood as prima facie evidence that he was John Martin. I could believe that a clever imposter might convincingly acquire the affectations, even the healing skills, of his subject. But no imposter, no matter how good, could acquire his subject's physical marks and scars. The two men *must* be the same person. And this premise left only one possibility. John Martin hadn't assumed the identity of Francis Schlatter. Francis Schlatter had once—and for a very specific reason—assumed the identity of John Martin.[32]

But could this hypothesis explain the healer's mind and motives, seamlessly, within the surrounding context of his life? Could it explain not only his past life but also his life going beyond? Whatever the results, the hypothesis had to begin with a set of questions: Why did Schlatter decide to return in 1897 rather than remain in hiding—either physically or by living under an assumed identity—until the final days of Daniel? Why did he take up a journey on foot down the Ohio and Mississippi Rivers? And why, after he came back into the public eye, did he deliberately—and obviously—provoke accusations that he was a fraud?

To address these questions as a detective might—because detectives are the boldest inquisitors of human behavior—I had to enter Schlatter's mind. At the very least, I had to understand the vision that had burned so brightly before him from the time of his 1893 pilgrimage. It was inspired by the Book of Daniel, and one set of verses, Daniel 9:24–27, seemed addressed specifically to him. "Seventy weeks are determined upon thy people and upon thy holy city," states the King James Version, "to finish the transgression, and to make an end of sins, and to make reconciliation for iniquity, and to bring in everlasting righteousness, and to seal up the vision and prophecy, and to anoint the most Holy." The prophecy continues: following *another* period of approximately seventy weeks, "the end thereof shall be with a flood, and unto the end of the war desolations are determined." In all, three years elapse between the divine warning and the apocalypse, and during a part of that time the Messiah would "be cut off, but not for himself." Assuming that Schlatter believed that the final days would occur during 1899, these prophetic events would have begun with his journey into Mexico in the spring of 1896—when the Messiah was "cut off" in a self-imposed exile, known only to himself.[33]

Taking my hypothetical "mind meld" with Schlatter further, it occurred to me that those three prophetic years of Daniel constituted sacred time. In other words, with his journey into Mexico,

Schlatter started on a path as sacred as his three-year pilgrimage. It would lead eventually to a worldwide war of destruction. Then, at the beginning of the new century, God would establish his kingdom. This may have been the reason for Schlatter's second pilgrimage down the Ohio and Mississippi Rivers. It not only fulfilled that portion of Daniel's prophecy relating to the Messiah's disappearance, but it linked the two pilgrimages into a spiritual whole, embracing a new Passion Story.

The audience for that story, however, would not be the present generation; rather, it would encompass those honest, common folk who survived the apocalypse of 1899. Freed from the oppression and corruption of their worldly masters, they would inhabit the glorious kingdom of New Jerusalem. It was for them that he would be anointed, as Daniel had it, as the "most Holy." But would the world then recognize and accept him as such?

In John 20:27, Jesus convinces Thomas of his resurrection by inviting him to touch the wound in his side—although Thomas *sees* that Christ, who has suffered death on the cross, stands before him. Schlatter, who was an intelligent student of the Bible, also realized that simply *appearing* before the masses who found themselves in a glorified kingdom of God would not convince the doubting Thomases among them. Thus he had to offer proof of his resurrection.

How would he do that? The answer came, again, from John 20:27. He would walk among believers and skeptics alike in the days between his death in Mexico and his exaltation in New Jerusalem. It stood to reason that he had to accomplish two things at once: he must return as the healer, but he must *not* be recognized for who he was. In other words, he had to convince the present world that he was a false prophet—and suffer the scorn, rejection, and persecutions attendant to that role—so that the future multitudes of New Jerusalem could accept the miracle of his resurrection. They would know that the Messiah had walked the earth while his bones lay in a Mexican grave.

Speaking to Ada Morley of the days to come, Schlatter said, "Father will not let my name die. Others will arise in my name and deceive many, but my name will thus be kept alive during my absence."[34] As a prophecy, it was astoundingly accurate, for he knew for a fact that *he* would emerge as a false prophet, and he would play that role well.

CHAPTER TEN

The Days of Daniel

"You will see. It's coming quicker than you think.
Father is going to take a hand in the affairs of men and they
will have cause to remember it for a long time!"[1]

FRANCIS SCHLATTER, LIFE OF THE HARP

SCHLATTER AND GILBERT arrived in Birmingham in the first month of 1899. As before, the healer began his ministry quietly and unostentatiously, setting up a box on the corner of First Avenue and Twentieth Street. Soon nearly four hundred people gathered around, and he began treating them in spite of lowering clouds and the threat of rain. One man who claimed to have been deaf for fifteen years walked away from the session amazed that he could now hear his ticking watch. Another, a black man whose "hearing apparatus" had stopped working, heard a great roaring when Schlatter placed his fingers inside the man's ears. Afterward he could hear as well as ever. Later, another man rejoiced that Schlatter had removed a "pain across his misery."[2] Other sufferers testified to cures, but some people walked away disappointed—as had always been the case.

When it started to rain, Schlatter and Gilbert returned to their rooms. There they sat down with a *Birmingham Age-Herald* reporter who had covered the healing session. "He is evidently of foreign birth," the reporter said, "as is betokened by his peculiar accent."[3] By now Schlatter's beard had fully grown back and blended with his long, luxuriant hair to recapture the Christlike demeanor that had been the hallmark of Denver's great healer.

At the time Schlatter and Gilbert arrived in Birmingham, a small cadre of street healers and fortune tellers had already been plying their trade for months. Schlatter's reputation, which had preceded him, gave them some concern, for the last thing they wanted was competition from someone who demonstrated true gifts. Rumor had it, for example, that while in Atlanta he had cured a crippled dog, who then trotted away following its owner, and the healer was afterward besieged by pet owners.[4]

Near the end of January another party came to Schlatter's rooms at 119 Twenty-First Street. He'd asked Gilbert to turn away most of his visitors; it was the only way he could get any rest. But when he heard women's voices outside, he told Gilbert to let them in. They were sisters, and the younger of them was a lovely, spirited, softly accented but self-assured woman eager to meet the healer. Her name was Luverna Comer.

Schlatter learned much about Luverna that afternoon. She was born and raised in Alabama and married a man named John Comer in the early 1880s. They had a son, Guy, who was now fourteen years old and living with other family members while attending school. Sometime after her husband's untimely death, about ten years earlier, she became seriously ill and sought treatment at Buffalo Lithia Springs in Virginia. Her condition grew worse, and she believed she would die, but at her lowest ebb the voice of Christ spoke to her and she was suddenly cured, astounding her doctors. As a result, she studied the Christ method of healing and practiced it in Chicago—and practiced it still. Healing had become her life's work.

"The minute I saw her," Schlatter wrote in *Modern Miracles*, "I was transformed. I could see in her the inspiration of my life."[5] After Luverna left, he couldn't get her out of his mind. He tried to forget her, he said, but finally gave in to the Father. At the first opportunity, he brought her back to his apartment. She came shortly before his scheduled healing session one morning, and he asked Gilbert to go down and prepare for the crowds. Then, when he and Luverna were alone, he proposed to her. "I was afraid to ask her in the old way for fear she would refuse, so I just said to her: 'I am going to make you Mrs. Schlatter; take this money and go to the station and buy a ticket and I will meet you at the depot at twelve noon. Get on another car so the people will not suspect anything, as this is too sacred to me to be written up in the papers.'"[6]

Amazingly, Luverna accepted. They got off the train in Cullman, Alabama, about forty miles north of Birmingham, and on January 31 they applied for a marriage license.[7] From there they traveled to Nashville to begin a new life together—and, as it turned out, with

FIGURE 19. Luverna Comer as a young woman,
about the time she experienced a healing vision
of Christ at Buffalo Lithia Springs in Virginia.
Following her marriage in 1899, she went by
the name of Luverna Comer-Schlatter.
Courtesy of the Comer Family.

the Martin family. In a single impulsive act, Schlatter abandoned his
thriving Birmingham ministry; his manager, Walter Gilbert; and
the healing campaign that had brought him several thousand miles
across the eastern United States. More than that, by his marriage,
whether he realized it or not, he instantly abdicated his role as a
Christ figure—for no matter how much the healer resembled the
venerable image of the Savior, Christ would always be seen as a
solitary figure who had put aside marriage. Schlatter's bride, Ada
Morley had said, was nothing other than humanity itself.[8]

Unpredictable as it was, nothing about his marriage precluded the
fulfillment of the prophecies of Daniel. In fact, it would have offered
him a chance to go into retreat a final time, awaiting the last days,
which he believed would ensue sometime that year. At least, that

was the impression Schlatter had given to Ada Morley, who wrote to Henry Miller Porter on May 25, 1899: "My mind is fixed on the fulfillment of Schlatter's promises this Summer."[9]

In the interim, the healer and his wife, Luverna, found what would seem to be a perfect honeymoon home. It was situated on the Cumberland River, "in the center of a beautiful park that had been once a lovely place when the South was in its bloom and the people lived in luxury." The park had gone to ruin, its once-symmetrical avenues of cedar trees and carefully pruned flowerbeds overtaken by new wild growth. "Old things shall pass away and all things become as new," he said—and in the spring of 1899, as he and Luverna looked out on the decayed residue of the antebellum South, those words would have had urgent meaning.[10]

Nothing in the course of current political and social events, however, pointed to an Armageddon-like clash between industry and labor—nor, for that matter, did the world at large seem on the brink of war and disaster. The late spring and summer of 1899 were particularly quiet, but perhaps it was the calm before the storm. In the meantime, Luverna became acquainted with Louisa Martin and her son Thomas, and Schlatter elaborated on the sketchy story he'd already told a reporter or two—that he came with his German-speaking Alsatian parents to Columbia, Tennessee, in 1858 and lived on Pulaski Pike for a number of years before returning alone to Europe to seek his fortune. Louisa and Thomas joined with him in the deception—and could do so, for Louisa Martin and her husband, Edward, had traveled widely, and quite possibly had lived in France.[11]

When word got out that Schlatter was living near Nashville, he and his wife began treating the sick and suffering in the city's haymarket square. During their honeymoon, they discussed joining together as a healing team, traveling from city to city, and how best to do it.[12] Schlatter had always been reluctant to speak with reporters, or to crowds, while Luverna practically lived to lecture. She naturally assumed the duties of manager, but with a higher purpose than the others—to promote her husband's work as a divine gift. As a healer herself, she was equipped to explain the inner workings of spiritual healing, and her role as a lecturer raised the level of his ministry above that of common faith healers.

After conducting healing sessions for a time, the couple left Nashville in September 1899 for Chicago. There they took rooms at the Palmer House, and Luverna noticed that her husband had become greatly troubled. He suffered from what the *Chicago Record* called "nervous prostration," and his wife arranged for a male nurse to attend to him. At one point Schlatter became enraged, threw a cuspidor at the nurse, and tried to jump out the window of their sixth-floor room.[13] Luverna was able to calm him down, but she had to wonder what might have driven him to attempt suicide. A day or so later, as they were walking on the street, he became so engrossed in an argument over money that Luverna simply turned around and walked away—unnoticed. When he discovered she was gone, he went back to the hotel, only to find that she had checked out. From South Bend, Indiana, she telegraphed the hotel's owner, William Palmer, to ask if the hotel staff could look after her husband until she returned to settle the bill.

Luverna thought Schlatter had gone temporarily insane, and his erratic behavior told her he was not the man she thought he was. After she returned to Chicago and reconciled with him, she spoke to reporters. "I have been asked many times," she said, "whether I have married the real Francis Schlatter or not. I believe that I have, and many people who knew him in Denver have said that he is the same. It makes no difference to me, however. I married Frank for love, and nothing else."[14] That was probably true—but it most certainly made a difference to her whether she had married the real healer or an imposter.

In fact, the stresses placed on the couple in the fall of 1899 only deepened over time. Luverna found herself in the position of having to defend her husband's disintegrating mental and emotional state in the face of others who wanted to protect her from the wiles of a charlatan, and Schlatter found himself needing his wife's guiding hand.

Chicago was the one place where Schlatter had been most vilified as an imposter, and Luverna understood that it was a toxic place for him now. Thus they left for Kokomo, Indiana, at the request and with the substantial support of a friendly benefactor, and remained there for several months. As if to ensure a protective environment, they invited Louisa and Thomas Martin to join them, and brought Luverna's son, Guy, into the fold as well.

For a while, things were quiet. Then, in early 1900 an episode occurred that testified to recurring trouble in the Schlatter household.

Luverna had her husband arrested for drunkenness and disorderly conduct, and he was thrown in jail.[15] She told reporters that he'd been taking brandy and opium as stimulants for exhaustion. Whatever it was, Schlatter had become deeply depressed. In spite of her belief that he was "a marvelous man, and ordinarily one of exalted goodness," she said, she was looking into divorce proceedings.[16]

Luverna didn't go through with the divorce, but the couple left Kokomo and took to the road. They seemed to be heading nowhere in particular, but the year 1900 would bring them directly to more bouts of drunkenness, arguments, breakups, and reconciliations in what would be a pattern of desperate need and discord in their marriage from that time on.

———————

BORDEAUX, TENNESSEE, lies in a floodplain of the Cumberland River that rises gradually to the higher suburbs north of Nashville. As I came off Briley Parkway, a beltway around the northern part of the city, and drove down Clarksville Pike heading toward the river, I expected to encounter a village of some kind, or at least a park or post office. I was almost to the Bordeaux Bridge (renamed for Martin Luther King Jr.) before I realized that Bordeaux wasn't *there*, in so many words. For all its long history, it remains an unincorporated area with a few scattered neighborhoods, commercial buildings, a hospital, and a small library.

I wanted to see where Louisa Martin had lived after her husband, Edward, died, and perhaps get a feel for her surroundings. From what I could tell, they were modest. One thing I realized from my short glimpse was that the home Francis and Luverna purchased along the Cumberland, surrounded by the vestiges of the Old South, was *not* in Bordeaux. There had been no big plantation houses or cultivated gardens here. Nevertheless, during the decade or so Louisa Martin lived in Bordeaux after leaving Columbia, she was well enough off financially to retain a maid who had been with her for more than twenty-five years.[17]

Whatever I knew about Louisa's background—and it was slim—came chiefly from her obituary and census records. She was born Louisa Matilda Sophia Gough in Newbury, a village in Berkshire, England, on November 19, 1833. The 1851 British census found her living with her mother, Sarah, and a servant girl in Barrington, eight miles southwest of Cambridge. Her father, Rev. Thomas Gough, an "independent minister," was not there at the time.

In 1859 Louisa married Edward Martin, and their first child, John E. (probably John Edward), was born shortly thereafter. Their second, Thomas Walton, came two years later. Both boys were born in England, but Thomas would later claim to be Canadian. They were living in Canada when the census taker found them in 1871, near Hamilton on the western shore of Lake Ontario. But, according to Thomas, his mother and father "lived under five different governments," of which three were England, Canada, and the United States.[18] Thus the Martins left England in the early 1860s, perhaps spending time on the Continent. In any case, from about 1870 on, they made their home in Hamilton, and in the early 1880s emigrated to the United States, moving to Columbia, Tennessee.

In 1883 Edward Martin & Sons, a construction company, picked up one of the most prestigious jobs in Columbia, the stonework for the Masonic Temple, a contract that would only have gone to a respected builder. In addition, Edward Martin was a thirty-second-degree Mason and a member of the lodge. By 1884 he was well established enough to assemble some fifty "artisans, mechanics and laborers and teams" to construct a plant for the Columbia Cotton Mills Company.[19]

When Edward died in 1886, he was buried in a cemetery next to McCain's Cumberland Presbyterian Church, about seven miles south of Columbia. Louisa left Columbia for the Nashville area, settling in Bordeaux. Her two sons joined her there, at least for a while. John appears once as a stonemason in the Nashville city directory in 1888, and Thomas as a stonecutter in 1892. But their whereabouts, and Louisa's, cannot be determined consistently through public records. In any case, her home in Bordeaux remained in the family's possession even after Louisa followed Francis and Luverna in 1900 to Kokomo—and then eventually to a permanent home in Miamisburg, Ohio, which she shared with Thomas.

That, in brief, was what I knew about the Martin family. But it was secondary to the main question I now pondered: when did Francis Schlatter come into their lives—and how?

That question preoccupied me as I drove from Nashville south to Columbia—so much so that I'd forgotten it was Sunday when I pulled up to McCain's Cumberland Presbyterian Church. It stood on a hillside above the highway—a simple, red-brick, gabled church that graced the landscape on which it was built. As I pulled up I saw a number of parked cars, their occupants making their way in fine clothes across a grassy field to the church.

I was not dressed properly to be in the company of Sunday worshippers. Nevertheless, brushing down my Levis, I went inside and spoke to the elder who was greeting congregants at the door. I briefly said I was looking for an early town resident and asked if I could wander through the church's cemetery.

"Sure," he said, not seeming to mind my Levis and T-shirt in the least. "But let me get you a list of the people buried here—and something about the church." He reappeared a few minutes later and placed several sheets of paper in my hand. "You're welcome to join us," he said, but I told him my time was limited. Even so, I took a moment to glance inside the worship hall. At the far end was a richly carved altar railing, a chancel, and a slim nineteenth-century Duncan Fyfe sofa behind the pulpit—a beautiful touch.

Outside, I ran through the burial list and quickly found the name of Edward Martin—but, as I fully expected, no François Schlatter. The cemetery spread out languidly, its modest white markers covered here and there with lichen and mineral rust. I wandered aimlessly among the gravestones for a few minutes but soon gave up. Without a plot map, I wouldn't be able to locate Edward Martin's grave easily. Nevertheless, I could imagine Louisa Martin and her two sons standing somewhere in this small cemetery more than a hundred years ago, a family without a father, ready to abandon Columbia now that Edward Martin & Sons was no more. Virtually nothing of their lives here survived but a few legal records, a gravestone I couldn't find, and a tapestry of folklore woven together in *Modern Miracles of Healing.*

Standing in McCain's cemetery, I suddenly felt awash in doubt. In this place the counterhypothesis seemed to prevail—that John Martin, a one-time mason and aspiring sculptor, had convinced his mother and brother to go along with his impersonation of Schlatter and all the lies that went with it. Here was his home—at least for most of the 1880s. After his father's death, Martin may have wandered west. He might even have become Schlatter's disciple in Denver—perhaps the shadowy L. E. Ryan—and on the healer's disappearance he might even have been sent to Manitou as a decoy. All this was possible.

For a time I was once again suspended between two competing hypotheses, both of which hinged on the correct reading of the patient record in Good Samaritan Hospital. Did John Martin become Francis Schlatter, or did Schlatter, in his need for anonymity after leaving Mexico, take the name John Martin? And if he did so, when did Schlatter meet the Martins, and what happened to their eldest son, John? Did he die? Did he abandon the family? I couldn't escape the difficulties these questions posed—and they became even more puzzling when I came across the U.S. census for 1900, which found the Schlatters and Louisa Martin living in Kokomo.[20]

In the first place, the census stated that *both* Francis Schlatter and Louisa Martin arrived in America in 1884. This certainly wasn't true of Louisa, who came to Tennessee with Edward and her two boys prior to 1883, the year her husband built the Masonic Temple in Columbia. Next, it listed both Francis and Louisa as natives of Germany, even though Louisa was born in England. And last, it stated that Louisa had given birth to four children, only two whom were living. This would seem to suggest that she had two sons and perhaps two children who died in infancy. But it could also mean that Francis Schlatter was the census taker's informant, since he often claimed to have had a brother and sister who died in Ebersheim.[21]

Thus the lies written into the 1900 census could well have come from Louisa's son John—acting as Francis Schlatter—for the benefit of his wife, Luverna. But one final piece of information didn't fit. When the census taker asked him about naturalization, he gave a remarkable answer. As I studied the record, each box in the Naturalization column pertaining to other members of the family was blank—meaning, since this was true throughout the census, that they were native-born or naturalized citizens. Only *his* had an entry—the abbreviation AL, for Alien. Why would Louisa's son John, who had entered the United States with the rest of the family two decades earlier, cast doubt on his own citizenship? It was a mystery, or perhaps a mental slip made by a man who never forgot he was Alsatian, or under what nation-state Alsace found itself—which was then Germany.

Furthermore, his claim that both he and Louisa came to the United States together in 1884 was curious. It was divorced from

any apparent motive to deceive. What would Schlatter gain by making the year of Louisa's arrival in America the same as his? It might
have been a mistake, but I doubted that. Two mistakes had already
been corrected on the form—Louisa's birth year, from 1840 to the
accurate 1832, with corresponding corrections to her age, and her
father's country of origin, from something now indistinguishable to
"Germany."

No, 1884—I believed—was deliberate. Schlatter stated quite specifically in *Modern Miracles* that he entered the port of New York in
May 1884.[22] Did he arrive with Louisa Martin—he an immigrant
but she merely returning from her family home in England to her
husband in Tennessee? And was he beholden to her for bringing
him to America? The notion was perhaps a bit of a stretch, but the
facts in Louisa's obituary, which her son Thomas prepared, lent
themselves to reasonable speculation. Louisa Martin's father, Rev.
Thomas Gough, had operated a sailor's mission in London. Was
it possible that the Goughs took in a young French boy in 1871, orphaned and speaking no English, but intelligent, whom they educated in British schools and sheltered in their own home as a son? If
so, Francis Schlatter, their young charge, would have been forever
indebted to the family.

IN SEPTEMBER 1899 Ada Morley was concerned that she had misunderstood Schlatter's prophecy. "The allotted days of Daniel will
have been numbered by November," she wrote Henry Miller Porter,
"unless I again take a wrong basis from which to compute. I am sure
Schlatter has spoken the truth. He repeatedly told me he could not,
would not die and I am very sure he will fulfill those words." She
went on: "I am anxious to see that great day for mankind—it will
be glorious, for his powers will be vast enough to adjust wrongs and
oppression."[23]

By early 1900 Schlatter's reputation had become vastly diminished since the height of his fame in 1895. Had he chosen to take
his ministry to Chicago, New York, and Europe, as he proposed, he
would likely have become a renowned healer. And if, at the same
time, he had taken his Populist message to the world, with its warn-

ing of divine retribution for two thousand years of inequality and injustice, he might have enlisted thousands of followers to his cause.

But instead of shaping his own destiny in the earthly realm—that is, becoming a spiritual leader with a social mission—Schlatter took on an otherworldly role as God's instrument of divine justice, the harp in the hand of the harper. Change would thus come from God alone, and the event would be catastrophic destruction and a new creation of biblical proportions. But what if God failed to act?

The prospect that God had abandoned him was surely on Schlatter's mind by the early months of 1900, as his mental state continued to deteriorate. Of course, he had once cautioned Morley against expecting a precise time for the fulfillment of Daniel's prophecy. "Don't you remember there are no dates in the Bible?" he said. "Time is all one—time and eternity are the same to Father." But they were not the same to the earthbound healer, for whom the vision of New Jerusalem was slipping away.

In May a reporter in Parkersburg, West Virginia, came across the drunken healer in a bar and played him up as a pathetic figure.[24] Luverna was back at the hotel packing her valise to return to Kokomo. In a fit of anger, Schlatter had struck her and torn several of her shirtwaists when she refused to give him drinking money. He ended up at the bar anyway, begging for drinks—and managed to find a benefactor who gladly paid for the entertainment of watching his comrades set the healer up with phony sufferers. "Schlatter would remove his slouch hat," a reporter wrote, "turn his eyes to the ceiling, and place his hands alternately on his patient's wrists and the back of his neck. 'Now, ain't you vell?' he would inquire"—in what the reporter called a "broken German dialect"—and the patient would delight in exaggerating his miraculous recovery.[25] One of the customers tried to get Schlatter to admit that he was Jesus Christ. When the man had almost gotten a confession to that effect, he hollered: "Well, if you're Jesus Christ, how in the hell do you come to be in this barroom?"[26] When the general hilarity died down, Schlatter said that the man didn't understand.

When his alcoholic binge ended in Parkersburg, Schlatter returned to Kokomo, and Luverna took him back. She would continue to do so after every episode, even when he ranted, destroyed her possessions, and beat her. She saw him as an extraordinary man with a divine gift, and she regarded his alcoholism as an aberration that momentarily drew him away from his inherent goodness. But she also found herself unable to deal with him when he became drunk and abusive, so she left him often. In the fall of 1900, while in Sandusky, Ohio, Schlatter fell to drinking again, and Luverna wrote him from the train: "Sorry, dear one, that I had to leave you. But the Master called me and His voice had to be obeyed . . . . I have been a true wife and will always be. You will find me in heaven your true and devoted wife. I give up everything this day to God. I love mother and brother Tom. I am sorry I lost my temper, but you will forgive me, won't you, dear? But your drinking almost made me insane at times."[27]

By the end of the year the couple were in Washington, D.C., and the healer gave the *Washington Post* an extended interview. The *Post* reporter found Schlatter to be humble and "unobtrusive in manner," but a formidable figure with his long hair and beard, stooped shoulders, and expression of sadness that could be thought to "imitate the likeness of the Saviour."[28] Schlatter spoke at length about his religious beliefs. "I was born and reared a Roman Catholic," he said, "but I have long since renounced that faith. I do not believe that God ever intended that the people of the world should be divided into religious sects as they are now."[29] He went on to express a pantheistic theology that would have been roundly condemned by the Catholic Church: "My church is the open air and my altar is the hillside, and my doctrine is freedom. That is the simplest and purest religion. It is the religion of Jesus as taught in the Scriptures."

A few weeks later he took up the question of religion again — and carried it further. Typically thought-provoking, Schlatter argued that Christianity had introduced sin into the world, and "sin is so much preached to the young that they become eager to taste it."[30] A true Christian, he said, is a man the world considers a heathen. Take, for example, the Indian, who worships the Great Spirit, lives day to day, and will not lie to his fellow man. "In his simplicity and nearness to nature he knows nothing of sin."

The healer, the reporter concluded, "has radical ideas."

It was true, but none that he expressed currently about sin and Christianity were as radical as those in *The Life of the Harp* — which foretold the end of civilization as people knew it. Recently, in fact, the *Washington Post* had published an article reflecting on the healer's

1896 visit to Ada Morley's ranch, taken from an interview with a Washington friend and confidante of Morley's. The friend had in her possession a few of the healer's gray hairs, "which Mrs. Morley gave her as a miser doles out his treasure, as a specific against bodily ills." In this article, for the first time, the public learned the details of Schlatter's prophecy. "A little war begun by the United States," he had apparently told Morley, would eventually lead to three years of universal war and bloodshed "as the world had never known." In the end, the healer would appear and "his kingdom would be recognized."[31]

But no such war had occurred, and it was now going on five years from the inception of the "days of Daniel" prophecy. "To the world," the *Post* stated, "Francis Schlatter had fallen a victim to his honest beliefs, but his disciples look for his coming, and with him the banners of peace, good will, and humanity."[32] As a matter of fact, Ada Morley had already revised her expectations. When she read stories about the Boxer Rebellion in China, she thought the beginning of the apocalypse was at hand. The healer's prophecies, however belatedly, were coming true—"every one, step by step, slowly unfolding."[33]

Nevertheless, the only realistic unfolding taking place in Schlatter's life was a plan to form a partnership in New York City with Benno Hollenberg, a neurologist he had befriended. They initially met in Memphis, where Schlatter had emerged in March 1897—and Hollenberg was the man who introduced the healer to the boarders in Cleveland a month or two later.[34] Why they did not form a partnership then is unknown—perhaps because Schlatter believed he had a grander mission to fulfill. At any rate, they reunited at the Christian Alliance mission on Forty-Second Street in early March 1901, where the Schlatters were holding sessions, and they discussed the idea of a establishing a treatment center combining medicine, osteopathy, and divine healing. Traveling to Albany, the Schlatters and Hollenberg incorporated the Francis Schlatter Institute with capital funding of fifteen hundred dollars.[35] Provisionally established in New York at Hollenberg's home on Lexington Avenue, the permanent center would have two floors, one for the doctor's practice and the other for the divine healers. "They have never made anything out of their wonderful gifts," Hollenberg said, "and I think it is time they did."[36] The doctor, who was working on an "absolute cure" for yellow fever, would be the organization's driving force: "They refuse to accept money for their services," he said. "I shall accept it for them."

A curious *New York Journal* reporter decided to explore the story. When he arrived to interview the healer, Luverna led him upstairs. "Mr. Schlatter has just taken a bath," she said, "and as his hair is so long, it takes some time to dry. I am afraid he will catch cold, and so I keep him out of drafts."[37] Indeed, the healer's hair fell almost to his waist, but the reporter noticed it was thinning on top. His beard was "pointed and trimmed," resembling the usual portraits of Christ, but the reporter didn't think this man was Denver's great healer. For one thing, he said, the original was Teutonic and had a German accent. This Schlatter "is apparently an Englishman" who had spent time in London and Redhill, Sussex, "which seems to destroy any possibility of his being the genuine Schlatter." Asked if the *Journal* could take his photograph "with a view to establishing his identity," the healer refused.

Schlatter could be abrupt with reporters. He'd already granted permission for photographs, once in Canton in 1897 and a few weeks later in Chicago. And he would soon have several made—if he hadn't already—in New York City at the Newman Studio.[38] But if he *were* the true healer, what he might want *least* of all was to allow a common press photograph of himself to end up in the hands of his Denver disciples—not because it might show him to be a *different* man, but the *same*. What if his friends and supporters in Denver suddenly realized that the healer was alive? Then the comforting cloud of doubt and hope that surrounded them would fall away, and they would want to know—perhaps *demand* to know—why the Messiah would abandon his divine mission to establish such a venal monument to egotism as the Francis Schlatter Institute.

Perhaps, most of all, they would want to know why he hadn't *returned*. But, for the true healer of Denver, to return would be impossible. There was only one way the Messiah could return—and that was in glory.

CHAPTER ELEVEN

"A True Account . . ."

A true account of the life, works and
wanderings of Francis Schlatter, the healer.

MODERN MIRACLES OF HEALING

O
N JULY 3, 1901, police were called to the Florence Apartments
at 335 Central Park West.[1] There they found Francis Schlatter
drunkenly raving that he was Jesus Christ and his wife, Luverna, packing her trunk to leave. In spite of the dark circles
around her eyes, she refused to issue a complaint for her husband's
arrest. The luxury apartment included a grand piano, mirrors on
the walls, and expensive furniture—all perhaps provided by Benno
Hollenberg. The "divine healer" railed that he had healed twenty
thousand people since his marriage, including European royalty,
and that he was of royal blood himself. To all this his wife assented,
but she was paying more attention to her packing. Asked where she
planned to go, she answered sarcastically—to Cairo, Egypt, to join
the Holy Family.

Francis, however, was the first one out the door, and Luverna
found herself calling on the police again to go in search of him. Late
that afternoon, when he returned and had sobered up, the couple
packed their clothing and left for Washington, D.C. Luverna told
friends that she would place her husband in a hospital for treatment.[2]
With their departure, hopes for the Francis Schlatter Institute joined
those of the fading New Jerusalem.

So, too, were Luverna's hopes for getting help for her husband.
Two weeks later, in Washington, he stood on a bench in the city's
Central Union Mission, exhorting the homeless and destitute men to
rise up. "With his jet black hair streaming over his gaunt shoulders,"
said the *Washington Times*, "Schlatter, gesticulating wildly with his

brawny hands, endeavored for nearly two hours to excite the transient guests of the mission, by urging them to follow him to the Capitol building on the hill, which he himself, the mighty Schlatter, would
completely destroy, he said, by the almighty power given him."[3]

The mission's director, no stranger to the ravings of madmen,
became alarmed only when Schlatter's apocalyptic message inspired
waves of agreement among the mission's inmates. The director tele-
phoned the nearest police station, and officers took the "radical"
speaker away.[4] He was charged with insanity. "Schlatter, the once
mighty," said the *Times*, "was locked in a dark and gloomy cell within
which to continue his earnest appeal for a riot."

The day after his arrest, Schlatter was committed to St. Elizabeth's Hospital for the Insane.[5] It didn't help when he said "I am
going to England to claim the estates of the Duke of Devonshire"
and accused his wife of absconding with fifty thousand dollars of his
property.[6] He lingered in the mental hospital for a few days while
doctors examined him. In spite of his behavior, they found him to
be sane, and on his release he was sentenced to thirty days in the
workhouse for vagrancy. As officers checked him in, he pleaded with
them not to shear off his locks. They honored his request.[7]

While Schlatter served his time in the Washington, D.C., workhouse, Luverna returned to New York City. There she stayed with
the family of E. E. Barney in a four-story walkup at 44 Bradhurst
Avenue, but hearing of Schlatter's release they took her to their
home in the country. Schlatter had no trouble tracking his wife to
the Bradhurst home, and there he "haunted the neighborhood day
and night," the family maid said.[8] He refused to believe that Luverna was no longer there. After a night or two of complaints from
neighbors, the maid called the police. They arrested him, and Magistrate Lorenz Zeller of the Harlem Police Court sentenced him to
three months in the workhouse on Blackwell's Island.[9] This time the
guards cut his hair.

Shortly after Schlatter's incarceration, a reporter met him in the
warden's office. The healer, dressed in a "dingy yellow jacket with
gray stripes and trousers of bed-ticking," seemed calm and self-
possessed.[10] "I accept this persecution cheerfully," he said, compar-
ing himself to Christ, who was persecuted before he was crucified.
"The fact that he was a divine man," the healer added, "could not
save him." Schlatter had received a letter from his wife, and he was

hopeful that they would eventually reconcile. "She is a connecting link in my work," he said. "I can't get along without her."

But by the time of his release, in December 1901, that hope was shattered. Luverna had filed for divorce in Washington, D.C., charging "cruelty, neglect and nonsupport."[11] Ever since her marriage to Schlatter, family members and friends had implored her to leave him. They tried to convince her that he was an imposter, and week by week his behavior seemed to validate their suspicions.[12] Now she was going through with it, not just threatening. He eventually came to understand this new state of affairs, and it crushed him. A few days after Christmas, in Wilkes-Barre, Pennsylvania, he tried to establish a new ministry without Luverna. "His name," stated a local newspaper, "well known, attracted people, but when they beheld a thin, sallow-faced, hollow-cheeked man, with close cut hair and a draggling mustache, their faith in the healer fled, and the few who underwent the laying on of hands experienced no benefit."[13]

Schlatter was well aware of the impression he made on sufferers. "They used to think I looked like Christ," he said, "and that gave them faith. Now with my hair gone and my wife gone, and the lawyer's notification of divorce proceedings just received, I am a broken man."[14] That he was, indeed. He had nowhere to go.

When he recounted this part of his life in *Modern Miracles*, Schlatter resorted to lies and obfuscation. He said nothing about the two jail terms, one in Washington and the other in the workhouse on Blackwell's Island. Nor did he mention that he was shortly thereafter thrown into jail in Hagerstown, Maryland, for vagrancy and served a long term there. Instead, he wrote: "I became restless again and sold out my beautiful home, which nearly broke my wife's heart."[15] Most likely that home was the couple's honeymoon retreat on the Cumberland River, and probably sold for expenses. For one thing, Schlatter's defense attorney at the Hagerstown hearing was Palmer Tennant, a well-known and presumably well-paid lawyer.[16]

After serving his time in the Hagerstown house of detention, Schlatter wandered from place to place. "The Father," he wrote, "did not want me to settle down. He had something else for me to do."[17] Whatever that was, it didn't rise much above the level of another aimless journey with little to show for it but a series of unremarkable healings. But while Francis journeyed throughout the East, Luverna put off her plan to divorce him. She decided, instead, to determine whether he'd been honest in claiming to be the authentic healer. That, in short, was probably the test of her willingness to stay with him. At the very least she could put to rest the accusations of her friends and relatives.

In July 1902 Luverna traveled to Denver. She went directly to the Fox home, introduced herself as Francis Schlatter's wife, and sat down with Mary Fox. It was undoubtedly an awkward meeting. For one thing, Mary's husband, Edward, had disappeared. He had been deeply affected by the news of Schlatter's death in 1897, Mary said, and over time he lost interest in his freight business, local politics, friends, and even his family. Things went downhill financially. Then, about a year earlier, he'd left Mary for an eccentric religious zealot named Amanda Leach, who had been known to search Denver for "cripples" to bring to the healer in 1895. When Mary discovered his whereabouts in Louisville, Kentucky, she had him brought to Denver and committed him to an insane asylum. But that was all past history, and he was now gone forever.[18]

As she sat listening to Mary Fox, Luverna may have been aware that she was a vivid touchstone to the source of Edward Fox's madness. On top of that, Luverna was now proposing that her husband, Francis Schlatter, was alive. In other words, all of the pain and suffering that Mary Fox had gone through as a result of her husband's obsession with the healer could have been avoided years ago — if the healer had simply returned. Now, it seemed, it was too late.

Luverna asked questions. Mary answered them honestly. When their meeting came to an end, Mary wasn't at all sure whether Luverna's husband was the real healer.[19] Luverna had mentioned several things that seemed to fit the circumstances of the healer's visit — but seven years had passed. Mary believed that most of the specific details Luverna mentioned could have appeared in the two books that came out afterward — Harry Magill's *Biography of Francis Schlatter* and Ada Morley's *The Life of the Harp in the Hand of the Harper*. And yet — as she later said — although Schlatter was "one of the purest of men, there was cunning in him." He'd often told her that he could easily disappear, and he'd have no trouble throwing people off his track. She was left to wonder: "Had he done this?"[20]

For her part, Luverna came away satisfied with Mary Fox's answers. Whatever she learned — be it physical features, pieces of intimate knowledge of events, or idiosyncrasies of behavior — she was now convinced that her husband was the true healer of Denver. And in spite of his constant drunkenness and abhorrent behavior toward her, she returned to him with a passionate goal. When she found him, and after they had reconciled, she proposed that he assume his rightful place as the renowned Francis Schlatter—and nothing could accomplish that better than a book that would put to rest any doubt about his credentials.

She also likely proposed that, when the book was published, he return to Denver, where she was certain his old friends and disciples would welcome him back. After seven years, it would be a great event—perhaps even greater than his healing ministry in 1895—and it would forever silence the imposters who had sullied his name since that time. Newspapers far and wide would cover such a triumphant return, and no doubt *The Life of the Harp in the Hand of the Harper* would be reprinted to great acclaim. It would bring his mission as a healer full circle, and it would be a stepping stone for an even greater ministry to come.

———————

THE WALK FROM Penn Station to the New York Public Library, guarded by its great stone lions, was little more than half a mile. Arriving from Philadelphia for the day, I'd planned to do some research on Benno Hollenberg's Francis Schlatter Institute, but I found almost nothing. Plus, it was a beautiful day, and I hated to waste it burrowed in a library's reading room—even one inside the great New York Public Library. So, with three hours to kill before I had to catch the train back to Philadelphia, I decided to take the subway to the apartment house Francis and Luverna shared in 1901, when their married life fell apart. I walked a block west to Times Square, then found a subway entrance a block beyond that, on Eighth Avenue.

But I stopped to gaze for a moment at the cinematic icon of New York City—Times Square—with its gigantic digital billboards, its sheer walls of glass, bright signage, outsized portraits, electric atmosphere, and waves of people walking the pedestrian plaza like an undulating river. Times Square was the only place I knew of that had a block-wide set of stands rising two stories high to allow visitors to look out over—Times Square.

The city didn't celebrate its glitz and material glory in the same way a century or so earlier, when the Schlatters lived there. But I wondered if Schlatter hadn't made his way to New York because that was where he expected the apocalypse to begin. At the very least, the city stood for all that he abhorred in modern civilization—the monopoly of wealth and power held in the hands of a very few and the visual flaunting of that monopoly in the city's great buildings, grand avenues, and giant docks. Ignatius Donnelly's fictional column of horror rose in Union Square, but Times Square captured for me the excessive worship of materialism that even Wall Street couldn't match. Here, I thought, was a place where an apocalyptic tower of destruction might be raised for a modern Messiah.

The subway trip to Ninety-Sixth Street put me a block or so from 335 Central Park West. But the five-story Florence Apartments, where the couple lived, had since been replaced by the twelve-story Turin in 1909—one of New York's distinguished apartment buildings at the time. While I couldn't get a glimpse into the bygone interior of the Florence, simply recrossing the street to the Central Park side was like stepping back into another era. A waist-high rock wall separated the park from the sidewalk and traffic, and I entered the park through the Gate of All Saints.

I decided to follow a meandering trail through the park. I could return to the Gate of All Saints or exit somewhere else. I still had plenty of time. In any case, I wanted to think about the consequences of defeat for visionaries like Schlatter and other end-times prophets and their followers. The most famous were the Millerites, followers of Baptist preacher William Miller, who believed that Christ would return in October 1844 and take them to heaven—in fact, they based their belief on the same passages from the Book of Daniel that later spoke to the cobbler Francis Schlatter. Then, in my own century, there were the followers of Jim Jones, David Koresh, and the Heaven's Gate cult—several hundred people who gave up their lives in fulfillment of their leaders' messianic prophecies.

Schlatter could have done the same thing—of that I was sure. However, it was only his true, honest, simple—even innocent—faith in the Father that prevented him from doing so. Not that he was without guile; he was highly intelligent and knew how to persuade others and protect himself. But he was fundamentally motivated by no earthly material or selfish goal, only the promise that he would be the Messiah of God's kingdom. And *that* wish was so outrageous and unobtainable that it had no frame of reference in the real world. Thus Schlatter had to be either childlike—for children leap to such extravagant claims—or insane.

As I walked along the path, I noticed a group of youngsters running toward a copse of trees near the park wall. Their teachers stood nearby, awaiting their discovery. It was an assignment of some kind, and I stood to watch. The trees were dense, and all I could see were flashing images of the kids running here and there. Then, suddenly, with a shout, they all returned with their prize. I couldn't see what it was, but their teachers were happy. Then they all proceeded on to another assignment.

Looking at that isolated group of trees, I contemplated the death scene in Mexico, and the unmarked grave the prospectors left behind. If Schlatter's New Jerusalem—the bright vision of children playing in a field of flowers—had crumbled to dust, all that remained was the evidence of his deception. In the past, whenever anyone asked him about the healer's death in Mexico, he'd said the reports were mistaken; he was never there. But when Luverna came to him proposing that he write a book and return to Denver, the prospect of the death scene would have surely come back to him.

Yes, people in Denver might be glad to see him—*after* they had made sure he conformed in all respects to the original healer. But then there would be inevitable questions: What about the reports from Mexico? Why had he abandoned his possessions? What happened to Butte? When did he come out of Mexico, and why had he begun healing in the East? Why hadn't he written to his old friends? Why had he waited so long to return? When did he expect the new dispensation to take place? All these questions, and more, faced him—posed by shrewd and thoughtful people like Clarence Clark, Joseph Wolff, and Rev. Myron Reed.

And what about Ada Morley? Hearing that he was in Denver, she would surely travel to see him. And what would he tell *her*? Would he say that he'd been biding his time in the East while awaiting the tribulation? This may, in fact, have been true—but then what about his erratic behavior, his dalliance with Margaret Ferris, and his marriage to Luverna Comer? Most important, what of God's plan to establish the city of New Jerusalem in the Datil Mountains, and the role the Father had prepared for the Messiah? The very last person the healer would have been able to face was Ada Morley, who had prepared his Gospel of New Jerusalem and expected it to be fulfilled.

For that matter, what about *The Life of the Harp in the Hand of the Harper*? It was a virtual blueprint of Schlatter's thought, from the roadmap of his destiny, laid out in his sister's visions, to his biblical prophecy of the apocalypse, and finally to his intimation that the Messiah would emerge reincarnate in the kingdom. All of that — now — would be seen as false hope, foolishness, and religious fanaticism. Accusations that he was a fraud he could bear, for he had done so since he emerged from obscurity in 1897 — but neither his current friends nor his wife would ever understand or accept the thought that he had staged his death in the wilds of Mexico. And if one followed the undeniable thread of *Life of the Harp*, it led to that scrub oak tree high in the Sierra Madre with its unmarked grave. In the mythical world of New Jerusalem, the spot would have been a shrine equal to Calvary or the Tomb of the Resurrection; but in the Babylon of the present, it stood for nothing more than a grave-robber's act of deceit.

SHORTLY AFTER THE Schlatters reconciled in July 1902, Francis wrote to Mary Fox. Based on what Luverna had told him, he expressed his sympathy over Mary's situation, including financial problems resulting from Edward's desertion. "I have heard all about your trouble," Schlatter wrote, "but the Father will help you out."[21] He asked her about Henry Hauenstein; gave his love to her daughter, Anna; and wondered if "that fellow Scott ever came back after I left." He also asked about "Father McNamarra," a name unknown in the records of the Denver Archdiocese, but Mary didn't challenge any of the facts in the letter. It concluded: "I am much obliged to you for treating my wife so lovely."

Late in the year, the Schlatters moved to Kalamazoo, Michigan, where Francis broke from his usual pattern of silence to give a lecture. People had asked him to speak, he said, and the Father had commanded him to do so. "If my conscience and the voice of God told me to arise from my bed at midnight and take a walk of five miles into the country or to do any other seemingly foolish thing," he said, "I would obey. I am not my own master. I follow the promptings of the spirit." His lecture topic was "How God Created Heaven and the Earth," and he had prepared a series of charts to guide his listeners, but in other respects he depended on God for inspiration.[22]

But the real reason the couple were in Kalamazoo was so that Schlatter could dictate the story of his life to Ella Woodard, a friend.[23] Ever since Luverna came back from Denver, she'd been pressing her husband to voice publicly that he was the true healer of Denver and to prove it by planning his triumphant return to the city where he achieved his great fame. Schlatter capitulated.[24] "We are coming to Denver in October," he said in his letter to Mary Fox, "the Father being willing."[25] By late January 1903 the healer announced in Chicago that he would soon be returning to Denver. In the interim, he had prepared a "true account" of his life. It would serve as the anchor of his campaign to reclaim his rightful place as Denver's great healer.

Most of the Denver press, left with good impressions of the long-ago healer, looked forward to the opportunity to resolve lingering questions about his death. "If he is the Denver healer," stated the *Times*, "he will be welcomed back with open arms. If he is an imposter this will be discovered in a twinkling."[26] The *Rocky Mountain News* thought the new healer lacked Schlatter's humility. "The real Schlatter," it argued, "was modest and could not be persuaded to talk about himself, while the present 'Schlatter' doesn't do much else."[27] The *Denver Post*—alone among the major dailies to take a combative stance—actually threatened violence if the healer turned out to be a fraud. "Colorado people have had all they can stand of these . . . reincarnated Christ humbugs," it wrote. "It may be that Schlatter has made up his mind to pose as a martyr, in which event he could not select a more trying ordeal than to venture back here."[28]

In the midst of all the speculation, one man of simple faith wrote to Schlatter in Chicago about his affliction. The man, William Hicklin, was a former shoemaker who had contracted blood poisoning after a mine accident years earlier. He had stood on crutches for two days in the line at the Fox home, and he finally received the healer's touch. Hicklin had wanted to return for another treatment, but was too late; the healer had disappeared. After writing, Hicklin received a clean linen handkerchief in the mail, and he placed it on his sore leg. His leg was improving, he said, and he believed that the healer was still alive.[29]

———————————

WHEN I FIRST SAT DOWN in 1991 to read *Modern Miracles of Healing* in the Library of Congress, I noticed that someone had made pencil notations in the book's margins. The long-ago reader — perhaps Ada Morley's Washington friend — had written the words "All garbage" next to a crucial part of the story. It was here the book's author told of abandoning his mission into Mexico after the death of his beloved horse Butte.[30] This episode epitomized the connection between the old Schlatter and the new. "All garbage" was true — but for the wrong reason. The author of *Modern Miracles*, I believed, wasn't an imposter trying to link his life to Denver's healer; instead, he was Francis Schlatter doing his best to sever that link.

As I saw it, Schlatter faced a dilemma. On the one hand, he had to satisfy Luverna's renewed belief in him — that he would vindicate himself to the world. On the other hand, he had to disassociate himself from the man who went into Mexico to await God's calling. These two imperatives must have played on his mind as he sat down with Ella Woodard in Kalamazoo to dictate the book. He knew that his contemporaries wouldn't care what he said. But he also knew that his old supporters in Colorado and New Mexico would study every word — and, in no uncertain terms, this book was for them. His not-so-simple task was to convince them that he was an imposter while asserting to everyone else that he was the genuine healer.

In this respect *Modern Miracles of Healing* might be regarded as a masterful — and, in this case, entirely necessary — manipulation of story and audience. As its author knew from reading Ada Morley's *Life of the Harp*, the route of the healer's two-year tramp set the geographical points of what she envisioned as a gigantic cross superimposed upon a map of the American West — north from Denver to Cheyenne, east to Hot Springs, west to the California coast, and east again to New Mexico. At approximately the center of the cross lay Datil, where the healer would return to establish New Jerusalem after his descent into Mexico. Morley's map, titled "Symbolic Outline of Pilgrimages," didn't actually show Schlatter's route of travel, but the healer in 1903 knew exactly what it was. Why, then, would he have described a route six years later that departed substantially from the original?

Applying the two routes to Morley's map, I could see immediately two areas the healer in 1903 wanted to avoid when he revisited his pilgrimage. One is the tramp across Kansas, and the other is his avoidance of any proximity to Mexico. In the first instance, Schlatter had learned with a shock that his long walk to Hot Springs had been in vain, for his spiritualist mentor, Helen Wilmans, had not been there to meet him. Looking back on that experience while dictating *Modern Miracles*, he may have decided to pursue another path, one that took him directly to Throckmorton and Hot Springs on his trail of suffering, then with a bizarre imaginative leg back into Kansas.[31]

The second instance of historical revisionism has him passing through the Llano Estacado, the Staked Plains, well north of the border with Mexico, which Schlatter followed for a time on his way west in 1894. This radical alteration of the original route conforms to the healer's changed circumstances in 1903, for now he had every reason to disassociate himself from Mexico. But it leads him to follow a reverse course along the Atchison, Topeka & Santa Fe, heading west toward California rather than east to New Mexico in 1895. The entire reconstructed pilgrimage of 1903 bespeaks a convoluted plan to reject parts of the original sacred route while holding on to a semblance of its original significance.

Most important, the author of *Modern Miracles* turns the pilgrimage Schlatter undertook ten years earlier into a mess of confused wanderings that bears no connection to the guiding hand of God. Few readers of *Modern Miracles* at the time would have noticed this. But anyone who had studied the healer's pilgrimage in the *Life of the Harp* would be highly aware of it. In fact, there is nothing of Schlatter's divine calling in the pilgrimage story as told in *Modern Miracles*. And for good reason: the destiny that shaped Francis Schlatter's every move while he wandered the American West in the nineteenth century had disappeared in the benign birth of the twentieth. The messianic fire had burned out—and with it Schlatter's faith in an apocalyptic solution to centuries of oppression.

Yet it is the same narrative voice speaking here, no different in its simplicity than in the *Life of the Harp*. In one passage Schlatter writes of waking up one night on the prairie to find himself in a nest of cottonmouth moccasins. "I could not get out," he says. "They were running all about me and over me but did not harm me. I believe they knew that I was their friend. I did not feel afraid for the Father was with me."[32] In spite of the obvious—to us—intentional deception, rationalization, and manipulation of events, the Schlatter of *Modern Miracles* speaks with disarming candor. In describing the vision that led to his pilgrimage, he offers an image of Jesus that hardly conformed to the sensibilities of Victorian society. The Savior, he states, rose out of a ball of flame that had come through the open window of the cobbler's shop. "He did not look like the pictures that the artists have painted of him," he writes. "He had a very dark skin, a fine developed face and form, and was almost nude. He had a covering over him that looked as if it was made of platted grass and woven by hand."[33]

Similarly, in spite of the highly imaginative and circuitous pilgrimage in *Modern Miracles*—almost none of it truthful, except perhaps the steamer voyage from San Diego to San Francisco—there are also moments of utter sincerity and believability. One of these relates to Hot Springs, and it is the most intriguing anomaly in the book. After arriving at the resort—in *Modern Miracles*—the cobbler visits the army reservation hospital and befriends a sergeant major who cannot walk. Schlatter gets permission from the head of the military reservation, one Colonel Little, to treat the soldier.[34] Then, leaving the hospital, he finds shelter in a saloon set up for homeless men run by the proprietor, whose name is Gunther, and when he escapes from jail he meets up with another Hot Springs resident named James Galagher, who travels with him for a while.

As I was to learn, all three men lived and worked in Hot Springs. Colonel William J. Little administered the Hot Springs army reservation when Schlatter was there; J. A. Gunther operated a saloon; and James R. Galagher spent his life in Hot Springs and is buried in Greenwood Cemetery, not far from the center of town.[35] Altogether they form an oasis of verifiable fact in what is otherwise—to modern eyes at least—an imposter's story.

To be sure, several other factual statements in *Modern Miracles* might be true. Schlatter refers to Juan Garcia, in whose home the *Albuquerque Daily Citizen* reporter Will Hunter first encountered the healer—but one could argue that the posthumous healer came across a copy of the newspaper. He speaks of meeting a few notable people in Denver, unpublicized, such as Judge Robert Kerr and Mrs. Archie Campbell Fisk, but he may have found some obscure reference to them. And he states that the boy on Ada Morley's ranch was named Carl Gardner, the son of a ranch hand, but the last name could have been a mere guess.[36] In most of these cases, the refutation rests on the absence of convincing independent evidence. But not that of Little, Gunther, and Galagher in Hot Springs, Arkansas. This isn't information easily obtainable from reading, research, or guess-work. It comes from firsthand knowledge, or from talking to some-one who was there at the time — and remembering every detail.

But to what purpose? If the author of *Modern Miracles* was an imposter, I thought, he must have been someone close to Francis Schlatter. Furthermore, he must have been planning to impersonate the healer from a very early period, at least months before news of Schlatter's death spread across the country. If so, then, why would he undermine his calculated study and preparation with ignorant as-sumptions or deliberate falsehoods? These could be found through-out his book, but they might be illustrated merely in the lies he told about his horse, Butte — that he received Butte as a gift in Albuquer-que after his disappearance, that he named the horse Butte because "he was a beauty," and that, of course, Butte died short of reaching the border from drinking alkali water.[37] As the unknown Library of Congress reader penned, it was "All garbage."

Based on the evidence I now had, however, I believed that Fran-cis Schlatter — the original Schlatter — might have had a very good reason to include such minute, true details within a welter of lies. The names of Little, Gunther, and Galagher — and the story in which they played a part — might have been known to Morley and the small audience of ranch hands to whom the healer spoke during the winter months on Ada's ranch. "And the details he gave in conversa-tion," she wrote, "which he positively refused to give later when told to write the events for publication [in *Life of the Harp*], greatly inten-sified the mysterious tale of agony and suffering."[38] Perhaps — and I hoped it was true — this was a coded message to Morley, perhaps one of regret or apology that he could not return as he had promised.

In the end, however, the most compelling reason I believed Fran-cis Schlatter was speaking in *Modern Miracles* to his friend Ada Mor-ley came not through his words, in and of themselves, but the pe-culiarities of his expression. Scattered throughout the book are odd phrases that would not be natural to a native speaker of English. "I . . . was taken in and used very kindly by a family of Creek Indians," he says about his pilgrimage, and of the Fox family he says, "I could not have been used better"—where "used" is the chosen word rather than "treated." In places he opts for the definite article "the" where the indefinite article "a" would be more appropriate: "At J. A. Summer's home, I ate the hearty supper"—a linguistic feature common in Schlatter's pilgrimage account in *The Life of the Harp*. Elsewhere, he uses odd diction ("I went to him and asked him for the place [that is, *job*]"), transposition of words ("They offered me large sums of money to induce me, but I did not feel this way inclined"), or incorrect prepositions ("Both of them took lessons of my wife"). These and other awkward departures from conventional English represent what one German-language scholar calls "interference from German."[39]

Francis Schlatter studied English constantly as a young man, but the lingering characteristics of his native Alsatian German remained with him his entire life. They appear often in *Life of the Harp*, and Ada Morley made particular note of his "quaint humor and queer expressions."[40] Only a few peculiarities of German grammar and diction appear in *Modern Miracles*, but enough are present to seriously question the proposition that its author was an English-born boy who grew up in Hamilton, Canada, and later lived in Columbia, Tennessee. Instead, it seemed more reasonable to believe that its author, who had so passionately jumped up to tear down an American flag in Philadelphia or tried to raise an army of indigents to attack the Capitol in Washington, had been forced to give up his messianic past and abandon his argument with the world.

CHAPTER TWELVE

God's Leading

I had another leading to walk through the
country again and heal wherever I was led.[1]

MODERN MIRACLES OF HEALING

F RANCIS SCHLATTER never made his promised appearance in
Denver. In late October 1903, however, he did begin a journey west, on foot, with a pet spaniel and a few dollars in his
pocket.[2] Luverna was nowhere to be found. She may have left
him again, perhaps after his failure to make good on his promise,
or he might have simply walked away from their Chicago home,
following God's calling.

Coincidentally, at the same time that Schlatter began his new
walking journey to the West, the books that the Alsatian cobbler had
left in the care of Albert Whitaker ten years earlier showed up in a
Denver bookstore.[3] They consisted of German textbooks on geology,
chemistry, metallurgy, and mechanical engineering. The Schlatter
of old, it seems, had been a devoted student of the sciences before
embracing psychic healing and biblical prophecy.

In this respect, the purpose of Schlatter's walking pilgrimage of
1903 was curious. "In 300 years," he told a reporter, "this country
will have exhausted its agricultural lands if something is not done to
open up the deserts of the great West. I have given this matter much
thought, having spent days without either food or water in crossing
the alkali sands."[4] Moreover, he had fashioned a way to change the
landscape of the West so that it could be more fruitful and produc-
tive. Having abandoned his messianic past, as I believed he did, he
embraced the notion that humans could alter their environment and
reform their institutions, something he had utterly rejected in his
conversations with Ada Morley. Nor was his idea for making the deserts of the West arable merely a version of the nostrum "rain follows

the plow." He had a plan to treat the soil itself—with nitrates. A few years later, he developed a nitrate production plant, and Luverna claimed that he had taken out patents on the Schlatter Airabon Soil Rejuvenator, though none exist in the Patent Office.[5]

Wherever his current journey took him, however, Schlatter's whereabouts for the next six years remains a mystery. In 1909, as a result of Charles McLean's death and subsequent speculation over the Denver healer's fate, Schlatter reemerged from his and Luverna's place of retreat in Battle Creek, Michigan. For the past few months he had withdrawn from public healing to take up a new interest, a connection between healing and metaphysics that he called the "key note" theory. Schlatter told the *Battle Creek Enquirer* reporter that he'd spent considerable time studying the arts and sciences, and his theory derived from the connections between music and chemistry. Everyone, he said, is attuned to a certain musical key. "For instance, all great musical composers are in the key of C. The great artists are in D, and the literary lights in E. Only the genius is attuned in a perfect key, the ordinary mortal being a little in discord."[6] Schlatter himself was in the key of F, he said, and when he encountered a sufferer in the same key, the healing was immediate. If not, it might take a while to become fully effective.

Schlatter also discovered twelve extra notes between the recognized notes. "For instance," said the *Enquirer*, "between C and C sharp there are still twelve tones that can be detected by the trained ear. Mr. Schlatter states that he expects to construct an instrument that will interpret these delicate notes. Our present music, he says, is harsh, because the tones do not graduate as they should were these newly discovered notes employed."[7] In fact, Francis and Thomas seemed to be at work on such an instrument, for in the 1910 U.S. census a few months later, Thomas's occupation was listed as producing a "musical chart."[8] Nor was the chart theoretical. Francis was already giving lessons in his key note system at a home in Battle Creek. Of some 144 "complete lessons," he was offering twelve "lectures" or courses.[9]

In spite of their serious ongoing marital conflicts, Luverna loved and admired her husband without reservation. Whenever she left him, it was with great reluctance, and she held out faith that they would reconcile again. Something like this happened shortly after their stay in Battle Creek, for when Schlatter was arrested in Toledo, Ohio, on April 10, 1910, for defrauding a woman of five dollars, he was almost certainly alone—and probably divorced.

The arrest of Francis Schlatter, occurring so soon after the widespread attention given to Charles McLean's death, led the Toledo police to contact Denver authorities. They sent a letter asking about the man's identity, along with a police report and mug shot of the derelict healer. "A photograph of the fellow came with the letter," stated the *Denver Post*, but "he does not bear the slightest resemblance to the real Schlatter, . . . who is generally believed to have died shortly after leaving this city."[10] It was quite true—the man in the mug shot had a rash of stubble, short hair, a drooping lower lip, and pendulous earlobes. His eyes, which the police report described as hazel, shone black in the harsh light of the police photographer's flash powder. Nothing about him, except perhaps the peculiar contour of his lips, resembled the heavily bearded, clear-eyed, upturned head of the healer of Denver. But he bore a distinctive hourglass mark on the right side of his nose (which the Atlanta witness had confused with the left), and the police report confirmed that he had a cicatrix on his left forearm.

The Toledo healer escaped jail time by returning the money he had taken from his victim, and continued to wander until Luverna eventually found him again. As in their separation following his abusive behavior in New York, they reconciled in a year or two and were remarried near her son Guy Comer's Nebraska home in November 1912.[11]

The war years interrupted the couple's healing work and consequently kept them out of the newspapers. They dipped under the surface of public attention while Jacob Kunze and August Schrader emerged to make Schlatter's name synonymous with sensationalism, burlesque piety, and mail fraud. During this time, according to Luverna, Francis joined three other men in buying mules throughout the West for the war effort while she volunteered for the Red Cross.[12] Afterward, in 1920, he went to work for Thomas, who had started a monument company in Miamisburg, Ohio. "He is a very fine sculptor and carver," Luverna said about her husband, "and did some beautiful work for his brother."[13] Luverna's words recall the occupation Schlatter gave to the Good Samaritan intake nurse—

"sculptor"—and raise the prospect that he met the Martin boys and their father in Columbia, Tennessee, during the mid-1880s, perhaps taken there by Louisa.

By 1921, having produced a flyer portraying her husband as a distinguished elder statesman, clean-shaven and with tufted locks barely suggesting his once-rich mane, Luverna set out to recapture the glory of their past ministry together—which had, in fact, never been at the heights Francis reached before they met.[14] (Interestingly, the flyer refers to the healer's birth in Alsace, France, rather than Germany, which suggests that the posthumous Schlatter was aware of the province's shifting nationalities over time.)

Then, from their Chicago home, they began another campaign throughout the Midwest. "There are times when we give open air demonstrations," she wrote, "sometimes in Masonic halls, Methodist churches, Episcopal churches, Spiritualist churches."[15] They did not wander from one city to the next as in former times. Instead, they waited for an invitation to arrive from a minister who learned of them through a church member.

Most of these gatherings were small. Then in April 1921 a sudden upsurge of interest turned the West Side Spiritualist Church in Columbus, Ohio, into a mecca of healing. In three days the number of sufferers mushroomed from fifteen to seven hundred. "Dr. Schlatter," the *Ohio State Journal* reported, "met and treated a continuous stream of humanity, bent, broken and ailing. An overpowering silence filled the church, broken occasionally by sobs, and even hysterical laughter, from afflicted persons."[16]

Once again—and perhaps for the first time since McLean's death in 1909—the local press took a sympathetic look at the healer. He was a "little less than average height," said the *Journal* reporter, "slenderly built, and slightly stooped." He carried with him a scrapbook of some five thousand newspaper clippings from his travels. Ever since God spoke to him at his cobbler's bench in Denver, Schlatter said, "I have obeyed his call. I suppose that I have healed more than 500,000 people in this country and Europe." The number—typically—was exaggerated, but he likely treated some 250,000 people over twenty years' time, with another 100,000 people observing the healing sessions. He was modest, however, in accounting for his healing powers. "It's just a gift from God," he said. "Some people

FIGURE 20. Luverna Comer-Schlatter during
the early 1920s, when she often had to go in search
of her wandering husband. Courtesy of the
St. Louis Post-Dispatch.

are gifted along musical lines, some are artists. It is my good fortune
that I can heal."[17]

The Columbus ministry, unpretentious as it was compared to
Schlatter's great campaigns of the past, recalled in miniature the so-
lemnity and grandeur of scenes from Albuquerque, Denver, Canton,
Chicago, and Atlanta. It was to be Francis Schlatter's final act as a
healer of multitudes, surrounded by the press and watching countless
sufferers come under his touch. He was sixty-five, probably impaired
by years of drinking and the ravages of chronic tuberculosis, and
losing his grip on reality. Luverna probably admitted more than she
meant when she told a *Journal* reporter: "I have to look after Dr.
Schlatter. He's just like a baby in business matters and everything
else. He is devoted to nothing but his work and I have to tell him
when to eat and sleep."[18]

LUVERNA HAD LONG HOPED that she could draw Francis away from the grip of spiritualism, which had occupied him for as long as they had been together, and into her own denomination, the Episcopal Church. Although she had struggled in earlier years—and won—against conservative Chicago clergymen who frowned on spiritual "Christ-centered" healing, the Episcopal Church had made some strides in the past two decades.[19] In fact, a couple of Boston priests had begun a holistic healing program similar to Hollenberg's neuro-spiritual Francis Schlatter Institute. The Emmanuel Movement of the Boston-based Emmanuel Episcopal Church combined spiritual, psychological, and physical approaches to healing, and Luverna saw it as a great opportunity for bringing Francis into the fold. Its originators, Rev. Elwood Worcester and Samuel McComb, borrowed on the emerging field of psychology and the established principles of New Thought to address spiritual, physical, and moral disorders.[20]

The Columbus healing sessions had exhausted the healer.[21] Arguing that he needed a rest, Luverna took Francis to Boston, where he could recuperate and perhaps meet with Reverend Worcester.[22] Whether or not a meeting actually took place is uncertain, but Luverna had already established a solid connection with the Episcopal leader. After persistent encouragement, Francis agreed to set his sights on confirmation in the church a few months later, in the fall of 1921.

Then, on June 25, while the couple rested on Cape Ann, about thirty miles northeast of Boston, Francis went on an errand to the village of Gloucester and never returned.[23] A day or two later he sent a letter on stationery from New York's Commodore Hotel stating that he planned to attend the spiritualist camp at Lily Dale, New York—the center of American spiritualism. He planned to give a healing demonstration there. If anything was certain, it was that Francis, in spite of his wife's carefully laid plans for him, intended to remain a powerful medium in the body of American spiritualists.

The next message came as a shock. Francis sent a telegram to Thomas Martin from Montreal stating that he was planning to sail to England. He intended to meet with James Moore Hickson, an An-

glican lay healer who had created the Society of Emmanuel, a movement roughly similar to Elwood Worcester's but emphasizing prayer
as the main healing agent. A few days later Luverna heard that Francis was still in Montreal—this news coming from a stranger in St.
Louis, W. M. Howe, whose name was unfamiliar to Luverna but
obviously not to Francis, for he had sent Howe the telegram directly
with instructions to contact his wife.

At the time, Francis was staying in Montreal's exclusive Windsor
Hotel. He had plenty of money—five hundred dollars in traveler's
checks—and may have been waiting for passage on the next ship
bound for England. Meanwhile, Luverna remained headquartered
in Boston's YWCA, and she was upset that her telegrams to the
Windsor went answered. She also objected to the suggestion by Boston police that her husband had abandoned her. "The thought of desertion is impossible," she said. "My husband and I are companions.
We were perfectly happy at our little cottage at Annisquam. We have
so much in common, and our work draws us together."[24] Indeed, she
managed to contact Francis, and he made arrangements to meet her
in Columbus, Ohio, where she had returned from their interrupted
idyll on Cape Ann.

Then disaster struck. On July 25, as Francis was boarding a ship
heading home, a U.S. immigration official refused him passage to
the States.[25] On the passenger manifest information card, the ship's
doctor entered a diagnosis of "constitutional psychopathic inferiority," and Schlatter was taken into custody by Canadian immigration
officials. He had suddenly become a man without a country—or
nearly so. On the manifest card, he had given his birthplace as
Alsace-Lorraine and a Canadian official wrote to Luverna that they
intended to deport her husband to France. Indeed, if Francis were
British born, this would have been the time to say so.

The reasons for his confinement were unclear. Aside from the
doctor's evaluation, which probably took place because Schlatter
listed himself as a "divine healer," the justification for holding him
ranged from his inability to pay his hotel bill to healing in a public
park without a license. Complicating the entire episode—but a key
to his troubles in Montreal—was the fact that Canadian officials
mistook him for Jacob Kunze, who with August Schrader had just
five years earlier been extradited to Los Angeles to stand trial for
mail fraud.[26]

By the time Thomas Martin paid the hotel bill, any real pretext for holding Francis ended. But until American immigration officials approved his return he remained in custody. With deportation to France a continuing threat, Luverna sent a letter to U.S. Attorney General H. M. Daugherty, a native of Columbus, for help in getting her husband back.[27] Initially she was confident that Daugherty would find evidence that Schlatter's father came to America in 1858. "It will take just a little time for me to find where he took out his papers," she wrote. In the meantime, she made the case for her husband's long residency in the United States, his status as a property owner, and his large following as a healer. She also addressed any objection based on the ship doctor's diagnosis by arguing that Schlatter had a house in Bordeaux (Louisa's old home) about two miles from Nashville. "If it should turn out to be so unfortunate that Mr. Schlatter is not well," she wrote Daugherty, "suffering from a nervous breakdown from overwork, there is a beautiful home there waiting for him where he can be nicely taken care of, and a loving wife and tender wife to care for him."[28]

None of Luverna's efforts to convince U.S. authorities prevailed. On September 7 the State Department's legal office reported that "from the testimony taken by the Montreal office of the Bureau of Immigration, it appears probable that Schlatter is not an American citizen."[29] As a result, it recommended that he be deported to France but allowed to reapply with proof of citizenship. Fortunately, Luverna had no idea that the State Department had rejected her appeals — for, in the end, it didn't matter. The Canadian government, with the assistance of U.S. commissioner John Clark, had released Schlatter from custody more than a week earlier.[30] He was now — ironically enough — in Hamilton, Canada, awaiting word about his prospects of returning to the United States.

Schlatter soon returned to the United States, probably through the good offices of John Clark. It had been a close call. At first, Luverna had planned to go to Montreal to assist her husband, but a lawyer advised her to stay home. If Francis had been deported, he said, she'd be deported along with him — for Canada's laws didn't allow for the separation of husband and wife. And if Francis had been deported to France alone, there was no guarantee that he'd ever return — even if she went there to get him. There was simply no documentation that he was an American citizen.

ON JULY 7, 1922, ten months after Schlatter's brush with deportation, Luverna sat in Denver's Oxford Hotel, once again searching for her wayward husband. "He has wandered off this way before," she told a reporter, "but he has always kept in touch with me, and I have prayed for him and felt that he was all right. But this time I have prayed and prayed and nothing has come of it."[31] Later, overtaken by apprehension and despair, she cried: "I am afraid — I — Where are you, Francis?"

Schlatter's latest disappearance, Luverna explained, grew out of a disagreement three weeks earlier. Francis wanted to travel from their Chicago home to California. "You are too old to make such a trip," Luverna told him. "You can't stand it."

"I have got to make it," he replied. His destination was Los Angeles, but mainly he wanted to see Denver. It had been twenty-seven years since he left, he said. All day they had discussed his trip — probably argued over it — and that evening Francis went out for a walk. He didn't return. The next morning, Luverna received a note from her husband stating that he was driving with a man whom he'd once healed. Later the *Post* learned that the argument wasn't just about travel plans. In one of his last letters, Schlatter wrote that "he was tired of hearing about religion and was going to Pikes Peak to forget about it."[32]

The search took Luverna from Chicago to Colorado Springs, then Denver, then Salt Lake City, where she had hoped to bring her husband into the Episcopal Church.[33] "I have visited many cities in search of him," she said, "but was never able to get in touch with him. I was informed that he was in Kansas City . . . and that he had gone from there on an automobile trip with a man whom he cured many years ago."[34] Again, she lost track of him and decided to remain in Kansas City, where she signed up to work for Unity Temple, the home of Unity, a rapidly growing religion that developed out of nineteenth-century New Thought and promoted a message of Christian universalism and spiritual healing.

She was there on October 16 when news of her husband's death arrived. He had been living only 250 miles away, in St. Louis — and in the company of a strange woman. Whatever thoughts raced through her mind as she packed a bag and ordered a cab to Union Station, uppermost perhaps was her belief that spiritualists had finally won. She had fought hard on behalf of her husband over the past twenty years—battling imposters who would deny him his rightful place as Denver's great healer, against spiritualists who saw him as a medium rather than a man of God, and even against his own tendency to follow God's "leading" without word or warning into thin air. Now her struggle had come to an end.

When Luverna arrived in St. Louis the next morning, she learned from Evelyn Hartman, owner of a rooming house at 5861 Easton Avenue, that Francis had been living for several days with a woman he'd called his wife. Yet yesterday noon, looking ill and with a bad cough, he had asked Hartman to send for Mrs. Schlatter in Kansas City. His condition worsened quickly, and by six o'clock that evening the healer's companion used Hartman's telephone to call a neighborhood doctor, who arrived too late to save the dying man. The woman then arranged for a nearby funeral home to pick up the body and without further notice returned to the room, got her handbag, and left. No one knew who she was or where she went.

Distraught and angry, Luverna at first believed Francis had been murdered. She searched the two rooms the couple occupied and claimed to have found drugs there. "They got him," she told a reporter, openly accusing his spiritualists followers.[35] Police went in search of the strange woman, whom someone identified as Madelyn Black. But even as Luverna spoke to the press, the coroner was conducting an autopsy at the nearby George L. Pleitsch funeral home, where the body had been taken. He concluded that Luverna's husband had died of a hemorrhage brought on by acute tuberculosis, and the police immediately dropped their investigation. Luverna accepted the finding, but she was furious to learn that her husband's body had been embalmed, after the autopsy, without her knowledge or consent. As she told the deputy coroner at the inquest the next day, Francis had *raised* people who had been pronounced dead.[36] Now, with the embalming, he couldn't possibly raise himself.

Luverna didn't testify formally at the inquest, which was held at the coroner's office in downtown St. Louis, but the doctor, a police officer, and Evelyn Hartman did. Nevertheless Luverna gave information for the death certificate that no one else could: Schlatter was sixty-six, born in France on April 29, 1856, and made his living as a lecturer. She added that he was a chemist and gave his father's name as Edward Schlatter. Throughout their lives together, Luverna never understood the name of her husband's true father, François, or his mother's name, Madeleine.[37]

What happened next will probably never be explained. A day or two after the coroner's inquest, Luverna left St. Louis and abandoned her husband's body to the Pleitsch funeral home, never once looking back. Or so it appeared. Perhaps she'd been so humiliated by the scandal and disgusted by her husband's behavior that she washed her hands of him in death. But given her love for him and her perpetual willingness to forgive him, that was not likely. Something went wrong.

Oddly, the death certificate states that Schlatter's burial took place two months later, in Miamisburg, Ohio, on December 15, 1922. This, then, was the *intention*. Thomas Martin lived in Miamisburg with his wife, Catherine, and was still active in his cemetery monument business. Even if Luverna wanted nothing to do with her husband's body, Thomas would have seen to its proper interment and given it a marker. Furthermore, his relationship with Luverna was excellent; after his wife died, Luverna and Thomas lived together for a time.[38] The only reasonable explanation for their lack of interest or curiosity in Schlatter's body is that they believed — or were led to believe — it had somehow been destroyed.[39]

ON MAY 7, 1945, just as Germany suffered a crushing defeat at the hands of Allied forces, *Newsweek* reported that St. Louis health officials had discovered several unburied bodies — all well preserved — in funeral parlors and makeshift morgues around the city. One was that of a sixty-year-old woman named Maud, who had been dead forty years. Another belonged to "Deaf Bill" Lee, dead thirty years. Another was a Chinese baby girl believed to have died in 1895, and a fourth was that of Jim Fields, a black man whose upright corpse stood sentinel near the Chinese infant's coffin in a cluttered warehouse. The final body, which health authorities found in the Pleitsch funeral home, was that of Francis Schlatter, a faith healer who died in 1922. It had lain remarkably well preserved in an open basement coffin for twenty-three years.[40]

Besides the brief national attention *Newsweek* gave to the story, the discovery of these forgotten dead was of passing interest in the triumphant news of Germany's defeat. A few articles had already appeared in St. Louis newspapers, yet the *St. Louis Post-Dispatch* treated the episode lightly. While city health inspectors hastily removed the bodies to the Municipal Cemetery, the newspaper commented that the law requiring a reasonable length of time for burial might be "something less than forty years." Even the small mystery surrounding the body in the Pleitsch funeral home failed to generate much curiosity. "At the time of his death," stated the *Post-Dispatch*, "he was said to be a famous occult healer, but this claim was disputed."[41]

It is a coincidence — but a compelling one — that Schlatter's body went into the basement of the Pleitsch funeral home in 1922, the same year that Edgar Hewett placed the healer's copper rod in the basement of the Palace of the Governors. And it's notable that both remained effectively hidden from the world for more than twenty years, one by virtue of having been forgotten and the other from a fear that Schlatter's mysterious relic would inspire a cult following.

When Schlatter's body went into the Municipal Cemetery in 1945, the tale of his copper rod — and the legend of his death that it represented — was just beginning to take on a new life. In fact, it may have been the catalyst for the meeting of Agnes Morley Cleaveland and Edgar Hewett in the Palace of the Governors in Santa Fe. The copper rod was central to Hewett's story. His chapter in *Campfire and Trail* served as the coda to Schlatter's fate for a generation of writers and readers, and though the rod played a lesser role in Cleaveland's *No Life for a Lady*, it was equally as poignant. But what did it *really* represent — except as a folkloric object belonging to a forgotten messiah?[42]

If Francis Schlatter came out of Mexico in 1896, spent a few days under an assumed name in Good Samaritan Hospital, and emerged a few months later as Francis Schlatter in Memphis, the purpose of the copper rod is undeniable. It was the single-most important possession left at the death scene atop Tinaja Canyon, for it would resist wind, rain, and the elements to prove, without question, that the skeleton was the Messiah's. That was its practical purpose. But it had a larger significance. If Schlatter had indeed planned his death, in his mind the rod would have come to be celebrated, in New Jerusalem, as the equivalent of the cross of Jesus — a memento mori that rose above all others. In either cases, it was an object of deception. But since Schlatter acted at the behest of the Father, in whose hands the healer was but an instrument, it might well be considered an object of *divine* deception.

Francis Schlatter Cyclus

MOUNT LEBANON CEMETERY lies about eight miles northwest of where the Pleitsch funeral home once sat on St. Charles Rock Road, an extension of old Easton Avenue. The suburbs and transportation corridors have grown up around it, pinching it on all sides. Just over a broad hill that forms the high point of the cemetery lie the runways of the St. Louis International Airport. But in spite of the erosion of its territory and the impinging world of steel and concrete surrounding it, the cemetery evokes a sense of peace, quiet, and natural serenity. About halfway up a gradual hillside rising to the northwest, a section of land called the Garden of Faith features a flat marker bearing no individual names. It is the burial plot of the nameless.

At last, I thought, Schlatter and his unburied companions had finally found a dignified home here. The inner-city Municipal Cemetery, in which the bodies had been placed in 1945, had to make way for an apartment complex about fifteen years later, and Mount Lebanon Cemetery agreed to find space for them. But the land it had designated as a potter's field was soon appropriated for the Mark Twain Expressway, which became one of the first stretches of Interstate 70 in the nation. The details of the land transfer and sale are unclear, and the temporary disposition of the orphaned souls from the Municipal Cemetery even more shadowy.[1] Nevertheless, when I finally visited Mount Lebanon in 2012, the staff guided me to the secluded spot in the Garden of Faith where the marker sat, then left me alone.

While there I brought along my copy of Otis B. Spencer's *Francis Schlatter Cyclus, in Twelve Numbers: Ye Holy Man and His Works*, a small devotional booklet of words and pictures expressing the belief that Schlatter was the second coming of Christ. I kept this rare 1896

FIGURE 21. Women wait in line at the Fox home in Denver, 1895.
Otis B. Spencer, who firmly believed in Schlatter's divinity, produced
twelve grainy images from his early-generation Kodak camera for his
ribbon-bound booklet, *Francis Schlatter Cyclus: Ye Holy Man and His Works*,
privately printed in 1896. So far only a handful of booklets are known
to exist, and none of Spencer's images, taken without official sanction,
has previously seen print. Booklet in author's possession.

treasure in an old leather binder of about the same period. Only one
picture in the book is of Schlatter; all the rest are groups of men,
women, and children waiting in line to see the healer. The blurry
Kodak photos give a timeless, mythic quality to the scene. On one of
the halftones in the book, somewhat jarringly, someone had written
"Mom" in blue ink. She is standing with several dour-looking white
women in satin-bow hats and dark clothing while behind her, also serious but with an unambiguous pride and dignity, is a black woman
in a long dress, dark shawl, and unadorned hat.

I thought of Ada Morley at the Fox home. She was forty-two then,
younger than most of these women, and lived twenty years beyond

the winter she spent with Francis Schlatter. Had it not been for her, and her remarkable literary talent, Schlatter's ideas about the corruption of the modern world, the coming apocalypse, the return of the Messiah, and the establishment of New Jerusalem would never have emerged as a comprehensive vision of the end times in the late nineteenth century—or Francis Schlatter as a modern-day prophet in the biblical tradition. Moreover, only one chapter in *The Life of the Harp*—Ada Morley's "Teachings in Retirement"—reveals the true scope of Schlatter's plan. Morley thus became not only the healer's disciple but the medium through which his mind and motives could be understood more than a century later.

She wasn't the only medium, however. Just as Ada Morley urged Schlatter to tell the story of his pilgrimage, which was the centerpiece of *The Life of the Harp*, Luverna Comer-Schlatter persuaded her husband to proclaim his rightful title as the true healer in *Modern Miracles of Healing*. Had it not been for her, the final act of Schlatter's modern-day Passion Story—which I believed played out in the bitter ashes of a new century—would never be known. At the same time, Luverna was the unwitting inspiration for one of the most remarkable books in American letters—an autobiography whose author deliberately undermined his own veracity.

Without these two midwives, and the books they delivered, little of historical importance would have followed from the bright blaze of Schlatter's 1895 fame. As it was, both books found their way to oblivion, as did the newspaper articles about Schlatter's imposters that ended up in a scrapbook put together by Thomas Dawson at the Colorado Historical Society. But the historical legacy of an event is not always obvious. History does not recognize manifestations of the divine—since they are *always* confined to the religious imagination. And history never will, because the apocalypse, if it ever *did* occur, would spell the end of history. However, we *can* study the power of human imagination, like Schlatter's, which sought a world beyond history—New Jerusalem—and the consequences that ensue, whether personal or social.

I paid my respects to the man who lay beneath the gravesite's flat granite marker. It read: "This is the final resting site of the unknown remains from the potter's field known as the New City of St. Louis Cemetery. Relocated 1995." The fact that one hundred years had passed from the healer's rise to fame to his long-delayed interment at Mount Lebanon struck me as compelling. So did the souls—people very much like those he touched over the years—who joined him there. They were like the people he touched in life: a white woman named Maud, a black man named Jim Fields, "Deaf Bill" Lee, and a Chinese baby girl, who died—as it happened—in 1895.

The Evidence Trail

I N 1945, after *Newsweek* announced the discovery of unburied bodies in St. Louis, Millard Everett, a columnist for the *Denver Catholic Register,* attempted to track down information about the St. Louis healer's identity. He made a few calls and looked at one or two documents, but he came away disappointed. "The trail has grown cold now," he wrote in the *Register* of June 7, 1945, "and the meager records yield few details." Yet at the time Everett wrote these words, a critically important document for determining the identity of the St. Louis healer lay only a few blocks away in the newspaper archives of the *Denver Post.* The *Post,* forever on the lookout for sensational news about Schlatter, had obtained the document from the Toledo, Ohio, police department more than three decades earlier.

On April 8, 1910, Toledo police arrested a man who gave his name as Francis Schlatter. He was charged with fraud and booked. During the arrest procedure, station officers photographed him and entered information on a standardized form that included typical body measurements and physical characteristics. His residence was given as Miamisburg, Ohio, and his nationality ("Descent") was listed as German—"speaking English." Based on these facts, we know him as the healer whose purported family members—mother Louisa and brother Thomas—lived in Miamisburg, Ohio. He was also the man who identified himself as John Martin in Cincinnati's Good Samaritan Hospital in 1896, the author of *Modern Miracles of Healing* in 1903, and the healer who died in St. Louis in 1922. Given his consistent life history from 1896 to 1922, but also acknowledging his tenuous identity, I will refer to him here as the "posthumous" Schlatter.

The 1910 police report, including detailed front and profile mug shots, is a rare document providing many points of physical evidence for determining whether this man was the original Francis Schlatter.

BUREAU OF IDENTIFICATION.

Gal. No. *1958*   Dept. of Police – Detective Service.   Neg. No. *1958*

Name *Francis Schlatter*   Color *White*

Alias

Residence *Miamisburg Ohio* Occupation   Descent *Germ. Eng.*

Crime *Obt. Money False Pre.*   Date of Arrest *4-8th 1910*

Officers *Howard D.B.*   Dist. No. *2.B.*

Sentence *Case Settled.*   Date *4-16-1910* Judge *Austin*

Previous criminal record *Wanted*

Numerical Order.	Marks, Scars and Moles.
I	*Tat F.S. Left forearm front 4.0 ~ elbow*
II	*Tat female head & bust right forearm front 4.0 ~ elbow*
III	*Obl. cic. left side neck 4.0 below lobe ear*
III	*Cic. forearm 1.0 to left of med line - hair line*

Name *Francis Schlatter*

Height	1 m *67.5*	Head, Length,	*19.2*	L. Foot,	*23.6*	Circle		Age *54* on
Eng. Hgt	*5' ft. 6" in.*	" Width,	*13.9*	L. Mid. F.	*10.9*	Periph. 2		*4-29-10*
Outs. A.	1 m *66.0*	Length		L. Lit. F.	*8.2*			Born at
Trunk,	*90.0*			L. Fore A	*43.9*	Pecul. *Germany*		

Incl. *Ver.*	Ridge *Ver.*	Border	Chin *Reg.*		
Hght *M.*	Base *Cle.* Root *dep.*	Lobe	Mous. *—* Beard *—*		
Width *M.*	Length / Projection / Breadth	Teeth *Fair*	Hair *Gray*		
Pecul.	*Mys. M gt. M.*	Wt.	Complexion *M. florid*		
	Pecul.		Build *Slender*		

Measured at Toledo, Ohio. { Date *April 11st 1910* By *R.F. McKey.*

FIGURE 22. Toledo, Ohio, police report on Francis Schlatter, 1910. Data in this document, both visual and quantitative, offer the only known sources of physical comparison between this twentieth-century Schlatter and the healer of Albuquerque and Denver in 1895. Francis Schlatter Collection (10029142), History Colorado.

Over the past twenty years, five forensic experts have examined it, along with other photographs, and four of the five experts have concluded that the man in the Toledo mug shots is not the original healer. Their opinions rest on everything from the Toledo healer's pendulous earlobes, which do not appear in photographs of Denver's healer, to differences in facial structure based on biometric measurements. Only one forensic expert, the late Michael Charney of Colorado State University, determined in 1994 that it was highly probable the two men were the same. The other experts were Dr. Robert Pickering, then at the Denver Museum of Nature and Science, who commented in 1996 on the pendulous earlobes; Dr. Barry Bullard, chief scientist for the Institute for Forensic Imaging (IFI) at Indiana University–Purdue University, Indianapolis, who conducted a study in 1998; Stephen Mancusi, a certified forensic artist who worked for nearly thirty years for the New York City Police Department, who provided a detailed report in 2009; and Dr. Robert M. George of Florida International University, a physical anthropologist with an expertise in craniofacial identification, who also conducted his study in 2009. The reports of all but Pickering's unrecorded comments can be found at www.vanishingmessiah.com.

The approach taken by the experts highlights their methodological differences. Drs. Bullard and George, for instance, based their findings solely on measurement. Except for the placement of markers, no subjective judgment played a part in their analysis. Their conclusions were based on the degree to which those measurements approximated one another—and they were not close enough to warrant a positive finding. Both scientists doubted the healers were the same, but they pointed out that the angle of the faces in the comparative samples affected the reliability of the experiment. Dr. George concluded that the comparison between the Toledo healer and an 1895 image of Schlatter (Figs. 7 and 22) was "inaccurate due to head tilting and foreshortening problems." Dr. Bullard's findings were similar. Furthermore, he said, "the scientific community . . . have not come to a conclusion that facial biometric measurements alone can be used to identify a given human being."

Although Stephen Mancusi also conducted measurements, his approach relied primarily on careful observation and an artist's understanding of facial anatomy. As with the other forensic experts, Mancusi cautioned that "in most cases, facial image comparisons will not yield definitive results," only a "degree of possibility." While he acknowledged certain points of similarity, Mancusi argued that definitive dissimilarities in the eyes, ears, and noses of the two healers could not be explained "by age or pose perspective." Michael Charney came to the opposite conclusion—years earlier—asserting that the probability the two healers were the same "is very high." Yet his approach, like Mancusi's, relied upon close study and an eye for detail rather than measurement exclusively.

Forensic science is a tool that combines with documentary evidence and contextual clues to provide a comprehensive understanding of an event, usually a crime, casualty of war, or natural disaster, and the identification of victims. It can also be used, as here, to confirm or disprove a claim that one person—known or unknown—is identical to another, usually someone of historical importance. In many of these instances, historically, the likeness in a photograph is the only body of evidence available. But when a wider field of evidence exists, it must also be brought to bear on the subject. In itself, the Toledo police report of 1910 contains significant factual information beyond the mug shots, but other documents, such as the coroner's report of 1922, add to the picture of the Toledo healer's identity.

To begin with, eyewitnesses in 1895 noted that Schlatter's eyes were generally blue-gray—variously described as "deep blue," steel gray and bright gray, "pure blue," "light blue," and "deep-set blue." The police report describes the Toledo healer's eyes as *hazel*, and the coroner's report as *blue*. The consensus over all the reports would be that both men had light blue to hazel eyes—though in the mug shot they appear darker, perhaps from the room's lighting or an aberration of the flash.

Reports of the healer's height in 1895 vary so widely that they are unreliable—from 5 feet 5 inches to 6 feet—and he stood slightly bent over, presumably from chest pain caused by chronic tuberculosis, which both men seemed to share. The most reliable assessment comes from Dr. Mary Ingersoll, in whose Denver boardinghouse Schlatter lived as a cobbler in late 1892 and early 1893. She stated that he was about 5 feet 9 inches (*Rocky Mountain News*, July 18, 1895). The 1910 Toledo police report gives a height of 5 feet 6 inches, but in 1922 the St. Louis coroner measured the postmortem body at 5 feet 9 inches—a more accurate and reliable measurement.

In 1895 witnesses testified to the unusually large size of Schlatter's hands (*Denver Republican*, September 19, 1895), which appear in Figure 5. Measurements taken of the Toledo healer in 1910 reveal a remarkably large hand size based on length of the left middle and little fingers — 4.3 inches (10.9 cm) and 3.2 inches (8.2 cm), respectively. To indicate how large a hand this suggests, in an anthropometric study conducted by the U.S. Army in 1991, measurement of the middle finger (digit 3) in over one thousand men found that the maximum length in the entire group was 4.1 inches (10.5 cm). Thus, by scientific measurement, the Toledo healer's finger length and corresponding hand size would have fallen somewhere in the 99th percentile of the population (for the report, see Thomas M. Greiner, "Hand Anthropometry of U.S. Army Personnel," U.S. Army Natick Research, Development, and Engineering Center, Natick, MA, December 1991).

Toledo police measurements of the healer's feet, on the other hand, indicate that they were small — 9.3 inches long (23.6 cm) for the left foot. This would appear to be a major departure from that of the 1895 healer, who had shoes made for him in Albuquerque that measured 13 inches long by 4¾ inches wide (*Albuquerque Morning Democrat*, July 27, 1895). However, a portrait of Schlatter taken a day earlier (Fig. 5) shows him wearing rather small shoes, although with one toe worn through. Schlatter believed he was growing physically as well as spiritually, even at nearly forty years old, and claimed he was six feet tall. If there were a great disparity between the size of his hands and his feet, it might well have been an embarrassment for him — and an inducement to falsify his shoe size, which could easily have been done, since he was a cobbler himself.

As is discussed in the text, two eyewitnesses, three years apart, independently observed a small mark on the right side of Schlatter's nose. One of them, Lillian Middaugh, saw the healer in Denver in October 1895, and the other eyewitness (*Atlanta Constitution*, November 22, 1898) observed the same mark on both Schlatter's nose in 1895 and on the posthumous healer during his Atlanta ministry of 1898. (Incidentally, I came across the *Atlanta Constitution* article in 2012, exactly twenty years after finding Middaugh's comment in 1992. They were but two factual needles in a haystack of some four hundred newspapers.)

The Atlanta eyewitness also noted that both the Denver and posthumous healers bore a cicatrix, or fleshy scar, on the left forearm — another precise mark of identification that shows up in the Toledo

FIGURE 23. Close-up of William A. White portrait
of Francis Schlatter, made on October 19, 1895,
showing a dark portion within the shadow at the
right of nose bridge that might be the "slight mark"
Lillian Middaugh described in her letter to the
Canton Repository of October 20, 1895. William A.
White, Library of Congress, LC-USZ62-46226.

police report (Fig. 22, last line under "Marks, Scars and Moles").
Without Lillian Middaugh's statement, the claims of the Atlanta eyewitness would be without merit for he — or she — could have been
an ally of the posthumous healer who merely attributed his physical
characteristics to the Denver messiah. But, significantly, Middaugh's
1895 observation validates the Atlanta eyewitness's of 1898, and by
extension we can trust that the Atlanta eyewitness observed the cicatrix on Schlatter's forearm in 1895 as well. In this way, the Toledo
police report, though it applies only to the posthumous healer, can
be positive evidence of a connection between the two men.

None of the remaining physical measurements in the Toledo police report or the 1922 coroner's report offer reliable comparisons
with the healer of Denver. Nevertheless, we can conclude that the
posthumous healer and Francis Schlatter shared three common
features — blue or blue-hazel eyes, inordinately large hands, and two
discrete marks or scars. To this we may add a comparative facial
geometry that is not grossly out of proportion, body type and height

of corresponding size, and a tendency in both men to bend slightly when standing. An argument could be made, as it was by Dr. Pickering, that the Toledo healer's pendulous earlobes distinguish him inalterably from Schlatter (Fig. 3). Yet it's important to note that earlobes can become distended with age (see, for example, R. Azaria, M.D., et al., "Morphometry of the Adult Human Earlobe . . . ," *Plastic and Reconstructive Surgery* III [June 2003]: 2133).

As discussed in the text, both healers privately shared certain characteristics of behavior, background, and personality—among them a deep interest in spiritualism, a habit of wandering off without warning, and residual German patterns of speech and accent, which would not likely be found in a native-born American or naturalized citizen of British ancestry. Although only observed secondhand, through historical documents, these characteristics combine with forensic results to define the larger body of evidence over the question of the posthumous healer's true identity.

To this broader forensic picture we must add the posthumous healer's deep knowledge of Francis Schlatter's life and activities—of events, people, and places—much of which was not available to him through published documents. In fact, his intimate awareness of Schlatter's healing ministry in Denver raises the possibility that he was a close confidant or disciple of the healer who decided, after Schlatter's disappearance, to begin his own career as an imposter. However, once we look holistically at the personal characteristics of both men, it seems highly improbable that a close associate of Schlatter's would be a veritable doppelgänger. The simpler explanation—using Occam's razor—is that the two men were the same.

1856		Francis Schlatter born in Ebersheim, Alsace, France
1871		Leaves Ebersheim for Paris and London
1884		Arrives in America (possibly)
1892	Sept.	Comes to Denver
1893	July	Begins pilgrimage
1895	July	Arrives in New Mexico and begins healing
	Sept.	Begins healing at Fox home in Denver
	Nov.	Disappears
1896	Jan.	Arrives at Morley ranch
	March	Departs Morley ranch
	May	Crosses border into Mexico
	August	John Martin in Good Samaritan Hospital
1897	March	Schlatter (Martin) heals in Memphis
	May	Prospectors find skeleton in Mexico
—POSTHUMOUS EVENTS—		
	June	Schlatter (Martin) asserts he is healer in Cleveland
	July	Begins healing ministry in Canton, Ohio
		Ada Morley publishes *The Life of the Harp in Hand of the Harper*
	August	Elopes with Margaret Ferris
	Sept.	Healing ministry in Chicago
	Dec.	Ada Morley investigates healer's death in Mexico
1898	July	Schlatter jailed in Philadelphia for destroying American flag
1899	Jan.	Marries Luverna Comer
1901	July	Committed to St. Elizabeth's Hospital in Washington, D.C. Sentenced to Blackwell's Island in New York City
1902	July	Luverna Comer-Schlatter meets with Mary Fox in Denver
1903	Feb.	*Modern Miracles of Healing* published
1906		Edgar Hewett discovers Schlatter's possessions in Mexico
1922		Hewett acquires Schlatter's copper rod Schlatter dies in St. Louis boardinghouse
1945		Bodies discovered in St. Louis and buried in Municipal Cemetery

ASIDE FROM THE two key sources of this study, *The Life of the Harp in the Hand of the Harper* (abbreviated as *LH*) and *Modern Miracles of Healing* (*MM*), the following abbreviations will be used for frequently quoted newspapers in citation form:

AMD	*Albuquerque Morning Democrat*
CR	*Canton (OH) Repository*
DP	*Denver Post*
DR	*Denver Republican*
DT	*Denver Times*
RMN	*Rocky Mountain News* (Denver)

Prologue: Where the Mirages Are Born

1. *DP*, November 14, 1895.

2. *AMD*, July 17, 1895. Tomé Hill is not mentioned specifically in the newspaper article—only that two boys found a man lying atop a "black mountain." However, the only mountains visible from this part of the Rio Grande valley are the Manzano Mountains to the east and the Ladron Mountains to the southwest—both of them too far away to have fit the story. In 1999 I investigated the "black mountain" and realized it was Tomé Hill, a geological mound covered with black volcanic rock southeast of Las Lunas. Tomé Hill has long been considered a sacred place, not because of Schlatter but as an important amalgam of cultures—ancient Puebloan, Spanish, and modern—along the venerable El Camino Real. Today, hundreds of pilgrims flock to Tomé Hill on Good Friday, some making the steep climb to three large crosses that form an iconic Calvary at the summit.

3. Ibid., July 21, 1895.

4. Ibid., July 17, 1895.

5. *RMN*, August 9, 1895.

6. *DT*, September 16, 1895.

7. Joseph Emerson Smith, quoted in the *Denver Catholic Register*, August 28, 1941.

8. Gene Fowler, *Timber Line: A Story of Bonfils and Tammen* (New York: Covici, Friede, 1933), 220.

9. Agnes Morley Cleaveland, *No Life for a Lady* (Boston: Houghton Mifflin, 1941; reprint, Lincoln: University of Nebraska Press, 1977); Edgar L. Hewett, *Campfire and Trail* (Albuquerque: University of New Mexico Press, 1943).

10. Norman Cleaveland with George Fitzpatrick, *The Morleys: Young Upstarts on the Southwestern Frontier* (Albuquerque, NM: Calvin Horn Publishers, 1971), 25–26.

11. Marriage license, Floyd Jarrett and Ada M. Morley, November 20, 1884, Jackson County, Missouri (Provo, UT: Ancestry.com., Missouri Marriage Records, 1805–2002). For Jarrett's abandonment of the family, see Cleaveland, *No Life for a Lady*, 36.

12. Cleaveland, *No Life for a Lady*, 223.

13. Ibid., 224.

14. Ibid., 225.

15. Hewett, *Campfire and Trail*, 69.

16. Ibid., 72.

17. Ibid., 74.

18. Cleaveland, *The Morleys*, 26.

19. Around 1939 or 1940 Hewett told Erna Fergusson, a noted New Mexico writer, essentially the same story of the copper rod that he later published in *Campfire and Trail*, but with a few notable differences: he and his guide were *not* standing on the site of an unmarked grave when he learned about the dead man, nor was the gravesite anywhere near the village in Fergusson's account. Instead, Hewett and his guide, he told Fergusson, were in Casas Grandes at the time, along with a horse wrangler who accompanied them. They went to see the village mayor, who showed them the healer's possessions. This man's son, not the original mayor, was the person who sent Hewett the copper rod sixteen years later, and an agreement was openly made between the two to exchange the rod for funds to hire a schoolteacher. Fergusson also related one unusual fact that didn't make it into *Campfire and Trail*—that townspeople believed the copper rod contained gold inside, and someone attempted to cut into the base—or larger—end (Erna Fergusson, "The Prophet Who Disappeared," Erna Fergusson Papers, 1846–1964, MSS 45 BC, Box 10, Folder 12, Center for Southwest Research, University of New Mexico).

20. Some of the details of the discovery mentioned here have been taken from other newspaper articles of the time, especially *RMN*, June 6 and 7, 1897, and *DT*, June 11, 1897. Morley's inscription, as given in the *Denver Times* article, is incorrectly dated "3-24-97."

21. The other prospectors were George Look, F. G. Stanley, and Frank Barnum.

Chapter One: The Denver Cobbler

1. *DT*, October 7, 1895, quoted in Harry B. Magill, *Biography of Francis Schlatter, the Healer, with His Life, Works, and Wanderings* (Denver: Schlatter Publishing, 1896), 19.

2. *LH*, 165. In 1895 Schlatter stated, somewhat mysteriously, that his first

journey "carried him to the west" over the line of the Union Pacific Railroad. He may have walked at least part of the way from Lincoln, Nebraska, to Denver in 1892 (*AMD*, July 17, 1895). Albert Whitaker recounts his first meeting with Schlatter in "Solve Mystery," *RMN*, February 1, 1903.

3. For biographical information on Pomeroy, see *Dictionary of American Biography*, vols. 15–16 (New York: Charles Scribner's Sons, 1946), 53; Eleanor C. Kilbourn, "Dream of Two Builders Coming True," *Mountain States Monitor*, November 1922; and "Brick Pomeroy—Fabulous Failure," *Denver Post Empire Magazine*, July 5, 1959. For information on Pomeroy and the Atlantic-Pacific Tunnel, see *Pomeroy's Advance Thought* (February 1894): 23, and Sid Stall and Marge Stall, "The Great Atlantic-Pacific Tunnel," *Denver Post Empire Magazine*, November 16, 1975.

4. Two modern overviews of spiritualism are Slater Brown, *The Heyday of Spiritualism* (New York: Hawthorn Books, 1970), and Ruth Brandon, *The Spiritualists: The Passion for the Occult in the Nineteenth and Twentieth Centuries* (New York: Alfred A. Knopf, 1983).

5. Sources vary on the year of Schlatter's arrival, and he was inconsistent as well. He claimed to have left France for America in 1881 (*AMD*, July 17, 1895) and in 1877 (*RMN*, July 18, 1895; *DR*, August 23 and September 19, 1895). But in *Life of the Harp* (176), he gives the year of his arrival as 1884.

6. *New York Herald*, September 23, 1895; *RMN*, October 5, 1895.

7. *New York Herald*, September 23, 1895.

8. Ibid.

9. New York State Vital Records Index, Registration 22102, National Archives and Records Administration (hereinafter NARA). Search conducted by David Kerkhof, librarian, Suffolk County Historical Society. Courtesy Conger Beasley Jr.

10. *New York Herald*, September 23, 1895.

11. Petition filed July 28, 1891. Volume 469, Record 170, Petitions for Naturalization Filed in New York City, 1792–1989, New York, NARA (Provo, UT: Ancestry.com). The document is an index file, likely made out in the 1930s, to an earlier petition for naturalization submitted in 1891 in one of the districts of New York. Presumably the petition was granted and a certificate sent to Schlatter unless circumstances intervened.

12. Albert Whitaker, letter to the editor, *RMN*, February 1 and 18, 1903.

13. *RMN*, July 18, 1895; obituary in *RMN*, September 21, 1916. For a description of homeopathy as practiced in Denver, see Robert H. Shikes, M.D., *Rocky Mountain Medicine: Doctors, Drugs, and Disease in Early Colorado* (Boulder, CO: Johnson Books, 1986), and Steve Grinstead, "Alternative Healing at the Crossroads: Denver's Homeopathic Hospital Succumbs to Modern Medicine," *Colorado Heritage* (Summer 2005): 19–29.

14. *RMN*, July 18, 1895.

15. Ibid.

16. In a provocative analysis of American religion, *A Republic of Mind and*

Spirit: A Cultural History of American Metaphysical Religion (New Haven, CT: Yale University Press, 2007), Catherine L. Albanese argues that a plethora of beliefs, many of them interrelated, like New Thought, spiritualism, and mental healing, came to dominate the religious imagination in the nineteenth century in contradistinction to evangelicalism and mainstream denominational religion.

17. Helen Wilmans, *The Blossom of the Century* (Atlanta: Foote and Davies, 1893), 103.

18. Interview with J. B. Stansell, *Chicago Tribune*, November 17, 1895.

19. This international symposium met from August 25 to October 15, 1893, at the Chicago Art Institute in conjunction with the World's Columbian Exposition.

20. *Chicago Tribune*, November 17, 1895.

21. Ibid.

22. Schlatter's relationship with Helen Wilmans might seem distant at best on the surface, since he was an unknown cobbler and she an influential exponent of New Thought who had just published a book on the subject. Yet he knew Marcus "Brick" Pomeroy's friend Herbert George, publisher of the Populist newspaper *The Road* (later *The New Road*) who was closely allied with Wilmans and may have given Schlatter a copy of *The Blossom of the Century*. George could also have informed Wilmans of the cobbler's intellectual and spiritual gifts as well as his interest in psychic healing. Thus it is not such a leap to think that she might have agreed to meet Schlatter in Chicago, or, when that became impossible, in Hot Springs, Arkansas. See "Schlatter," *The Road*, September 28, 1895. For a brief account of Helen Wilmans's life, see http://helenwilmans.wwwhubs.com.

Like many practitioners of psychic and spiritual healing, Wilmans became the object of early twentieth-century Progressive reformers who considered these practices unlawful—in her case, she was charged with "absent treatment," or healing by distance. Whether or not she advocated this in the early 1890s, it came close to Schlatter's belief that he could heal through the medium of a letter or object, just as the Father had commanded him to do on the day of his vision in 1893. Given their mutual interests, and mutual friends, a meeting would not have been unusual at all.

23. *Chicago Tribune*, November 17, 1895. In this quotation, I have capitalized "Street" in "Seventeenth Street" to conform to current usage.

24. Albert Whitaker, letter to the editor, *RMN*, February 1, 1903, mentions the two cigar makers.

25. For an excellent overview of the silver panic of 1893 and subsequent depression as both affected Denver, see Stephen J. Leonard and Thomas J. Noel, *Denver: Mining Camp to Metropolis* (Niwot: University Press of Colorado, 1990), 102–13.

26. *RMN*, July 18, 1895, and February 1, 1903. McClelland states that, according to Mrs. Lamping, Schlatter took the valise to the "Atlantic and

Western depot"—but no such depot existed. This obviously referred to Whitaker's office at the Atlantic-Pacific Railway Tunnel Company in Denver's Railroad Building.

27. Francis Schlatter, "The Two Years' Pilgrimage," in *The Life of the Harp in the Hand of the Harper*, ed. and comp. Ada Morley (Denver: privately published, 1897), 13–14.

28. Ibid., 165.

29. Ibid., 127–28.

30. Ibid., 129.

31. Ibid., 127.

32. The first eight children of François and Madeleine Schlatter are listed in Gil Alonso-Mier's *François Schlatter: l'homme aux 100 000 guérisons* (Paris: Arqa éditions, 2006), 101. They are Ignace (born in 1836), François Joseph (1839), Martin (1840), François Antoine (1842), Madeleine (1845), Marie-Anne (1848), Régine (1851), and François (1853), who died early.

33. *LH*, 141.

34. Ibid., 160.

35. Ibid., 158.

36. Ibid., 161–62.

Chapter Two: Pilgrimage

1. *LH*, 80.

2. *RMN*, February 1, 1903.

3. *LH*, 29

4. Ibid.

5. Ibid., 17.

6. Ibid., 30.

7. Ibid., 31.

8. Ibid., 16.

9. Ibid., 38.

10. Ibid., 40. Original copy: "to-morrow."

11. Ibid., 42.

12. Ibid., 40. Original copy: "any one."

13. Ibid., 48.

14. In *Life of the Harp*, Schlatter states that the stream into which he sank was a tributary of the Washita River (48), but he meant the Arkansas River, which flows eastward through the state of Arkansas to the Mississippi.

15. Ibid., 49.

16. Ibid., 50.

17. Ibid., 51

18. Ibid., 52. Original copy reads: "bed bug."

19. Conger Beasley Jr., *Messiah: The Life and Times of Francis Schlatter* (Santa Fe, NM: Sunstone Press, 2008), 47.

20. *LH*, 52.

21. The kangaroo court episode appears in *Life of the Harp*, 52–54.

22. Ibid., 57.

23. Ibid., 56.

24. Ibid., 58. More than one version of this story exists. Schlatter neglected to mention anything about working in the deputy's home in *Life of the Harp*, but Harry Magill, in *Biography of Francis Schlatter* (22–23), took this information from Schlatter's interview with a *Denver Times* reporter in 1895. Magill was incensed that the deputy sheriff had "virtually resurrected slavery and trifled with the law," but Schlatter never expressed resentment over this clearly inappropriate use of prisoner labor.

25. Magill, *Biography of Francis Schlatter*, 24. The original sentence continues: "I asked Him why He made me go in that direction, when before it had always been the other way, but He told me to go on; it was not for me to quarrel with the Father, so I obeyed."

26. *LH*, 60.

27. Schlatter told reporters in 1895 that he had begun to comprehend his destiny through visions he experienced in the Hot Springs jail. While there, he said, "I had visions during many nights[.] In one night I beheld thirty-five. They were like a panorama, following one after another. They showed me clearly events which have already been fulfilled and others yet to come. The work is to be greater." Magill, *Biography of Francis Schlatter*, 26.

28. Ibid.

29. *LH*, 65; Magill, *Biography of Francis Schlatter*, 27.

30. [Charlie Reuben Stedman], *Life of Francis Schlatter, the Great Healer or New Mexico Messiah* (Denver: privately published, 1895), 6.

31. Ibid.

32. Stedman, *Life of Francis Schlatter*, 7; Magill, *Biography of Francis Schlatter*, 31. In *Life of the Harp*, Schlatter speaks of "devils" (70).

33. Joseph Emerson Smith, reminiscence in *Denver Catholic Register*, July 24, 1941. Smith indicates that this story came to the *Denver Post* by telegraph in the summer of 1895, and that the *Post*'s editor wanted him to meet with Schlatter and verify it. Smith saw Schlatter often during the 1895 healing sessions, but never stated whether or not the story was true.

34. *LH*, 79.

Chapter Three: The Desert Messiah

1. Fitz-Mac (Fitzjames McCarthy), "The 'Christ Man' of Denver," *The Great Divide* 12 (November 1895): 253.

2. The full story can be found in "Imitator of the Christ in New Mexico," *AMD*, July 17, 1895. Will Hunter wired a condensed article to Denver's *Rocky Mountain News* on the sixteenth, and both papers came out with a story

the next day. Then, on August 4, the *News* published Hunter's original story, under his byline, with a some variations and additional material ("What Gift Has This Man of Marvels?").

3. *AMD*, July 21, 1895; *RMN*, August 4, 1895.

4. *AMD*, July 23, 1895.

5. Ibid., July 18, 1895; *RMN*, July 18, 1895.

6. *RMN*, August 4, 1895.

7. *AMD*, July 21, 1895; *RMN*, July 21, 1895. For information on Melchior Werner, see *History of New Mexico: Its Resources and People* (Los Angeles, Chicago, New York: Pacific States Publishing, 1907), 529, and Howard Bryan, *Albuquerque Remembered* (Albuquerque: University of New Mexico Press, 2006), 99. Melchior's wife, Josefa, and Schlatter's stay at her home are mentioned on page 203 in Bryan's book.

8. Quoted in Thomas J. Steele, S.J., *Works and Days: A History of San Felipe [de] Neri Church, 1867–1895* (Albuquerque, NM: Albuquerque Museum, 1983), 108.

9. *AMD*, July 20, 1895.

10. *RMN*, August 7, 1895.

11. Ibid.

12. *AMD*, July 27, 1895; see also ibid., July 26, 1895.

13. Ibid., July 25 and 27, 1895.

14. Ibid., July 27, 1895. For Schlatter's comment about the photographer's broken plates, see *RMN*, August 24, 1895.

15. Many newspaper articles from 1895 include physical descriptions of the healer, and they vary widely. Here's a sampling. *Height:* 6 feet (*AMD*, July 17, and *RMN*, August 4), 5 feet 9 inches (*RMN*, July 18), and 5 feet 9 or 10 inches (*RMN*, August 23). *Eye color:* deep blue (*RMN*, August 4), steel-gray (*RMN*, August 24), pure blue (*DT*, September 18), and light blue (*DR*, September 19). *Hair:* brown (*RMN*, July 17) and black, tinged with gray (*RMN*, August 24). *Hands:* large and soft (*DR*, September 18), rough (*DT*, September 18), unusually large (*DR*, September 19), and large, soft, and flexible (*DT*, October 3). *Feet:* 13 inches by 4¾ inches (*AMD*, July 25), shoes enormous (*DR*, August 23), and broad (*DR*, September 19). *Teeth:* prominent gap in upper teeth (*AMD*, July 21), and two missing upper teeth (*RMN*, August 4, and *DR*, August 23).

16. *History of New Mexico*, 1040. For an account of Hadley's evening with Schlatter, see *AMD*, July 27, 1895.

17. *History of New Mexico*, 534, 541.

18. Ibid., 546–47, contains a lengthy biography of Summers as well as his portrait.

19. *Progressive Men of the State of Montana* (Chicago: A. W. Bowen, n.d.), 58–59. Bovard, who served for several years as a mission superintendent in New Mexico for the Methodist Episcopal Church, eventually became presi-

dent of Montana Wesleyan University. See also Rev. Thomas Harwood, *History of New Mexico Spanish and English Missions of the Methodist Episcopal Church from 1850 to 1910* (Albuquerque, NM: El Abogado Press, 1910).

20. *AMD*, August 10, 1895. Will Hunter's questioning of Schlatter also appears in the same newspaper article.

21. Ibid., August 11, 1895.

22. Ibid., August 10, 1895.

23. Ibid., August 13, 1895.

24. Fitz-Mac, "The 'Christ Man' of Denver," 253. Later published in *Life of the Harp*, 90.

25. *AMD*, August 16, 1895; *RMN*, August 16, 1895; *DT*, August 17, 1895.

26. *AMD*, August 18, 1895. Original: "every one."

27. Ibid.

28. Ibid., August 21, 1895.

29. Ibid.

30. Ibid., August 22, 1895. Will Hunter, who reported the story, stated that Schlatter asked the Indian in Spanish if he had a handkerchief, and the man replied no. Then a woman in the room offered hers. It's possible that Schlatter was familiar enough with Spanish to ask such a question, though Hunter also suggested that the healer could speak Zuni (*AMD*, July 23, 1895), which is unlikely.

31. Ibid.

32. Ibid.

33. *Santa Fe Daily New Mexican*, August 22, 1895; *AMD*, August 23, 1895; *RMN*, August 23, 1895.

34. *Denver Catholic Register*, July 24, 1941.

35. Ibid.

36. Ibid. I have changed the numeral "40" to the word "forty" in the original quote.

37. Ibid.

38. Ibid.

39. Ibid.

Chapter Four: Healer of the Multitudes

1. Joseph Wolff, "The Healer in Denver," *LH*, 104.

2. All four of Denver's major newspapers covered the story of Schlatter's arrival, which appeared in each paper on August 23, 1895.

3. *Santa Fe Daily New Mexican*, August 22, 1895; *RMN*, August 23, 1895; *DP*, August 23, 1895. The *Denver Post* was the first to refer to "Smith" as L. E. Ryan and stated that he met the healer in Colorado Springs. This mysterious figure is first mentioned in the *Rocky Mountain News*, August 23, 1895, as hailing from Salida, Colorado; he was also said to be from Colorado Springs (*DP*, August 23, 1895), and joined the healer in Albuquerque (*RMN*, Septem-

ber 22, 1895) as a railroad man (*RMN*, September 20, 1895). In addition to the train ride, he stayed with Schlatter at the Union Hotel on arriving in Denver and slept with him for two nights afterward (*RMN*, August 24, 1895).

4. *DR*, August 23, 1895.

5. *DP*, August 23, 1895. The *Denver Republican* quoted Schlatter slightly differently: "No, indeed, I never have been married. I have no family. I have no relatives."

6. *Denver Catholic Register*, June 21, 1945. I am indebted to Patrick Fraker for finding Kern's name in the Colorado Springs city directory for 1940.

7. *RMN*, August 24, 1895.

8. *DP*, August 23, 1895. In the original, the quote reads: "It is in here, in here."

9. Ibid.

10. *DT*, August 23, 1895.

11. *AMD*, August 11, 1895.

12. *Santa Fe Daily New Mexican*, August 22, 1895; *RMN*, August 23, 1895.

13. The healer stated he would resume healing on September 16 and leave for Chicago six weeks later (*RMN*, September 8, 1895); would leave for Chicago on November 16, and a ticket had been sent for his use (Ibid., September 17, 1895); would never return to Denver once he "starts for the lakes" (*RMN*, September 22, 1895); was directed by the Father to go to Chicago (*DT*, October 3, 1895); would gather disciples and establish a church at a later time (*DR*, September 19, 1895); and would probably visit England and France (*RMN*, September 8, 1895).

14. *RMN*, September 16, 1895.

15. Thomas F. Dawson, "Francis Schlatter—Denver Healer of the '90s," *The Trail* 11 (October 1918): 12–13.

16. Ibid.

17. Ibid., 13.

18. *DT*, September 16, 1895; *RMN*, September 17, 1895.

19. Millard Everett, "Smith Scooped on Story of 'Healer' because of Accident on Mountain," *Denver Catholic Register*, July 31, 1941. Schlatter's clothing is described in the *Denver Times*, September 18, 1895. Smith's story of his fall and subsequent scolding by his editor is recounted in the *Denver Catholic Register*, July 31, 1941.

20. *DT*, September 16, 1895.

21. *RMN*, September 17, 1895.

22. *DT*, September 16, 1895. Harry Webber appears in a photograph taken during Schlatter's healing sessions by W. A. White, the event's "official" photographer. See Magill, *Biography of Francis Schlatter*, facing page 163.

23. *DT*, September 17, 1895. All other quotes from the second day's healing session are from the same source.

24. *DP*, September 19, 1895.

25. *DT*, September 18, 1895.

26. Ibid., September 17, 1895.

27. *DP*, September 19, 1895. I removed a comma after "Christ."

28. *RMN*, September 17, 1895.

29. *DT*, September 19, 1895.

30. *RMN*, September 23, 1895.

31. *DP*, September 18, 1895.

32. *RMN*, September 23, 1895.

33. Of the seventy or so cases described in Denver newspapers, some 30 percent mentioned rheumatism and another 25 percent paralysis—which likely referred to limbs too painful to move and thus, in most cases, was probably also due to rheumatism or arthritis. Six percent of the sufferers complained of deafness, 10 percent of blindness. The remaining 30 percent consisted of people with various ailments, including skin cancer, kidney stones, tuberculosis, heart failure, asthma, breast cancer, tumors, and mental illness. The sampling is not scientifically valid, but it does offer a rough glimpse at the distribution of ailments people brought to the healer.

34. *DT*, September 19, 1895.

35. Ibid.

36. Ibid., October 12, 1895.

37. *RMN*, November 12, 1895. Schlatter's complete wording, after the man asked why, is "Shall I tell you, do you desire me to tell you right here, before all these people?"

38. *DR*, November 13, 1895. From time to time Schlatter borrowed the archaic language of the King James Version of the Bible.

39. In Matthew 12:25, Jesus rebukes the Pharisees, who have accused him of casting out demons in Beelzebub's name. He makes it clear that only God has that power. Schlatter turned the passage on its head. "In these latter days," he states, only Beelzebub can cast out devils, while servants of God, like himself, cannot.

40. *DR*, October 26, 1895.

41. *DT*, September 21, 1895. One doctor, Mary E. Bates, took a distinctly enlightened view. She planned to investigate the healer for herself; was not prejudiced against him or for him; and thought there "might be certain kinds of human tribulations and ills" he could help.

42. *RMN*, October 7, 1895.

43. Ibid.

44. Books on this subject are too numerous to catalog, but two good studies are Robert C. Fuller, *Alternative Medicine and American Religious Life* (New York: Oxford University Press, 1989), and Norman Gevitz, ed., *Other Healers: Unorthodox Medicine in America* (Baltimore: Johns Hopkins University Press, 1988).

45. *RMN*, October 18, 1895.

46. *DT*, October 22, 1895.

47. *DP*, October 19, 1895.

48. Charles R. Stedman, "A True Story of the Early Life of an Eastern Boy and His Accomplishments in the West," 130–37, unpublished memoir in my possession. Stedman wasn't the only writer to plagiarize newspaper accounts. Harry Magill borrowed large chunks from Denver's newspapers for his *Biography of Francis Schlatter*.

49. *RMN*, October 20, 1895.

50. *DP*, October 19, 1895.

51. *DR*, October 22, 1895. Other newspaper articles dealing with the handkerchief scam are *DT*, October 26, 1895; *RMN*, October 30, 1895; and *RMN*, November 11, 1895. The final postponement to November 14 is mentioned in the *DT*, November 4, 1895.

52. *DR*, October 24, 1895.

53. *RMN*, November 8, 1895.

54. *RMN*, November 11, 1895.

55. Ibid.

56. Ibid.

57. Ibid.

58. Dawson, "Francis Schlatter," 13.

59. *RMN*, November 28, 1895.

60. Dawson, "Francis Schlatter," 14. The owner of Kuykendall's had a different recollection about Butte's purchase—and much closer to the event—than Clark did more than twenty years later. The owner said that Clark told him he needed a "perfectly gentle" white horse. The owner "thought at once of 'Old Butte,' and when the horse was brought in from the pasture he was just the one wanted by Mr. Clark" (*RMN*, November 28, 1895). I have modified the punctuation in the original sentence, adding a comma after "yes" and replacing a semicolon with a period and new sentence.

61. *RMN*, November 11, 1895.

62. *DT*, September 26, 1895. I have changed "O" in the original to "Oh."

63. *DR*, November 11, 1895.

64. *RMN*, November 11, 1895.

65. Ibid.

66. *DT*, October 22, 1895.

67. Paul Gale Chappell, "The Divine Healing Movement in America" (Ph.D. diss., Drew University, 1983), 73.

68. Ibid., 274.

69. *DT*, October 22, 1895. The original text reads "hold onto Him" and includes the spelling "Saviour."

70. *Colorado Springs Gazette*, November 13, 1895.

71. *RMN*, November 15, 1895.

72. Ibid., November 14, 1895.

73. Ibid.

74. *DP*, November 15, 1896.

75. The note is reproduced in the *Rocky Mountain News*, November 15, 1895; W. T. Stead, "The Story of Schlatter, Healer of the West," *Borderland: A Quarterly Review and Index* 3 (1896): 65.

76. *RMN*, November 14, 1895. Joseph A. Connor, a grain merchant from Omaha, and his party also tried to get a hearing with Schlatter. They wanted him to stay over in Omaha for a few weeks before continuing on to Chicago. Connor fared no better with Fox than the St. Louis man (*RMN*, November 14, 1895; *DP*, November 14, 1895); but the healer treated Connor's fifteen-year-old daughter for asthma, which Connor believed would be a permanent cure (*RMN*, November 15, 1895). I have changed punctuation here, replacing a comma with a period and new sentence, and adding a dash.

77. Ibid.

78. Ibid.

Chapter Five: "Father takes me away"

1. *RMN*, November 15, 1895.

2. *DP*, November 14, 1895.

3. *Denver Catholic Register*, June 21, 1945. According to Millard Everett, the *Register*'s regular columnist who had interviewed Joseph Emerson Smith about Schlatter in 1941 and maintained a vital interest in the healer, this was the first time Leonard Kern had ever told the story of that nighttime flight.

4. *DP*, November 14, 1895.

5. Ibid.

6. Ibid.

7. Ibid.

8. *Denver Catholic Register*, August 28, 1941.

9. Ibid.

10. Ibid. The original uses an Arabic numeral for "eleven."

11. *RMN*, November 15, 1895.

12. Clarence Clark directly stated that this meeting took place to address the selling of places in line (*RMN*, November 18, 1895). However, since Clarence Clark, Joseph Wolff, and the Foxes all knew that Schlatter would disappear that night, and were committed to helping him, the meeting was more likely a final planning session for the deception they were about to launch. This became apparent to at least one reporter two weeks later, who wrote: "It has been the opinion of quite a number of persons that Mr. Clark knew more of the healer than he has been willing to make known. He has stated at different times that he did not know the whereabouts of Schlatter, but it is [improbable] that the healer has not communicated with any of his Denver friends since leaving the city. The programme was for Schlatter to journey by slow stages to New Mexico without attracting the

attention of the public but he was too well known to get off so easily" (*RMN*, November 28, 1895).

13. Alexander Rooney established his ranch in 1860. Although the size of its acreage has been considerably reduced since then, it received a Centennial Farm Award in 1987 as one of Colorado's oldest continuously operating historical ranches. Listed in the National Register of Historic Places, the ranch remains in the hands of the Rooney family—now five generations from its founder. For an inside look at the history of the ranch and its past and present owners, see "Historic Rooney Ranch: Established 1860" (2006), http://www.rooneyscustomfloors.com/history.html.

14. *RMN*, November 17, 1895.

15. *DP*, November 15, 1895; *RMN*, November 15, 1895. Much of the information about Rooney's invitation came from shoemaker John Boucher, who knew Schlatter well in 1892–93 and became acquainted with Alexander Rooney at that time too. It's entirely possible that Rooney was a part of the conspiracy, allowing people to believe Schlatter was on his ranch. In fact, Joseph Wolff set up an elaborate ruse in Boulder that convinced a *Denver Times* reporter that the healer was at the Wolff home—a story that may have caused the newspaper considerable embarrassment (*DT*, November 22, 1895).

16. *RMN*, November 15, 1895; *DP*, November 15 and 16, 1895; *DT*, November 16, 1895.

17. *RMN*, November 16, 1895.

18. *DT*, November 16, 1895. The story of a man registering himself in a Beatrice, Nebraska, hotel as Francis Schlatter can be found in the *Denver Post*, November 15, 1895.

19. *DP*, November 16, 1895.

20. Ibid., November 18, 1895.

21. Charmaine Ortega Getz, *Weird Colorado: Your Travel Guide to Colorado's Local Legends and Best Kept Secrets* (New York: Sterling Publishing, 2010), 24. See also "The Tolstoi of the West," *Kansas City Star*, August 5, 1905.

22. Charles N. Whitman, the owner of the LS Ranch in Tascosa, Texas, purchased the healer's new saddle from the Leonard-Scheck Saddlery Company in Denver. He and Clarence Clark spent $120 for Schlatter's horse, clothing, and gear (*RMN*, June 12, 1897).

23. *RMN*, November 24, 1895; *Pueblo Chieftain*, November 24, 1895.

24. *RMN*, February 1, 1897.

25. Ibid., November 23, 1895.

26. *Colorado Springs Gazette*, November 28, 1895.

27. *RMN*, November 28, 1895.

28. *Albuquerque Daily Citizen*, December 13, 1895. The *Daily Citizen* states that, after spending the night in Springer, New Mexico, Schlatter left for Ocate, several miles southwest, on his way to Albuquerque. But it's much more likely he traveled northwest to Cimarron, then took the Cimarron

Canyon freight road up into the Sangre de Cristos to Moreno Valley. There he visited Elizabethtown, which lay at the valley's north end, then crossed the valley and made his way down Taos Canyon to Ranchos de Taos.

29. *Santa Fe New Mexican*, December 31, 1895. For some reason, this story did not appear until the end of December 1895, but it describes a visit that took place in Velarde (also called La Joya), in the southeastern tip of Rio Arriba County, about December 12. Velarde's location, between Taos and Española, puts Larragoite's ranch squarely on Schlatter's path down the Rio Grande, and events before and after pinpoint the visit in early December. Another element of confusion is that the *existing* town of La Joya, Socorro County, lies well south of Albuquerque—which doesn't make sense in the context of Schlatter's journey. Confirming evidence comes from the *Santa Fe New Mexican*, December 28, 1895, which states that Mariano Larragoite, "of Velarde, Rio Arriba county," entertained Schlatter.

30. *Santa Fe New Mexican*, December 31, 1895.

31. Ibid.

32. In *Life of the Harp*, 118, Schlatter states that his journey from Denver to Datil took exactly seven weeks and six days, placing his arrival on January 7. Ada Morley also confirmed January 7 as the date of the healer's arrival, and she gave March 29 as the date of his departure (*RMN*, June 12, 1897).

33. Puzzled as to how Schlatter could have found her ranch, she asks, "You must have seen the men who had my letter to Mrs. Summers inviting you to rest here?"—to which he answers, "No" (*Life of the Harp*, 116).

34. *AMD*, February 13, 1896. The article states: "The night he left Denver he mailed a letter to one of his nearest friends in Albuquerque, telling the latter when and where to meet him, near the little Mexican village of Peña Blanca."

35. *Santa Fe New Mexican*, December 31, 1895.

36. Newspapers contributed to the confusion over Schlatter's whereabouts at the end of December and into early January. Several state incorrectly that he visited Gallup. The December 28 *Albuquerque Daily Citizen* predicted that Schlatter would stop by Gallup "in the vicinity of Fort Wingate." The next day Portland's *Morning Oregonian* said that he was already there. Then, on January 2, the *Santa Fe New Mexican* stated that Schlatter spent New Year's Day on a ranch four miles from Gallup and planned to go to Mexico and into South America. If so, he could not very well have been seen by an eyewitness, as he was, heading south from Acoma on December 31. The only possible way he could have visited Gallup on New Year's Day would have been to take the railroad there and back, along with his horse, which is highly unlikely.

37. *RMN*, January 14, 1896. The *Albuquerque Morning Democrat* of January 3, 1896, states that Schlatter "was at San Jose, close to Cubero on the line of the Atlantic & Pacific." This was most likely La Vega de San Jose, about ten miles west of Cubero Station and ten miles north of Acoma.

38. *RMN,* January 14, 1896.

39. Ibid.

40. *Santa Fe New Mexican,* January 30, 1896.

41. Ibid. In the original, "sir" is not capitalized. All quotes from the conversation between Sol Block and Francis Schlatter are from the same source.

42. Ibid. Based on his conversation with Block, Schlatter expressed an odd, and certainly heretical, understanding of these fundamental Christian concepts. He believed that, presumably on the Day of Judgment, souls in hell would be released and have an opportunity to reform. However, those in purgatory or heaven remained there forever. Thus he turned the traditional functions of hell and purgatory on their heads, and denied the role of purification and release that gives purgatory its name.

43. Ibid. The novelty of this interpretation for its time was noted by Mary Sullivan, an archaeologist at the Colorado Historical Society. "Reasons for abandonment of large portions of the Southwest have probably been around since the ruins were discovered," she wrote, "but [not] seriously discussed in print, as far as I know, by anthropologists or archaeologists until the second decade of the 20th century.... [Schlatter] seems to have beaten the 'experts'...by some 17 years!" (Mary Sullivan to David N. Wetzel, email message, September 14, 2010).

Chapter Six: Winter Retreat

1. *Longmont (CO) Ledger,* June 18, 1897.

2. In 1897 Morley alluded to the people living on the ranch the year before as "myself, the cook, [and] the cowboys, down to the German boy we had" (*RMN,* June 12, 1897).

3. *LH,* 113.

4. Ibid., 114.

5. The early pages of Morley's chapter "Teachings in Retirement" in *Life of the Harp* contain a number of initially obscure allusions to a "pledge made to my higher self" in Denver; the Via Dolorosa; the death of fear; a "higher death"; and Paul's conversion on the road to Damascus. Taken together, they combine to suggest that Ada's answered prayer to see Schlatter again, and to serve as his host, involved giving up something from her past. I can only conclude that this was her grief-driven search for meaning, often tinged with skepticism toward traditional Christianity ("Then I realized the situation and saw defeat," 115).

6. Ibid., 113.

7. Henry Wood, *Ideal Suggestion through Mental Photography: A Restorative System for Home and Private Use Preceded by a Study of the Laws of Mental Healing* (Boston: Lee & Shepard, 1893).

8. Fergusson, "The Prophet Who Disappeared."

9. *LH*, 121.

10. Ibid., 125.

11. Ibid., 127.

12. Ibid., 167.

13. Ibid., 122–23. Morley refers here probably to the adepts, or "masters," who appear in theosophical thought, which postulates that all religions have their origin in a now-lost primordial system of unified belief. The true standard-bearers of this ancient religion, either undying or reincarnated, are the mystic adepts. See Bruce F. Campbell, *Ancient Wisdom Revived: A History of the Theosophical Movement* (Berkeley: University of California Press, 1980).

14. *LH*, 123. I have changed the spelling in the full sentence from "O, no" to "Oh, no."

15. Ibid., 163.

16. Ibid., 131.

17. Ibid., 138.

18. Ibid., 124.

19. Ibid., 159.

20. Ibid., 129.

21. Ibid., 130.

22. For Schlatter, the "kingdom" does not refer to the Kingdom of God, or heaven, but to the one thousand–year earthly reign of God that many Christians today call the "Millennium." This he regarded as heaven, a state of mind, which becomes an external reality in the New Jerusalem (Ibid., 135).

23. Cleaveland, *No Life for a Lady*, 112–13. Agnes Cleaveland states that "an old friend and business associate of my father's" became a court-appointed guardian of the estate. This was Manly Chase, but after a serious falling out with Chase, her mother, Ada, relied on Henry Miller Porter, with whom she corresponded regularly. She appealed to Porter for justice in the civil case over her property, not for herself but to protect the children's inheritance, specifically in letters dated September 6 and 18, 1900 (Box 7, File M, Collection 501, Henry Miller Porter Papers, Colorado Historical Society). See also Darlis A. Miller, *Open Range: The Life of Agnes Morley Cleaveland* (Norman: University of Oklahoma Press, 2011), 29, for further information on this issue, including "a long, drawn-out legal battle…involving a succession of lawyers, guardians, and judges, to make certain that Agnes, Ray, and Lora had sufficient money for their support and education."

24. Agnes Cleaveland tells a story about Raymond's asking her to help him release the cattle from the partner's pen one night, and how close they came to injury and possibly death. See Cleaveland, *No Life for a Lady*, 190–93.

25. *LH*, 152.

26. Ibid., 149. I have made a significant word change in this quotation, since it is mistaken and makes no sense in the original. "There are the self-sold slaves," he says, referring to small trades people. "They are a different class from the industrial slaves," which refers to wage earners working for other companies. Then, in the original, he says: "The latter are now helpless, I know. Have I not been one?" Of course, he was a cobbler, working for himself, not a wage earner. Thus, I changed "latter" to "former" in the text.

27. A good overview of Populism—and still valuable after many decades, even if superseded by more recent books—is Richard Hofstadter's *The Age of Reform* (New York: Alfred A. Knopf, 1955). Hofstadter's analysis of anti-Semitism in the Populist movement has come under attack by recent historians as unfairly tarring a single group within a widespread evil, but he correctly identifies Populist anti-Semitism through a ubiquitous image in Populist literature—"a map of the world dominated by the tentacles of an octopus at the site of the British Isles, labeled: 'Rothschilds'" (78). This image appeared regularly in Herbert George's *The Road*, a distinctively Populist Denver newspaper, and one that supported Schlatter.

28. *RMN*, September 23, 1895.

29. Ibid., 150.

30. Ibid., 151.

31. Though there is no documentation for the statement that Morley made nocturnal notes of her conversations with Schlatter, the depth and character of detail in *Life of the Harp* suggest it. If she did, those notes may have been lost in the fire that took Agnes Cleaveland's home in Berkeley (Cleaveland, *No Life for a Lady*, 316–17).

32. Ibid., 151.

33. Ibid., 176.

34. Ibid. I have changed 'Caesar's Column' and 'Looking Backward' in this quotation to italics and removed the single quotation marks.

35. Ibid. I have removed the word "But" from the beginning of this sentence.

36. Ibid., 128.

37. Ibid., 140. In the original, the sentence reads: "It is the only solution of conditions, apparent inequalities."

38. Ibid., 141.

39. Ibid., 140.

40. Ibid.

41. Ibid., 170.

42. Ibid.

43. Ibid., 171.

44. Ibid., 141.

45. Ibid., 167.

46. Ibid., 184.

47. Ibid., 185.

48. Cleaveland, *No Life for a Lady*, 14–15.

49. *LH*, 185.

50. Ibid. I have modernized the spelling of "can not."

51. Ibid. 184. The original phrase is: "They have been talking it quietly…"

52. *Weekly Rocky Mountain News*, March 12, 1896.

53. *LH*, 186.

54. Ibid.

55. *Albuquerque Daily Citizen*, March 20, 1896.

56. Ibid.

57. Ibid. I have brought the spelling of "to-morrow" up to date.

58. Ibid., 189.

59. Ibid.

60. Ibid.

61. Ibid.

62. Ibid., 190.

63. Ibid.

64. Ibid.

65. Ibid., 129.

Interregnum: Into Mexico

1. *El Paso Times*, May 17, 1896.

2. Dispatches from the American consulate at Ciudad Juarez, Mexico, for the period August 10, 1891–October 13, 1897, Roll 5, Publication M184, NARA.

3. *RMN*, July 5, 1897.

4. *Colorado Springs Weekly Gazette* (quoting *New York Times*), June 17, 1897. I have placed a comma after "circulated beforehand."

5. *Denver Catholic Register*, August 28, 1941. This is the only known reference to medals inside Schlatter's coat. Whether religious or honorary, they obviously held some meaning for him.

6. *RMN*, June 6, 1897.

7. *George's Weekly* (formerly *The Road*), February 7, 1903. George states: "We knew Schlatter in his day and entertained him in our home."

8. In *No Life for a Lady*, Cleaveland treats her mother's belief in Schlatter, and her refusal to accept his death, with a certain amount of disdain. "She was now sure that a short-cut into the Eternal City was to be opened through the tortuous mountains of human struggle" (224).

9. *RMN*, June 12, 1897.

10. *Longmont (CO) Ledger*, June 18, 1897.

11. *RMN*, June 12, 1897.

12. *DR*, June 14, 1897.

13. *RMN*, June 12, 1897.

14. Ibid., June 21, 1897.

15. *DP*, March 29, 1903. Reporters for the *Albuquerque Morning Democrat* (July 21, 1895) and *Rocky Mountain News* (August 4, 1895) also noted the healer's missing teeth.

16. In all likelihood, Hewett met the *jefe politico*, or *alcalde*, G. R. Azeariel, in the Palacio Municipal in 1906 rather than in Azearial's home. For one thing, guardianship of the healer's effects—initially—was a legal responsibility. In summer 1897 much discussion had ensued about their disposition, including an auction. Schlatter's supporters in Denver—Clarence Clark, Charles Whitman, and Mrs. Lucien Scott—had made their interest in them known. As a result, Azeariel eventually offered them to the State Historical Society of Colorado, subject only to the decision of the district judge in Ciudad Juarez. Clark approached the historical society's director, Thomas Ferril, who sought Governor Alva Adams's approval, but nothing happened—perhaps because they had the same concern over sensational publicity that Hewett later showed for the Museum of New Mexico (*RMN*, June 21 and July 5, 1897; *DP*, September 7, 1897). By 1922, when Hewett returned to Mexico—this time to Nuevo Casas Grandes, not the old village—he found Azeariel's *son* in possession of the copper rod (Fergusson, "The Prophet Who Disappeared"). For literary purposes, in *Campfire and Trail*, Hewett simply collapsed father and son, and two different towns, into one. He was not, after all, writing history—though others took it as such.

17. Another Schlatter researcher, who had obtained the official investigative report, told me that the cause of death was murder—a "slashing wound." Phone conversation with G. Weston DeWalt, March 3, 1993.

18. *LH*, 173.

Chapter Seven: "These men were imposters"

1. Quoted in Dawson, "Francis Schlatter," 14.

2. *Cleveland Leader*, June 9, 1897. I have removed quotation marks and capitalization from "healer" in the boarder's comment. The wording in the original reply is: "In fact he is here present with us," and I have added the dash following "introduce to you."

3. For an excellent study of one group of the unemployed, Coxey's Army, see Carlos A. Schwantes, *Coxey's Army: An American Odyssey* (Caldwell, ID: Caxton Press, 1985).

4. Elias Ammons, "A Tribute to Thomas Dawson," *Colorado Magazine* (November 1923), 1, gives an overview of Dawson's life. My article, "Thomas F. Dawson: History's Journalist," in the Colorado Historical Society's newsletter, *Colorado History Now* (February 2002), 3, briefly discusses both Dawson and the Dawson scrapbooks, which contain the only known extant body of original newspaper articles on Schlatter's imposters.

5. Dawson, "Francis Schlatter," 14. From internal evidence, it's clear that

Dawson interviewed Clarence Clark in 1916, two years before he published the article.

6. Ibid.

7. The earliest extensive coverage of Schrader thus far can be found in the *Galveston (TX) Daily News*, particularly August 8, 11, 13, 14, 15, and 16, 1896. See also the *Perry (IA) Bulletin*, May 7, 1896. For comments about his clothing and apparel, see the *Galveston Daily News*, August 14, 15, 1896, and *Arizona Republican*, September 26, 1901. Information about his early life and background comes from the *Galveston Daily News*, August 15, 1896. On his early churches and the colonies of worshippers in New Mexico, see the *Arizona Republican*, August 14, 1905, and the *Oakland Tribune*, July 6, 1907.

8. *Galveston Daily News*, August 16, 1896.

9. *DT*, December 6, 1900.

10. *Anaconda (MT) Standard*, March 21, 1901.

11. Ibid. McLean came up with the burial-and-resurrection idea back in 1898, when he first began his ministry. See the *Perry (IA) Daily Chief*, May 12, 1898.

12. McLean's death in October 1909 generated newspaper coverage around the nation, perhaps more than any since Schlatter's death in Mexico twelve years earlier. While extensively treated in the *Denver Post*, October 21 and 22, 1909, many newspapers weighed in on the subject. See, for example, *Los Angeles Times*, October 22, 1909; *Omaha World-Herald*, October 22, 1909; and *Chicago Tribune*, October 22, 1909.

13. *Oakland Tribune*, October 25, 1909. Here Kunze discusses his first healings at age eight in Switzerland, and he claims that he healed ninety thousand people of yellow fever in Calcutta.

14. The earliest known accounts detailing the appearance of August Schrader with his partner, Jacob Kunze, are found in the *St. Louis Post-Dispatch*, May 7 and 8, 1908. The healers' subsequent travels and use of aliases are recounted in the *Fort Wayne (IN) News*, September 11, 1908, and *Denver Post*, May 9, 1909. They were also arrested for swindling a man of twelve hundred dollars to fund an expedition to Honduras in which they expected to find a twenty million–dollar treasure that would support their plan for a South Sea colony. See the *Nebraska State Journal*, August 27 and 30, 1910. News articles several months later linked the treasure with Francis Schlatter and the so-called Freeland Islands, thought to lie five hundred miles south of Tahiti. See the *Denver Times*, June 29, 1911, and *Marion (OH) Weekly Star*, July 1, 1911.

15. *Marion (OH) Weekly Star*, July 1, 1911. Kunze states that his mother's maiden name was Schlatter and his father's Dowie, and he tells an outlandish tale about being the brother of John Alexander Dowie, who founded Zion City in Illinois—and who was born and raised in Australia, not Switzerland. Kunze often went under the name of Dowie and seemed to be obsessed with the famous healer. For Dowie, see Philip L. Cook, *Zion City*,

Illinois: Twentieth-Century Utopia (Syracuse, NY: Syracuse University Press, 1996), and Chappell, "Divine Healing Movement in America," 283–340.

16. *Hastings (NE) Daily Tribune,* October 25, 1909. The healers borrowed the name of their island from *The Port of Missing Men,* a novel by Meredith Nicholson (Indianapolis: Bobbs-Merrill, 1907).

17. Schlatter's comments about making his way to the battlefields of France can be found in the *Denver Times,* April 4, 1916. For his arrest, see the *Denver Times,* May 13, 1916, and *New York Times,* May 28, 1916. Schrader's arrest in Los Angeles appears in the *Fort Wayne (IN) Sentinel,* June 12, 1916. For coverage of the hearing, see *New York Times,* June 14, 1916, and *Denver Post,* June 14, 1916.

18. *DP,* June 14, 1916.

19. *Reno Evening Gazette,* June 28, 1916.

20. *Mansfield (OH) News,* October 19, 1916; *New York Times,* October 29, 1916.

21. *Los Angeles Times,* February 28, 1917. See also the *Denver Post,* February 28, 1917, for another account of Schrader's death.

22. U.S. Department of Justice, Office of the Superintendent of Prisons, U.S. Penitentiary, McNeil Island, Inmate Case Files (1899–1920), Box 42, Record Group 129, NARA. Kunze served from March 18, 1917, to June 1, 1918, having had his eighteen-month sentence reduced to fifteen months for good behavior. The prison record indicates he had three sons: Frank, Emil, and Rudolph.

23. *DP,* October 19, 1922.

24. "Meet Me in St. Louis," *Newsweek,* May 7, 1945, 62.

25. For a look at Dawson's life, see Ammons, "Tribute to Thomas Dawson," 1, and Wetzel, "Thomas F. Dawson."

26. Francis Schlatter, *Modern Miracles of Healing: A True Account of the Life, Works, and Wanderings of Francis Schlatter, the Healer,* comp. Ella F. Woodard (Kalamazoo, MI: privately printed, 1903), 8. The chronology here is disjointed. The author probably means to say that he attended school in London after *returning* from Columbia, not before he arrived there at the age of two. *Modern Miracles of Healing* is now available online at the Internet Archive location https://archive.org/details/modernmiraclesof00schl. The website lists the book as "Falsely attributed to Schlatter."

27. Ibid., 9–10.

28. Ibid., 10. I have removed the comma from the original phrase "May, 1884."

29. Ibid., 50–51.

30. The church bombing of July 18, 1896, involved the illegal kidnapping of a wrong suspect, Tom McKee, across state lines; abuse of habeas corpus; judicial malfeasance; forced evidence; and biased news reporting. The actual bomber, twenty-six-year-old William Hinson, an irrational young man avenging the death of his sister, killed himself when police finally came for

him. The details can be found in *Portsmouth (OH) Daily Times,* July 2–August 31, 1896.

31. Good Samaritan Hospital, Cincinnati, Medical Records Office, 1896 patient record book, p. 580.

Chapter Eight: "Look at My Face"

1. *Chicago Tribune*, September 5, 1897.

2. *CR,* July 21, 1897.

3. Ibid., August 8, 1897.

4. Ibid.

5. Ibid.

6. Ibid., August 12, 1897. I have spelled out "25" in the quotation and corrected a typographical error, "yars" in the original.

7. Ibid., August 7, 1897.

8. Ibid., August 8, 1897. But a *Chicago Times-Herald* reporter thought differently. "In five minutes, by actual count," he wrote, "Schlatter received seven 25-cent pieces." The reporter projected the profits, at that rate, to be twenty-one dollars an hour. "Financially, Schlatter has struck it rich in Canton," he concluded (*DP*, August 9, 1897, via *Times-Herald*). But this was hardly true. The Canton healer later said that he paid his "secretary and manager" one hundred dollars per month each, which amounted, he said, to 25 percent of the proceeds, or eight hundred dollars a month. But he was toying with reporters—as he often did (*CR*, August 31, 1897).

9. *CR*, November 3, 1895.

10. Ibid., August 1, 1897.

11. *DP*, August 9, 1897.

12. *CR*, August 1, 1897.

13. Ibid. I have changed the wording of a later line, which originally begins, "Well, I tell you, that I believe…"

14. Ibid.

15. Ibid., August 8, 1897.

16. Ibid., August 11, 1897.

17. Mark C. Carnes, ed., *American National Biography*, Supplement 2 (New York: Oxford University Press, 2005).

18. *CR*, August 11, 1897.

19. Ibid.

20. Ibid.

21. Ibid.

22. Ibid., August 12, 1897.

23. Ibid., August 18, 1897.

24. *Pittsburgh Press*, August 20, 1897.

25. *CR*, August 18, 1897.

26. In my research, I haven't found any Ohio newspapers that made this claim.

27. *CR*, August 18, 1897. By her own admission, she *had* seen him. During the healing of her younger sister, Ferris spoke of a neighbor who had run away from home. "I remarked in a joking way," she told reporters, "that perhaps I would do the same. Schlatter laughed and remarked that it was not necessary for me to go alone. It was just an ordinary remark in fun."

28. Ibid.

29. *Pittsburgh Press*, August 19, 1897.

30. *Milwaukee Journal*, August 19, 1897; *North American* (Philadelphia), August 20, 1897; *New Orleans Daily Picayune*, August 20, 1897; *Morning Oregonian* (Portland), August 20, 1897; *Emporia (KS) Daily Gazette*, August 20, 1897; *Bismarck (ND) Daily Tribune*, August 20, 1897.

31. *Akron (OH) Beacon Journal*, August 20, 1897.

32. *CR*, August 21, 1897.

33. Ibid., August 14, 1897.

34. An article in the *Pittsburgh Press*, August 19, 1897, implied that Schlatter was after Ferris for her wealth.

35. *Cleveland Leader*, June 9, 1897. In this sentence, I have removed a comma after "November" and spelled out "Colorado" for "Col." in the original.

36. *CR*, October 20, 1895.

37. Ibid., August 19, 1897.

38. Ibid.

39. *MM*, 51–52. I have changed a semicolon following "could not speak" to a dash for clarity.

40. *CR*, August 29, 1897. For the role of G. C. McAllister, who invited the healer to Chicago and offered to put him and his managers up for two months at a hotel, see the *Chicago Daily News*, August 28, 1897.

41. The Manhattan Beach Hotel, formerly the Hotel Endeavor, sat on the southeast corner of Seventy-Fifth Street and Bond. Built to house members of the Christian Endeavor youth society during the World's Columbian Exposition in 1893, it had more than six hundred rooms and a courtyard larger in area than a football field, in the center of which sat a large, circular, airy pavilion.

42. *CR*, August 31, 1897.

43. Ibid.; *RMN*, August 31, 1897. For Rattlesnake Bill's Liniment, see Dan Hurley, *Natural Causes: Death, Lies, and Politics in America's Vitamin and Herbal Supplement Industry* (New York: Broadway, 2006), 23.

44. *Chicago Tribune*, September 5, 1897.

45. Ibid.

46. Ibid., August 30, 1897.

47. *CR*, August 31, 1897.

48. Ibid.

49. *Chicago Tribune*, September 5, 1897.

50. Ibid.

51. Ibid.

Chapter Nine: The Sparrow's Fall

1. Luverna Comer-Schlatter, "The Story as Told by Mrs. Comer-Schlatter," in *MM*, 118–19.

2. *Chicago Tribune*, September 5, 1897.

3. *Washington Post*, June 1, 1896.

4. Alfred Theodore Andreas, *History of Chicago*, vol. 3 (Chicago: A. T. Andreas, 1886), 542. Thacher was also a pioneer in the founding and expansion of the Baha'i faith in the United States, a belief he became acquainted with at the World's Congress of Religions at the Chicago World's Fair in 1893.

5. *St. Paul Globe*, November 29, 1896; Comer-Schlatter, "The Story as Told," 118.

6. Comer-Schlatter, "The Story as Told," 114.

7. Ibid. 118.

8. *MM*, 59. "It was said," he added, "that if we had them in line they would reach from Manhattan Beach to the City Hall, a distance of nine miles."

9. The story of Gilbert's introduction to the healer in Pittsburgh, and his later employment as manager, appears in *MM*, 58, 64ff.

10. Ibid., 62.

11. *Zanesville (OH) Courier*, January 12, 1898; *Zanesville (OH) Times-Recorder*, January 13, 1898.

12. *MM*, 65–66.

13. *Philadelphia Inquirer*, August 3, 1898.

14. Ibid., July 8, 1898. I have changed "did not" in the quote to "didn't."

15. Bill of indictment, No. 68, *Commonwealth v. Francis Schlatter*, August 2, 1898, Philadelphia City Archives.

16. *Reading (PA) Times*, August 4, 1898.

17. Ibid.

18. Ibid.

19. Bradenburg's obituary can be found in the *New York Times*, December 29, 1905; his museum in Philadelphia is mentioned in several sources, including the *New York Dramatic Mirror*, September 1, 1900, and September 12, 1903; and his work with Mr. and Mrs. Tom Thumb, mentioned on a coin, can be found in the *Numismatist* 11:11 (1898): 228. For the Jolson brothers at the Arch Street Museum, see Herbert G. Goldman, *Jolson: The Legend Comes to Life* (New York: Oxford University Press, 1988), 32.

20. *New York Dramatic Mirror*, September 12, 1903.

21. *MM*, 69.

22. *Evansville (IN) Journal*, September 13, 1898.

23. *Evansville (IN) Courier*, September 21, 1898.

24. Ibid., September 14, 1898.

25. Ibid., September 20, 1898. I have added commas after "besides" and in the phrase "Then, too." I have also joined two words into "sometime."

26. *Atlanta Constitution*, November 23, 1898.

27. Ibid., 75–76.

28. *Galveston (TX) Daily News*, August 8, 1896.

29. *Atlanta Constitution*, November 22, 1898.

30. *Evansville (IN) Courier*, September 20, 1898.

31. *Atlanta Constitution*, November 22, 1898. "Cleatrice" is a mispronunciation made either by the witness or the *Constitution*'s reporter. The correct term is "cicatrix," a scar or fleshy growth over a wound. The mysterious marks on the Atlanta healer's upper palate might have been a result of Schlatter's nearly exclusive diet of field corn during his pilgrimage. In *Life of the Harp*, he says that the skin of his mouth became worn off "from the long period of eating this dry, hard corn" (30).

32. Two deliberate falsehoods in *Modern Miracles of Healing*, Schlatter's claim that he was involved in a Parkersburg train wreck and arrested as a suspect in the Portsmouth church bombing (*MM*, 44–45), could very well be considered alibis by a man who feared his role in the Mexico death scene might be discovered. By linking himself to these events, in other words, he placed himself in the Ohio valley in the summer of 1896, far from Mexico. The claim would have made no sense as the argument of an imposter.

33. We cannot know, of course, whether Schlatter's interpretation of "seventy weeks" in Daniel's prophecy was literal or symbolic.

34. *RMN*, February 16, 1903.

Chapter Ten: The Days of Daniel

1. *LH*, 136

2. *Birmingham (AL) Age-Herald*, January 19, 1899.

3. Ibid., January 17, 1899.

4. Ibid., January 19, 1899.

5. *MM*, 89–90.

6. Ibid., 91. I have added the word "money" to the passage, and changed the original "twelve a.m." [he meant p.m.] to "twelve noon."

7. *Macon (GA) Telegraph*, February 2, 1899; marriage bond between Francis Schlatter and Luverna Coleman (she used her birth name rather than Comer, her previous married name), January 31, 1899, Cullman County Courthouse, Cullman, Alabama.

8. *LH*, 82.

9. Ada Morley to Henry Miller Porter, May 25, 1899, Henry Miller Porter Papers, Colorado Historical Society, Denver. I have added an apostrophe to the word "Schlatters" in the original.

10. *MM*, 93. The loosely rendered quote is from 2 Corinthians 5:17.

11. *Miamisburg (OH) News*, March 28, 1912.

12. *Ohio State Journal* (Columbus), April 23, 1921.

13. *Newark (NJ) Advocate*, September 8, 1899, citing the *Chicago American*; *Chicago Inter-Ocean*, September 8, 1899. The *Inter-Ocean* article makes it sound as if Schlatter's violent episode with the male nurse *followed* Luverna's departure, but logic doesn't support this order of events.

14. *Chicago Inter-Ocean*, September 8, 1899.

15. *Middletown (NY) Daily Press*, March 27, 1900.

16. *Logansport (IN) Reporter*, March 29, 1900.

17. Luverna Schlatter to Hon. H. M. Daugherty, attorney general of the United States, September 3, 1921, FBI case file M1085, Roll 954, FBI Case Files, 1908–1922, NARA.

18. *Miamisburg (OH) News*, March 28, 1912.

19. *Martin, E. v. Columbia Cotton Mills Company*, 1885, Maury County Archives, Columbia, Tennessee.

20. U.S. census, 1900, Center, Howard, Indiana, Roll 377, page 2A, enumeration district 0056 (Provo, Utah: Ancestry.com). The designation "alien" in the census is odd. In 1891 Schlatter submitted a petition for naturalization, which usually resulted in the award of a certificate (see chapter 1, endnote 11). He would not likely have forgotten his status after only nine years. It's possible the district court turned down his petition, though he had waited the required three years for residency. He might also have left for the West before his certificate arrived, leaving him in doubt about his naturalization status.

21. *MM*, 8.

22. Ibid., 10.

23. Ada Morley to Henry Miller Porter, September 13, 1899, Porter Collection, Colorado Historical Society. I have added "the" before the word "truth" and a comma after "glorious." For the sake of clarity, I have replaced "he" with "Schlatter" in the sentence "I am sure Schlatter has spoken the truth."

24. *Daily State Journal* (Parkersburg, WV), May 23, 1900.

25. Ibid. The original states: "Schlatter would then remove his slouch hat."

26. Ibid. In the original, "you're" is written "your'e" and the word "hell" is written as "H——l."

27. *Elyria (OH) Republican*, September 20, 1900. I removed a comma after the word "heaven" in the sentence, "You will find me in heaven, your true and devoted wife." This is not a suicide note, as the comma would suggest,

but a statement that her fidelity would extend into the afterlife. Likewise, her giving up "everything to God" probably refers to shedding her anger and emotional pain.

28. *Washington Post*, December 10, 1900. The original phrase is "imitate the lickness [*sic*] of the Saviour."

29. Ibid. Since Edward Martin was a high-ranking Mason—an organization inimical to the Catholic Church—it would have been odd for him to raise his sons Catholic. Thus it is difficult to believe that John Martin, not Francis Schlatter, would have made this statement. By the same token, Louisa (Gough) Martin was raised a Methodist. I have removed the word "of" in the sentence "That is the simplest and purest of religion."

30. *Williamsport (PA) Gazette and Bulletin,* January 16, 1901.

31. *Washington Post,* January 20, 1901.

32. Ibid.

33. Ada Morley to Henry Miller Porter, August 8, 1900, Porter collection, Colorado Historical Society. I have added the second comma to the original phrase.

34. *Cleveland Leader,* June 9, 1897.

35. *Marion (OH) Daily Star,* March 12, 1901.

36. *Lincoln (NE) News,* March 28, 1901, from the *New York Journal.*

37. Ibid. In the first sentence, I have changed "draughts" to "drafts."

38. The reverse side of Schlatter's portrait includes the words: "Newman Studio, New York. Photographers Association of America. Awarded at National Convention, 1897." Courtesy *St. Louis Post-Dispatch* archives.

Chapter Eleven: "A True Account . . . "

1. *DT,* July 8, 1901.

2. *New York Tribune,* July 4, 1901.

3. *Washington Times,* July 19, 1901.

4. *Washington Post,* July 19, 1901.

5. Ibid.; *Lima (OH) Times-Democrat,* July 19, 1901.

6. *Washington Post,* July 19, 1901.

7. *New York Times,* July 21, 1901.

8. *Scranton (PA) Tribune,* August 26, 1901.

9. *Hamilton (OH) Democrat,* September 3, 1901.

10. Ibid. I have removed a comma after "jacket."

11. *Baltimore Sun,* December 21, 1901.

12. *RMN,* January 30, 1903.

13. *Muskogee (OK) Phoenix,* December 30, 1901. The *Phoenix* got the story from the AP wire, sent out by an unknown Pennsylvania newspaper.

14. Ibid.

15. *MM,* 100.

16. *Hagerstown (MD) Mail,* January 11, 1902.

17. *MM,* 100–101. The original has a typographical error: "settled down."

18. *RMN,* March 17, 1901; *DT,* March 18, 1901; *RMN,* March 18, 1901.

19. *DT,* January 28, 1903.

20. Ibid.

21. *RMN,* January 30, 1903.

22. *Kalamazoo (MI) Gazette,* December 27, 1902.

23. *MM* (title page).

24. The idea that *Modern Miracles of Healing* grew out of Luverna's insistence that her husband prove himself to be the true healer is inferential, not documented. But it makes sense: whether or not her husband was in reality an imposter or the genuine article, it would not have been in his best interests—from his perspective—to expose himself in this way.

25. *RMN,* January 30, 1903. The article quotes a letter sent on July 20, 1902.

26. *DT,* January 28, 1903.

27. *RMN,* January 30, 1903.

28. *DP* editorial, quoted in *George's Weekly* (formerly *The Road*), February 7, 1903.

29. *RMN,* March 2, 1903.

30. This notation can be found on page 44 of the copy of *Modern Miracles of Healing* held by the Library of Congress. A digital copy of the entire book, complete with the penciled notations, is available at https://archive .org/details/modernmiraclesof00schi. As mentioned in an earlier note, this website describes the book as "Falsely attributed to Schlatter."

31. Following his escape from Hot Springs, the author of *Modern Miracles of Healing* states that he walked to Junction City, Kansas, and there "went into a Latter Day Saints' church prayer meeting. I healed several there [and] was offered money for the healing but I would not take it" (19). Newspapers in the Geary County Museum have so far failed to verify such an event, but the curious question is why Schlatter would stretch the truth several hundred miles to explicitly note such a healing—especially since *The Life of the Harp* makes no mention of Junction City but does of Manhattan, Kansas, only a few miles away.

32. *MM,* 21.

33. Ibid. 12.

34. Ibid., 16.

35. Ibid., 16–18. For research into William J. Little and others mentioned here, I am indebted to Donna Miner, who relied on the 1890 Reconstructed Census for Garland County, Arkansas; Greenwood Cemetery Records; and city directories—all available at the Hot Springs Historical Society. Other documents consulted include the *Hot Springs Sentinel* (Garland County Public Library) and the annual reports of 1893 and 1894, by William J.

Little, superintendent of the U.S. Reservation, Hot Springs, Arkansas, National Park Service.

36. Juan Garcia appears in *Modern Miracles of Healing* on page 35, Judge Kerr and Mrs. Fisk on page 40, and Carl Gardner on page 41.

37. *MM*, 40, 43.

38. *LH*, 126.

39. William D. Keel to David N. Wetzel, email message, January 15, 2014. A professor of German at the University of Kansas, Keel received his Ph.D. in Germanic linguistics and specializes, among other things, in German dialectology. Some of the examples he found suggestive of a German grammatical interference are (italics mine): "I went to him and *asked him for the place* [fragte ihn nach der Stelle]"; "*I did not feel this way inclined* [ich war nicht so geneigt]" — although the *feel*, Keel stated, is not German without a reflexive ("feel myself inclined") — and "He *had given up all hopes* [alle Hoffnungen aufgegeben] until his two daughters came to our meeting. Both of them *took lessons of my wife* [nahmen Unterricht von]." The phrases in the text, in order, are from *MM*, 20, 39, 35–36, 28, 52, and 86.

40. *LH*, 160.

Chapter Twelve: God's Leading

1. *MM*, 101.

2. *Los Angeles Times*, October 30, 1903.

3. *Denver Catholic* (later *Denver Catholic Register*), October 17, 1903.

4. Ibid. I have removed a comma after "agricultural lands."

5. Luverna Schlatter to Fred K. Nielsen, Solicitor's Office, U.S. Department of State, September 3, 1922, FBI case file, M1085, Roll 954, NARA.

6. *Battle Creek (MI) Enquirer*, October 24, 1909.

7. Ibid. I have removed a comma after the phrase "tones do not graduate as they should . . ."

8. U.S. census, 1910, Miamisburg Township.

9. Ibid.

10. *DP*, May 12, 1910. In the late 1980s Stan Oliner, a knowledgeable amateur historian and collector, came across the Toledo police report and mug shots in a pile of discarded photographs when the *Denver Post* moved its offices. He donated the materials to the Colorado Historical Society, for which he later served as curator of manuscripts.

11. Marriage record, Box Butte County, Nebraska, November 16, 1912, p. 358, No. 1717.

12. Luverna Schlatter to Fred K. Nielsen, September 3, 1921, FBI case file, M1085, Roll 954, NARA.

13. Luverna Schlatter to H. M. Daugherty, ibid.

14. One piece of information in this flyer (*St. Louis Post-Dispatch* Archives)

led to a decades-long puzzle—and a final intriguing coincidence. The flyer states that Schlatter, on his railroad trip from Albuquerque to Denver in 1895, had ridden "in a Special Car in charge of General Eames, who supervised the Ben Buller Estates." Over the years, I searched extensively for both "Eames" and "Buller" to no avail. Then, in 2010, Tim Blevins, manager of special collections for the Pikes Peak Library District, suggested to me that "Buller" might actually refer to General Benjamin Butler. I looked into Butler's life and discovered that his son-in-law was Adelbert Ames, former Civil War general and Mississippi governor and senator. Furthermore, General Ames supervised Butler's large estate, which was carved from the Mora Land Grant in New Mexico. Ames's private records show that he was, in fact, in New Mexico during the time of Schlatter's ministry there (Box 17, folder 2, Account books, Ames Family Papers, Sophia Smith Collection, Smith College). Altogether, the pieces of information here make for a remarkable coincidence—one made even more powerful by the "Buller" and "Eames" misspellings.

15. Ibid. The sentence originally had semicolons between the listing of churches.

16. *Ohio State Journal* (Columbus), April 21, 1921.

17. Ibid. I have lowercased "his Call" to reflect modern usage.

18. Ibid., April 23, 1921.

19. *St. Paul (MN) Globe*, November 29, 1896.

20. For a study of the Emmanuel Movement, see Sanford Gifford, *The Emmanuel Movement: The Origins of Group Treatment and the Assault on Lay Psychotherapy* (Boston: Boston Medical Library in the Countway Library of Medicine, 1998).

21. *Boston Sunday Advertiser*, n.d. [ca. July 24, 1921].

22. Ibid., ca. July 17, 1921, clipping in FBI Investigative Case Files, 1908–1922, M1085, Roll 954, NARA.

23. Ibid.

24. *Boston Sunday Advertiser*, n.d., FBI case file, M1085, Roll 954, NARA.

25. Passenger manifest information card, U.S. Department of Justice, Immigration and Naturalization Service, Washington, D.C. Copy in author's possession.

26. Luverna Schlatter to Fred K. Nielsen, Solicitor's Office, U.S. Department of State, September 3, 1921, FBI case file, M1085, Roll 954, NARA.

27. Luverna Schlatter to H. M. Daugherty, August 8, 1921, FBI case file, M1085, Roll 954, NARA.

28. Luverna Schlatter to H. M. Daugherty, August 5, 1921, enclosed in materials sent by Department of Justice to Department of State, August 15, 1921, FBI case file, M1085, Roll 954, NARA.

29. Internal report from Office of the Solicitor, U.S. Department of State, to director, September 7, 1921, FBI case file, M1085, Roll 954, NARA.

30. Luverna Schlatter to Fred K. Nielsen, September 3, 1921, NARA.

31. *DP*, July 7, 1922.

32. Ibid., July 9, 1922. The original states: "and he was going to Pikes Peak . . ."

33. *Salt Lake Tribune*, October 18, 1922.

34. *St. Louis Post-Dispatch*, October 18, 1922.

35. *St. Louis Globe-Democrat*, October 18, 1922.

36. *St. Louis Star-Times*, October 18, 1922.

37. Coroner's inquest, Case No. 1218, October 19, 1922, St. Louis, and certificate of death for Francis Schlatter (Missouri Bureau of Vital Statistics). Whether truly ignorant of Francis's Alsatian parents or in denial, Luverna somehow overlooked his statement in *Modern Miracles of Healing* that Edward was his *stepfather*, not his natural father (*MM*, 8). In any case, it's unlikely that Luverna's grasp of her husband's life and motives will ever be fully known.

38. U.S. census, 1930, Miamisburg, Montgomery, OH, Roll 1857, page 23A, enumeration district 0164 (Provo, UT: Ancestry.com).

39. Luverna Comer-Schlatter died on April 27, 1932, and is buried in Oakwoods Cemetery, Chicago (Illinois, Deaths and Stillbirths Index, 1916–1947 [Provo, UT: Ancestry.com]). Thomas Martin died in Miamisburg, Ohio, on August 24, 1939 (Probate Court of Montgomery County, OH, Case 86411).

40. *Newsweek*, May 7, 1945, 62.

41. *St. Louis Post-Dispatch*, April 26, 1945. The original quote uses a number for "forty years."

42. Thirty years later, in 1976, the copper rod became the symbol of a landmark agreement between the Museum of New Mexico and the School of American Research over ownership and use of their mutual collections (Kenn Ulrich, "Healing Rod Symbolizes Landmark Settlements," *El Palacio* 83:1 [Spring 1977]: 42–43). Then, another thirty years later, the rod was placed on public view in 2009 as a part of the Museum of New Mexico's new exhibition on New Mexico history following a renovation of the Palace of the Governors in the early twenty-first century (Frances Levine, "A Place Like No Other," *El Palacio* 114:2 [Summer 2009]: 41).

MUCH OF THE LITERATURE about Francis Schlatter has been forgotten or rendered ephemeral because the healer made such a brief mark on American history. Nevertheless, his legacy has been enduring, and from time to time researchers and writers have rediscovered him, written about him, and then seen their efforts, like their subject, lapse into obscurity. Nevertheless, the body of work about him warrants documentation if only because it reveals wide differences in how historians and biographers approach a legendary figure.

Aside from major works about Schlatter discussed in the text, a diverse literature on Schlatter appeared from the first decade of the twentieth century through the 1940s, when the healer was reborn through the efforts of Agnes Morley Cleaveland and Edgar Hewett. One of the earliest treatments of him can be found in a portrait of healers down through the centuries entitled *Fads or Facts?* by Mesha Rayon (Chicago: MS Publishing, 1908), a study of mystical healing that, in Schlatter's case, castigates doctors and ministers who dismissed him out of hand.

In 1910 the popular playwright William Vaughn Moody drew upon Schlatter's ministry in Denver to produce a play called *The Faith Healer*. A review of Moody's play in *The Independent* (May 5, 1910) panned it for not living up to the drama of the real thing—and, in the process, demonstrated the reviewer's fascination with the healer: "Whether he escaped from the crowd for rest and further spiritual vigils in the wilderness," the reviewer said, "or whether, having lost faith in his powers he fled in despair, will never be known." (Incidentally, Denver playwright Frank X. Hogan also produced a play about Schlatter in the early 1980s called *The Denver Messiah*, and Hogan left it up to the audience to decide the outcome.) Four years after Moody's play, Frank L. Packard published *The Miracle Man*, a novel about a group of ne'er-do-wells who attempt to exploit a deaf, mute, and blind healer and end up being transformed by him. The novel relates to Schlatter only tangentially, but it is an effective Christian parable in which the miracle man's death becomes the only way out of a predicament in which his now-reformed exploiters find themselves.

Thomas Dawson, who was intrigued enough about Schlatter to collect several newspaper articles on his imposters, interviewed one of the healer's closest friends and benefactors, Clarence Clark, in 1916. Dawson published the interview two years later as "Francis Schlatter—Denver Healer of the '90s," *The Trail* 11 (October 1918). Another intriguing account also appeared in 1918—Vance Thompson's article "Strindberg and His Plays" in *The*

Bookman: A Review of Books and Life 47 (June 1918): 361–69. Thompson states that Strindberg, whom he met in fin de siècle Paris, told him of befriending Schlatter in a Latin Quarter *crèmerie* in 1896—and proved it by showing Thompson a picture of Schlatter from that year's French edition of the *Review of Reviews*. "I feared him," Strindberg said, "and he pursued me—a strange and awful man." The man Strindberg feared—if, indeed, he really believed him to be Schlatter—was instead Paul Hermann, a German American painter (Evert Sprinchorn, ed., *Inferno, Alone, and Other Writings* [Garden City, NY: Doubleday/Anchor Books, 1968], 156–57, 341).

Also in 1918 Benjamin Warfield published *Counterfeit Miracles* (New York: Charles Scribner's Sons), a reasoned argument against the claims of faith healers. He mentions Schlatter only once and confuses him with one of his imposters, Jacob Kunze, who was convicted of mail fraud in 1916.

In 1921 Dr. C. S. Bluemel, a Denver physician, mentioned Schlatter in a lecture on faith healing in "Faith Healers, with Special Reference to Aimee Semple McPherson" (*Colorado Medicine* 18 [July 1921]: 143–46). Bluemel cited the case of Denver's "pioneer newsboy," Owens—a person Schlatter treated but "whose crippled form is daily seen on the streets at the present time." Bluemel accepted news reports that Schlatter had died in an insane asylum—a piece of undocumented hearsay—or was practicing in Nebraska at that time as either the original healer or one of his impersonators.

One of the most intriguing feature stories to appear on Schlatter during this period came in 1928 from Frank McClelland, a *Rocky Mountain News* reporter who had covered the healer in 1895 ("Denver's Famous Healer Francis Schlatter and His Many Imitators," *Rocky Mountain News* supplement, March 18, 1928). McClelland had managed to gain Schlatter's trust in 1895 even though he didn't believe the healer had divine gifts. Now, more than thirty years later, McClelland showed himself to be utterly confused by Schlatter's impersonators, but he fondly described a moment in 1921 when he demolished the claims of a hapless Schlatter imitator who tried to impress him.

Finally, Gene Fowler, a one-time Denver news reporter–turned–author, published a mock-heroic study of Colorado's famous historical figures, including Schlatter, in *Timber Line: A Story of Bonfils and Tammen* (New York: Covici & Sons, 1933). Fowler, whose masterful blend of history, legend, and personal experience could be considered a pioneering work in creative nonfiction, explored the world of Colorado's past through the lens of the *Denver Post* and its owners. He treats the healer respectfully.

The early 1940s, of course, saw the publication of Agnes Cleaveland's *No Life for a Lady* (Boston: Houghton Mifflin, 1941; reprint, Lincoln: University of Nebraska Press, 1977), in which "The Healer Comes to Datil" appears; and Edgar Lee Hewett's *Campfire and Trail* (Albuquerque: University of New Mexico Press, 1943), containing Hewett's "The Copper Rod"—both of which are discussed in the Prologue. In the same year that Agnes Cleaveland published *No Life for a Lady*, Haniel Long included a chapter on Francis Schlatter in *Piñon Country* (New York: Duell, Sloan and Pearce, 1941), part of a series edited by Erskine Caldwell called American Folkways. Long, a New Mexico writer, drew most of his material from *The Life of the Harp in the Hand of the Harper*.

Beginning in 1947 articles on Schlatter appeared from time to time in Sunday newspaper supplements, magazines, and periodicals. Richard Gordon's "Miracle Man" (*Rocky Mountain News*, October 26, 1947) draws upon Agnes Cleaveland's story of the healer and shows that Gordon had also read *The Life of the Harp*, an unusual feat for most feature writers. William Jones Wallrich, another writer familiar enough with *The Life of the Harp* to quote some of Schlatter's sayings from it, nevertheless relied upon hearsay and rumor in practically every other respect. His "'Christ Man' Schlatter" (*The New Mexico Historical Record*, Vol. 4, 1949–50) contorts the facts and mangles chronology while uncritically accepting "folkloric" statements as fact. Wallrich reworked his article twenty years later, but with little improvement, for *Frontier Times* (February–March 1971). Wesley B. French did a much better job of keeping his facts straight for "Denver's Mystery Messiah" (*Denver Post Empire Magazine*, September 30, 1951) and was the first writer to offer a few facts about Schlatter's imposters—even suggesting that the man who died in St. Louis in 1922 may have been the true healer. But, in the end, he states: "The case of Francis Schlatter, Denver's healer and messiah, remains an unsolved mystery."

In the mid-1950s Estella DeFord Graham postulated that Schlatter "was a modern saint," an assessment reflected in the title of her article, "Francis Schlatter—A Fool for God" (*Fate*, October 1955). Drawing substantially on Agnes Cleaveland's book, Graham took Schlatter's last words to Ada Morley seriously, concluding that if at some future date Schlatter and Morley played their roles in New Jerusalem in the Datil Mountains, "I would like to be there." Four years later, *Rocky Mountain News* drama editor Frances Melrose, who made a career writing historical features, reviewed Schlatter's life in "Denver's 'Messiah' of the 1890s" (January 11, 1959). She expanded on the story twenty-three years later in "The Mystery of the Faith Healer" (*Rocky Mountain News*, April 25, 1982).

In 1971 Olive Bertram Peabody mixed a substantial body of new fact with generous dollops of speculation in "Did Francis Schlatter Lose Faith?" (*The West*, April 1971), an intriguing question that she failed to address in the article itself. Like Wesley French, Peabody briefly followed Schlatter's imposters, ending with speculation that the St. Louis healer, whose body lay forgotten for twenty-three years, was Schlatter's. "It was a mystery within a mystery!" she wrote. Another writer to speculate on Schlatter's fate was Larry Cantwell ("The Healer in Denver," *Denver Westerners Brand Book*, 1971),

whose error-ridden article gets more right factually about Schlatter's imposters than it does about the healer himself. Cantwell reprinted the article
in the *Rocky Mountain Herald*, a historical tabloid, on October 27, 1973.

One of the best popular articles to appear on Schlatter is Alice Bullock's
"Francis Schlatter: A Fool for God" (*El Palacio*, March 1975), whose title,
a Catholic concept, borrows from Estella Peabody's. Bullock's conclusion
similarly leaves open the possibility of Schlatter's divinity. "If he were a
Christ or not," she wrote, "certainly his reception was consistent with what
could be expected if Jesus were to walk today in the market place." Bullock
is the first to incorporate Agnes Cleaveland's and Edgar Hewett's stories
into an account of the healer's last months. She repeated the story more
briefly in *The Squaw Tree: Ghosts, Mysteries and Miracles of New Mexico* (Santa
Fe, NM: The Lightning Tree—Jene Lyon, Publisher, 1978). In 1976 Ruth
Eloise Wiberg, in *Rediscovering Northwest Denver: Its History, Its People, Its Land-
marks* (Denver: Northwest Denver Books), relied on local materials, a bit of
dubious information, and her writer's imagination in recounting Schlatter's
colorful 1895 appearance in Denver's suburb of Highlands.

In 1978 Schlatter's biography reached what was likely its broadest audience as a segment of "Footnote People in American History" in David
Wallechinsky and Irving Wallace's *The People's Almanac #2* (New York: William Morrow). Contributing author Stephen G. Hughes wrote a balanced
account of the healer's life, noting early influences on Schlatter's thought
and recognizing the importance of *The Life of the Harp* to Schlatter's mission, though not mentioning it by name. Curiously Hughes states that "the
record of [Schlatter's] discourses was lost" when Ada Morley's ranch house
burned down—neither of which happened—but he otherwise makes a
cogent argument for the eclipse of Schlatter's story in the twentieth century.

The only well-documented, scholarly article to appear on the healer so
far is Ferenc M. Szasz's "Francis Schlatter: The Healer of the Southwest"
(*New Mexico Historical Review* [April 1979]), recently revised, retitled, and
included as a chapter in Szasz's *Larger Than Life: New Mexico in the Twentieth
Century* (Albuquerque: University of New Mexico Press, 2006). Szasz, who
died in 2010, remains the only American scholar to place Schlatter's life
and thought within the social, religious, and political context of the late
nineteenth century, a transition period that justifies the chapter's inclu-
sion in a twentieth-century study. He also touches upon, for the first time
since the 1897 publication of *The Life of the Harp*, the character of Schlatter's
mind—his interest in Populism, reincarnation, spiritualism, prophecy, and
New Thought.

Soon after Szasz's article appeared, Rev. Thomas Steele, SJ, elaborated
on Schlatter's emergence as a healer in New Mexico ("Brief Career of the
'Healer,'" *Impact: The Albuquerque Journal Magazine*, November 11, 1980). The
article emphasizes the battle of Albuquerque's newspapers over Schlatter's
character and motives. Steele concludes that Schlatter, while not a charla-

tan, was definitely "mentally unbalanced"—primarily for acknowledging that he was the Messiah. A year later, Steele offered a brief inside look at Schlatter through entries from the diaries of Albuquerque's Catholic priests, in *Works and Days: A History of San Felipe Neri Church, 1867–1895* (Albuquerque, NM: Albuquerque Museum, 1983).

Robert H. Shikes, M.D., gives a concise, accurate, and balanced synopsis of Schlatter's healing work in *Rocky Mountain Medicine: Doctors, Drugs, and Disease in Early Colorado* (Boulder, CO: Johnson Books, 1986), though he repeats C. S. Bluemel's unsubstantiated claim that the healer was reported to have died in an insane asylum. Mike Flanagan, writing a historical feature called Out West, pulled together standard published material for a short biography of Schlatter that is liberally sprinkled with errors and ends with typical unanswered questions about the healer's fate (*Denver Post*, December 20, 1987). More reliable, though drawing largely on Szasz, is a very brief account of the healer in Marta Weigle and Peter White, *The Lore of New Mexico* (Albuquerque: University of New Mexico Press, 1988).

In 1989 Norman Cleaveland performed an important service to the memory of Francis Schlatter by republishing his grandmother's *The Life of the Harp in the Hand of the Harper* in a volume called *The Healer: The Story of Francis Schlatter* (Santa Fe, NM: Sunstone Press). Cleaveland sandwiched the century-old work between his mother's "The Healer Comes to Datil" and Edgar Hewett's "The Copper Rod" from their respective books. Cleaveland's opinion of the healer is guarded: "Charlatan, miracle worker or deluded mystic?" he writes. "Few contemporaries can ever decide and history itself is not sure." In 1990 Stephen J. Leonard and Thomas J. Noel raised an equally intriguing question—that of "when Francis Schlatter died and where he is buried"—in their respectful nod to him in *Denver: Mining Camp to Metropolis* (Niwot: University Press of Colorado).

In 1992 a breezily written, anonymous article in *The Sights, Sounds, and Tastes of Denver* (vol. 1, no. 5) offered an overview of Schlatter's career—including the era of Schlatter's imposters—sprinkled with highly imaginative facts and invented conversations. Another article, this one by Tom Sharpe for *New Mexico Magazine* (March 1993), tells of Schlatter's death in Mexico but paradoxically includes the 1910 police mug shot of the "posthumous" Francis Schlatter (see Appendix), sans explanation. Another view, more concise and accurate, appears in Phil Goodstein's *The Seamy Side of Denver* (Denver: New Social Publications, 1993). A year later, Kenneth Jessen wrote a snippet of a biography on Schlatter for *Bizarre Colorado: A Legacy of Unusual Events and People* (Loveland, CO: J V Publications, 1994), which ignores current sources. On the other hand, the New Mexico historian Marc Simmons drew upon conversations with Norman Cleaveland to produce a remarkably clear, concise, and accurate overview of Schlatter in "Healer on Horseback" (*Santa Fe Reporter*, May 26–June 1, 1999). Keith Chamberlain took a different tack in 2004, concentrating exclusively on

Schlatter's Denver ministry in a well-written, in-depth, and informative look at the healer's work ("Francis Schlatter: North Denver's Mysterious Healer," *North Denver Tribune,* July 1, 2004).

In 2006 Gil Alonso-Mier, a French professor of English literature, published the first full-length work on Schlatter in more than a century. The first volume of this two-volume set, *François Schlatter: l'homme aux 100 000 guérisons* (Paris: Arqa éditions, 2006) consists of *The Life of the Harp* translated into French, and a biography; the companion volume, *L'Évangile de François Schlatter* (*The Gospel of Francis Schlatter*), contains Schlatter's thoughts and ideas as well as people whom he treated, his supporters, letters, and a reprint of Otis Spencer's *Francis Schlatter Cyclus.* The Alonso-Mier work, which argues for Schlatter's divinity, is a summation of sorts and a definitive assemblage of material on Francis Schlatter.

Conger Beasley Jr.'s *Messiah: The Life and Times of Francis Schlatter* (Santa Fe, NM: Sunstone Press, 2008) is notable as the first full-length English-language biography of the healer to appear in more than a hundred years. For that reason, it marks an important turning point in the public's awareness of Schlatter. Unfortunately, however, the book suffers from misquotations, inadequate documentation, and liberally inserted fictional material. Bill Blanning's *Denver's Extraordinary Faith-healing Messiah* (New York: Eloquent Books, 2009) is an unreliably transcribed compilation of articles from Denver's newspapers on Schlatter's healing ministry of 1895, but it contains no interpretation or analysis of events.

Perhaps fittingly, the latest publication on Francis Schlatter is a thoroughgoing study of his imposters. In "Marketing a Messiah: Denver's Divine Healer and His Inspiration of Entrepreneurs," in *Enterprise and Innovation in the Pikes Peak Region* (Colorado Springs, CO: Pikes Peak Library District, 2011), Tim Blevins ably expands our knowledge of Charles McLean, August Schrader, and Jacob Kunze—though he kindly left the task of uncovering the final posthumous Schlatter to me.

INDEX

animal magnetism, 79
Armageddon (or apocalypse), 100, 112, 128, 221; "a little war" by U.S. would spark, 189; occurring in 1899, 113, 123, 174, 175; unrealized, 189, 201. *See also* Daniel, book of
Armijo, Mariano, 58
Atlantic-Pacific Railway Tunnel Company, 19, 23
Audenried, Charles Y., 167

Battle Creek (Mich.), 206
Bellamy, Edward, and *Looking Backward*, 113
Bible, the (King James Version), 60, 79, 89, 109, 113, 151; copy of, found with skeleton, 7, 8, 13, 122; and "doubting" Thomas in Gospel, 175; no dates in, per Schlatter, 187; and reincarnation, 31, 113–14
Biography of Francis Schlatter. See Magill, Harry B.; see also *Modern Miracles of Healing*, subtitle of
Blackwell's Island (New York City), 192
Blavatsky, Helena, 109
Block, Sol, 102–3
bombing of church. *See* Portsmouth (Ohio), and church bombing
Bordeaux (Tenn.), Louisa Martin's home in, 159, 182–83, 212
Boucher, John W., 25
Bovard, Charles L., questions Schlatter about his divinity, 60
Bradenburg, Charles A., 170, 256n19

Brady Lake, Kent (Ohio), 151–52, 155–56
Bryan, William Jennings, 111
Buffalo Lithia Springs (Va.), 178, 179. *See also* Comer, Luverna
Bullard, Barry, 225
Bulmer, Thomas, 122
Butte (Schlatter's white horse), 84–85, 100, 108; in healer's escape, 91–92; in *Modern Miracles*, 144, 203; origin of name, 84; overloaded with gear, 117–18
Byrnes, John F., 161

Canton (Ohio), 149, healer. *See* Schlatter, Francis *posthumous*
Caples, Richard, 14
Capron, Adolphus B., 95
Casas Grandes (Mexico), 7–8, 13–14, 124–25, 234
Charney, Michael, 225, 226
Chicago World's Fair, 26, 134; and Ferris Wheel, 152
Christian Science, 26
church bombing. *See* Portsmouth (Ohio), and church bombing
Clark, Clarence, 13, 133, 197; holds special gathering for healer, 69–70, 111; investigates Schlatter imposters, 135; obtains Schlatter's horse, 84–85, 243n60; orders casting of copper rod, 98; role of, in healer's escape, 98
Cleaveland, Agnes Morley, 7, 12, 216; meets with Edgar Hewett in 1945, 5, 9
Cleaveland, Norman (son of Agnes), 5

Colonia Juárez, Mexico (Mormon settlement), 127–28
Columbia (Tenn.), 143, 145, 180–83; Masonic Temple in, 183, 185
Comer, Guy (Luverna's son), 178, 181, 207
Comer, John (Luverna's first husband), 178
Comer, Luverna (also Comer-Schlatter), 163, *179*, 197, *209*; attitude of, toward spiritualism, 210, 214; beaten by husband, 187, 191; as Chicago healer, 163–64; and "Christ method" of healing, 163, 178; death of, 263n39; and doubts about husband's identity, 181, 193–94; healed at Buffalo Lithia Springs, 164, 178; and husband's death, 214–15, 263n37; influence of, on husband's legacy, 221; marriage of, 178, 257n7; renews faith in husband, 194–95; searches for husband (1922), 213; visits with Mary Fox in 1902, 194–95
conspiracy. *See* disappearance of Francis Schlatter
copper rod, 5–9, *12*, 118, 122; as divine compass, 121; first seen at Gatza household, 98; meaning of, 216–17; at Museum of New Mexico, 9–11, 263n42; prospectors discover, 13–14; and spiritual strength, 6. *See also* Clark, Clarence; Hewett, Edgar
Corbin, "Aunt" Sally, 20–21
Crystola (Colo.) spiritualist community, 98

Daniel, book of, 112, 113, 116, 128, 174–75, 179; and verse 9:26, 115
Datil (N.M.), 5, 13, 102, 117; as promised site of New Jerusalem, 7, 115, 197

Daugherty, H. M., 212
Davis, Alexander Jackson, 20
Dawson, Thomas, 135, 141; scrapbooks of, 141–42, 221
DeSantis, Diana, 10–12
Dickinson, Edward, 85
Dickson, Laura, 165–66
disappearance of Francis Schlatter, 1–3, 90–98; conspiracy regarding, 95, 98, 244n12; departure at night, 91–92; reaction of crowd to, 92–93; reasons for, 95, 96
Donnelly, Ignatius, and *Caesar's Column*, 112–13, 196
Dowie, John Alexander, 86, 139
Driscoll, Dan, 38
Driscoll, Harry, 92
Dye, Tom, 57–58

Ebersheim, Alsace (France), 30, 31, 143, 185
Eddy, Mary Baker, 26
Elizabeth (Colo.), Schlatter discovered near, 97
Emmanuel Movement, 210–11
Everett, Millard, 223

Ferris, George Washington, 152
Ferris, Margaret (wife of George), 152; meets Schlatter *posthumous,* 152; elopes to Pittsburgh, 153–54; ends relationship, 154
Festival of Mountain and Plain, 81, 84
Fisk, Mrs. Archie Campbell, 203
Fitz Mac. *See* McCarthy, Fitzjames
folklore about Schlatter, 55, 56, 79; and discovery of healer's body, 7, 12; and horse Butte, 84–85
Foote, Frank M., and healing of daughter, 88
forensic analysis of two Schlatters: color of eyes, 226; differences in scientific approach, 225–26;

foot size, 227; hand size, 226–27; height, 226; marks and scars, 227–28; pendulous earlobes, 225, 229; and scope of evidence, 226. *See also* Schlatter, Francis; Schlatter *posthumous*

Fowler, Gene, 5

Fox, Anna (daughter of Edward), 68, 198

Fox, Edward, 56, 68, 83; brings Schlatter to Denver, 57; builds fence for crowds, 71; committed to insane asylum, 194; rejects St. Louis offer, 88–89; role of, in healer's escape, 91–94; tormented by news of healer's death, 122

Fox, Mary (wife of Edward), 68; receives letter from healer in 1902, 198; visits with Luverna Comer-Schlatter, 194–95

Francis Schlatter Institute (New York City), 189–90, 195, 210

Franco-Prussian War, 31–32

Galagher, James R., 202–3

Garcia, Juan, 53, 202

Gardner, Carl (mentioned in *Modern Miracles*), 203

Gatza, Charles, 98

Gaul, Maggie, 152

George, Herbert, and *The Road*, 122–23, 124, 236n22

George, Robert M., 225

Gilbert, Walter S.: called effeminate, 170–71; defends healer's authenticity, 172–73; as healer's manager, 165–66, 177–78, 179

God's leading, 115, 205, 214

Goff, Alonzo A. and Nancy Jane, healing letter of, *73*

"gold bugs," 110–11

Good Samaritan Hospital (Cincinnati), 144, 173–74, 216; patient

record in, for John E. Martin, 145, 185

Gough, Thomas, 183; operates sailor's mission in London, 186

Greenback movement, 20

Gunther, J. A., 202–3

Hadley, Walter C., 58

handkerchiefs (healing), 72; first use of, 62–63; fraudulent use of, 82–83, 95

Handy, J. P., 87–88

Hanley, Daniel, 95

Hartman, Evelyn, 214

Hauenstein, Henry, 56, 198; describes healing sensation, 56

healing. *See* spiritual healing

Hermosillo ranch (Datil, N.M.), *108*, 109, 116

Hewett, Edgar Lee, 5, 10; acquires copper rod, 9, 216; and Erna Fergusson, 234n19; meets with Agnes Cleaveland in 1945, 5, 9; and story of Schlatter's unmarked grave, 7–9

Hicklin, William, 199–200

Hickson, James Moore, 210–11

Highlands (Denver suburb), 3, 70, 81, *82*

Hollenberg, Benno, 133, 189–91, 210

Hot Springs (Ark.), 35, 38–39, 41, 202, 144, 201; jail in, 42–44; Schlatter's escape from, 45; in *Modern Miracles*, 202

Hunter, Will, 51–54, 58, 62, 63, 100–01, 202; questions Schlatter about his divinity, 60–61

If Christ Came to Chicago, by William T. Stead, 67, 134

Ingersoll, Luther J., 23–24

Ingersoll, Mary, 23–24, 58; estimates Schlatter's height, 24;

notices Schlatter's hacking cough, 24

Ingersoll, Robert G. (husband of Mary), 107

Jarrett, Floyd, 5

Jordan, E. B., 86; tries to discredit Schlatter, 86–87

Kalamazoo (Mich.), 198–99, 200

Karl (unknown German ranch boy), 105, 108, 247n2. *See also* Gardner, Carl

Kern, Leonard, 91

Kerr, Robert, 203

Keystone Hotel (Philadelphia), 166, *167*

Kidd, E. R., 149, 159, 164

Kipley, Joseph, 160, 162

Knapp, O. T., 165–66

Kokomo (Ind.), 181; U.S. census of 1900 in, 185–86

Kunze, Jacob, 138, *141*, 142, 169, 207, 211, 252n15; joins August Schrader, 139, 252n14; mail fraud hearing of, 139; sent to federal prison, 140, 253n22

Lamping, George, 28–29

Lamping, William (son of George), 28–29

Larragoite, Don Mariano, 100, 102

Law of Being. *See* Wilmans, Helen

leading. *See* God's leading

Lengle, Ed, 149, 159, 164

letters, healing, 72, *73*, 89, 200. *See also* Goff, Alonzo A. and Nancy Jane

Life of the Harp in the Hand of the Harper, The, 194–95, 198, 203, 221; compared to *Modern Miracles,* 201–2, 204; and description

of pilgrimage in, 36; map of Schlatter's travels in, *146–47;* no mention of spiritualism in, 156; radical ideas in, 188; Schlatter proposes title for, 6; "Teachings in Retirement" in, 111

Little, William J., 202–3

McAllister, G. C., 159

McCabe, John, 121

McCain's Cemetery (Columbia, Tenn.), 143, 183

McCain's Cumberland Presby-̓ terian Church, 183–84

McCarthy, Fitzjames, 61

McComb, Samuel, 210. *See also* Emmanuel Movement

McLean, Charles, 137–8, 142; death of, 138, 206, 208

Magill, Harry B., and *Biography of Francis Schlatter, with an Account of His Life, Works, and Wanderings,* 142, 194

mail (for Schlatter), 17, 84, 89; and mail fraud, 83, 139–40, 141. *See also* letters, healing

Mancusi, Stephen, 225–26

Manhattan Beach Hotel (Chicago), 159, 162, 163, 164, 255n41

Manitou (Colo.), 97, 157, 185; Schlatter sighting near, 97, 157

Manley, William P., 172

Manzanares, Rick, 124–28

Martin, Edward (husband of Louisa), 143, 180, 182–83; buried in McCain's Cemetery, 184; as Mason, 183, 259n29

Martin, John E. (first son of Louisa Martin), 157, 158; born, 183; in Good Samaritan Hospital patient ledger, 145; possible motives of, 169–70; as sculptor, 145, 184; as stonemason, 183. *See also* Good Samaritan Hospital; Schlatter, Francis *posthumous*

Martin, Louisa (née Gough), 145, 148, 180–83; born, 182; deception of, about Schlatter *posthumous*, 180; emigrates from Canada to Columbia (Tenn.), 183, 185; marriage of, 183; in Bordeaux (Tenn.), 182, 183, 212; in Kokomo (Ind.), 181, 185–86; reunites with Schlatter *posthumous*, 159; speculations about, 186, 208

Martin, Thomas Walton (second son of Louisa Martin), 143, 165, 180, 186, 210, 212, 223; and musical chart, 206; as stonecutter, 183; claims to be Canton healer's half-brother, 159; death of, 263n39; deception of, about Schlatter *posthumous*, 180; lives with Luverna Comer-Schlatter, 215; in *Modern Miracles*, 143; owns monument company in Miamisburg, 207, 215; settles in Miamisburg (Ohio), 215; and wife Catherine, 215

Martin, William K., 116–17

Martino, Silverio, 52–53, 55

Memphis (Tenn.), 144, 151, 164, 216; Schlatter *posthumous* begins healing in (March 1897), 159, 171

mental healing, 80

messiah, return of. *See* Schlatter, Francis; Schlatter, Francis *posthumous*

Miamisburg (Ohio), 183, 207, 215, 223

Middaugh, Lillian, 158, 173; observes mark on Schlatter's nose, 158, 227–28

millennium. *See* New Jerusalem

Miller, William, and Millerites, 196

Modern Miracles of Healing: A True Account of the Life, Works, and Wanderings of Francis Schlatter, the Healer, 142, 145, 146–48, 200, 223; compared to *Life of the Harp*, 201–2; copy of, in Library of Congress, 200, 260n30; mixture of truth and falsehood in, 142–45, 168–69, 184, 186, 193, 202–3, 257n32; narrative voice in, 201–2; no mention of spiritualism in, 156; and Parkersburg (W.Va.) train wreck, 257n32; peculiarities of expression in, 203–4, 261n39; pilgrimage in, 144, 200–201; and Portsmouth (Ohio) church bombing, 144, 145, 253n30, 257n32; as rare autobiography, 221; subtitle of, from Harry B. Magill, 142; title of, from Myron Reed sermon, 142

Morley, Ada McPherson, 5, 13, *116*, 197–98, 220–21; and capitalism, 109–10; and Daniel's prophecy, 115, 180, 186, 189; denies Schlatter's death, 7, 122–23; influence of, on Schlatter's legacy, 221; and New Thought, 105–6; and numerology, 29–30; offers relics of Schlatter's hair, 189; skeptical of death reports, 122–24; and social issues, 106–7; and theosophy, 248n13; travels to Mexico, 124

Morley, Agnes (Ada's daughter). *See* Cleaveland, Agnes Morley

Morley, Loraine (Ada's daughter), 6

Morley, Raymond (Ada's son), 6, 109, 248n24

Morley, William Raymond (Ada's husband), 5

Mount Lebanon Cemetery (St. Louis), 219–20
Museum of New Mexico, 5, 7, 9–10, 251n16, 263n42. *See also* Palace of the Governors

New Jerusalem, 7, 112, 115, 128–29, 175, 197, 216–17, 221; in Datil Mountains, 7, 197, 200; preceded by apocalypse, 112; role of, in human imagination, 221; unrealized, 187, 189, 191, 201
New Thought, 6, 25, 86, 210; and Unity, 213
Norris, William, 85
Nuevo Casas Grandes (Mexico), 125
numerology, 25, 29–30

Pajarito (N.M.), 53
Palace of the Governors (Santa Fe, N.M.), 5, 216; described, 9–10. *See also* Museum of New Mexico
Paralta (N.M.), 51–52
Paris Commune, 32
Parkersburg (W.Va.), 187; train wreck in, 187, 257n32
Pickering, Robert, 225, 229
Piedras Verde River (Mexico), 7, 9, 13
pilgrimage of Francis Schlatter, 35–49, 109, *146–47;* and imagined pilgrimage in *Modern Miracles,* 144, *146–47,* 200–201
Pleitsch, George L., funeral home, 214–15, 216
Pomeroy, Marcus M. ("Brick"): influence of, on Schlatter, 19–20; mining ventures of, 19, 23; and spiritualism, 20
Porter, Henry Miller, 180, 186
Portsmouth (Ohio), and church bombing, 144, 145, 253–54n30

prejudice: and Francis Schlatter, 70, 114; and Schlatter *posthumous,* 151, 169
progressivism, and spiritual healing, 140

Rattlesnake Bill, 160, 162
Reed, Myron, 70, 76, 111, 197. See also *Modern Miracles of Healing,* title of
reincarnation. *See* Schlatter, Francis, ideas of
Revelation, book of, 113, 115
Reynolds, Arthur, 160
Rice, James A., 154–55
Romero, Andres, 58
Rooney, Alexander, 96, 245n
Rooney Ranch: rumored to have concealed Schlatter, 96–97
Roosa, Frank, 139; extradites Kunze and Schrader from Canada, 140
Ryan, L. E. (unknown friend of Francis Schlatter), 67, 68, 71, 184–85, 240n3
Ryan, William, 21; death of, 21–22

St. Elizabeth's Hospital for the Insane (Washington), 192
St. Louis (Mo.), 213–15; Schlatter *posthumous* dies in (1922), 213; unburied bodies found in (1945), 215–16, 223
Sauerwein, Frank, 48, 108
Schlatter, Francis (*see also* Schlatter, Francis *posthumous*)
—*characteristics of:* archaic language, 79; clairvoyance, 57; clothing and dress, 53, 71; disappearances, 1–2, 27–28, 91–92; German accent, 26, 161; healing methods, 71–73 (*see also* handkerchiefs; mail); healing power,

89; medals of, inside jacket, 122, 250n5; missing upper teeth, 21, 38, 124; physical description, 21, 239n15; physical marks, 158, 173–74; portrait, *77*, *158*; possible tuberculosis, 24–25; speaks broken English, 161–62, 204; tolerance, 78; unusual shoe and hand sizes, 58; and wooden bead rosary, 122
— *ideas of:* astral projection, 27, 156; capitalism, 109–10; claims to be reincarnated Christ, 3, 45, 103, 112; divine destiny, 30, 44; hell and purgatory, 247n42; mother reincarnated, 114; Populism, 38, 46, 111; prejudice, 114, 169; prophetic healing, 24, 74; providence, 26–28, 84, 89; reincarnation, 31, 113–15, 169, 198; spiritualism, 20, 25; will return as Messiah, 45, 60–61, 100, 103, 221 (*see also* apocalypse; Bible; New Jerusalem)
— *life of (arranged chronologically):* early life, 31–33; in Long Island, 20–22; arrives in Denver in 1892, 19, 23; as cobbler in Denver, 23–29; departs Denver in 1893, 29; route of pilgrimage around West, 144; in Mojave Desert, 47, *48*; begins fast in New Mexico, 53; undertakes fast-breaking meal, 61–62; departs Albuquerque in private Pullman car, 63; in retreat at Hauenstein house, 68–69; opens ministry at Fox home, 71–73; to depart for Chicago on November 16, 69, 83, 87; called as witness in handkerchief fraud case, 83, 87; last day of healing in Denver, 1, 87; farewell letter,

90, 91, 92, 93; disappearance of, from Denver, 1–3, 90–98; journey south to New Mexico, 98–101, 246n29, 246n36; arrives at Morley ranch on January 7, 1896, 101, 106, 246n32; predicts possessions would be found in 1897, 123; on Mexican border, 121; effects of, 13–14, 251n16
Schlatter, Francis *posthumous. See also* Martin, John; Schlatter, Francis
— *characteristics of:* accepts money for his work, 150–51; accused of insincerity, 161; alcoholism of, 187, 188; arrogant and willful, 157; attempts suicide, 181; chemist, 215; crosses hands in healing, 150; defends drinking whiskey, 151, 157; dresses well, 160; hands, 171, 192; healing methods, 160–61; impulsive, 159, 179; lecturer, 215; physical description, 161, 170–71, *171*, 188, 190, 193, 207, 208, 225; physical marks, 158, 173–74, 207, 257n31; physically abuses Luverna, 187, 191; possible confidant of Francis Schlatter, 203; sculptor, 145, 184, 207–8; speaks perfect English (as described), 161, 190; tuberculosis, 209; unusual speech, accent, or dialect, 168, 170–71, 177, 187; use of handkerchiefs in healing, 149–50, 161; use of managers, 149, 157, 164–65; wanders off without notice, 205, 210, 213, 214
— *claims of:* abandons journey to Mexico when horse dies, 144; arrives in New York, May 1884, 143, 186; born to British royalty, 191, 192; boy on Morley ranch named Carl Gardner, 203;

and cottonmouth moccasins,
201–2; deer licks his hand, 151;
emigrates with parents to Columbia (Tenn.) in 1858, 143, 180;
pilgrimage across West, *146–47,*
200; pilgrimage down Ohio and
Mississippi Rivers, 144, 174, 175;
raised as Roman Catholic, 188;
that he is the healer of Denver,
167; that he is the messiah, 151,
191, 192; and vision of Jesus, 202
— *ideas of:* Christianity introduced
sin into world, 188; cultivating
western deserts with nitrates,
205–6; "key note" theory of
human harmonics, 206; prejudice, 169; spiritualism, 156, 210;
universalism and pantheism, 188;
unknown musical scales, 206
— *life of (arranged chronologically):*
claims to be Francis Schlatter,
142; Canton (Ohio) ministry,
150–55; scandalous affair with
Margaret Ferris, 151–55, 157;
Chicago ministry, 159–62, 163;
tears down American flag in
Philadelphia, 166–68; marries
Luverna Comer, 178–79; living in Kokomo (Ind.), 181–82,
185–86; and U.S. census of
1900, 185, 258n20; establishes
Francis Schlatter Institute, 189;
threatens to attack U.S. Capitol,
191; imprisoned in Blackwell's
Island, 192; writes Mary Fox
in 1902, 198–99; dictates his
autobiography in Kalamazoo,
199; publishes *Modern Miracles of
Healing,* 142; announces return
to Denver, 142, 199, 205; and
Schlatter Airabon Soil Rejuvenator, 206; arrested in Canton in
1910, 207; remarried to Luverna,

207; disappears in 1921, 210–11;
threatened with deportation,
211–12; disappears in 1922, 213;
dies in St. Louis in 1922, 142;
death certificate of, 215
Schlatter, François (father of Denver healer), 31, 215
Schlatter, Madeleine Deschamps
(mother of Denver healer), 31,
215; children of, 237n32
"Schlattertown," 83
School of American Research, 9,
10, 263n42. *See also* Museum
of New Mexico; Palace of the
Governors
Schrader, August, *136,* 142, 169,
172, 207, 211, 252n14; arrested for
mail fraud, 139; borrows idea of
New Jerusalem, 137, 169; death
of, 140; description of, 135–36;
partnership of, with Jacob
Kunze, 138–39, 207
Scott (acquaintance of Denver
healer), 89, 198
Scott, John R. K., 168–69
silver panic of 1893, 28, 46, 81, 110,
134
Simpson, A. B., and holiness movement, 86
Smith, Joseph Emerson, 4, 64–65,
71, 122; reports on Schlatter's
disappearance, 93–94
Snyder, Thomas C., 149–50
social gospel, and image of Christ
as reformer, 134
Southworth, Edward, 80
Spanish-American War, 166
Spencer, Otis B., and *Francis
Schlatter Cyclus,* 219–20
spiritual healing: and abortion, 78;
causes of, 79–80; Christ-centered, 210; effectiveness of,
80–81; and faith, 86; and kinds

of ailments in Denver, 242n33;
letters, *73*, 83–84; miraculous,
87–88

spiritualism, 25, 30, 140, 156, 210; in
Denver, 23; and Lily Dale (N.Y.),
210; origins of, 20; and progressivism, 140; Schlatter's interest
in, 22, 25, 26, 33, 68, 86, 111,
157, 210; shared by Denver and
Canton healers, 156–57, 229. *See
also* George, Herbert; Pomeroy,
Marcus; Wilmans, Helen

spiritualists, 20: at Brady Lake
(Ohio), 151; in Denver, 25

Sproul, J. W., 154

Stanley, L. H., 173

Stansell, J. B., 26–28

Stedman, Charlie R., 82

suggestion, power of, 79–80, 81

Summers, James A., 58, 63, 71, 123;
directs healer to Morley ranch,
101–2

Swedenborg, Emanuel, 20

Swingle, Billy, 107, 117, 118

Teller, Sen. Henry M., 111, 160

Teller, J. C. (senator's nephew), 160

temperance movement, 151

Tennant, Palmer, 193

Thacher, Chester I., 163, 256n

theosophy, 25, 113

Tilden, J. H., 80

Times Square (New York City),
195–96

Tinaja Canyon (Mexico), 13, 15,
129, 216

Toledo (Ohio) police report, 207,
223–29, *224*, 261n10

Tomé Hill (N.M.), 3, 233n2

Union Pacific Railroad, 39, 54,
234n2; allows sick employees
free passage to healer, 85

Union Square (New York City),
113, 196

Unity, 213

Velasquez, Jesus, 52

visions: of healing mission, from
Life of the Harp, 29–30; of healing
mission, from *Modern Miracles*,
202; of Schlatter's destiny, by
his sister, 30

Ward, Edward H., 154

Washington, D.C., 188, 191; and
planned attack on U.S. Capitol,
192

Webber, Harry, 68, 72

Werner, Josepha, 55–57, 58

West Side Spiritualist Church
(Columbus, Ohio), 208–9

Whitaker, Albert S., 19; gives
Schlatter money for journey, 35;
receives Schlatter's valise and
books, 29, 205

White, William, 1, 2, 4

Whitman, Charles N., 98, 122; role
of, in healer's escape, 98

Wilmans, Helen, 25, 142; and
Blossom of the Century, 25, 109;
influence of, on Schlatter, 25–25;
and the Law of Being, 25–26;
as possible object of Schlatter's
journey, 35, 42, 201; and spiritualism, 25–26, 201

Wolff, Joseph, 98, 197; role of, in
healer's escape, 98, 244n12,
245n15

Woodard, Ella, 199, 200

Worcester, Elwood (Emmanuel
Movement), 210, 211

World's Congress of Religions, 26

Zeller, Lorenz, 192